The Submarine
PIONEERS

The Submarine
PIONEERS

RICHARD COMPTON-HALL

SUTTON PUBLISHING

First published in 1999 by
Sutton Publishing Limited · Phoenix Mill
Thrupp · Stroud · Gloucestershire · GL5 2BU

British Library Cataloguing in Publication Data
A catalogue record for this book is available from the British Library

ISBN 0-7509-2154-4

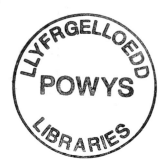

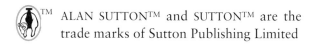

For Eve, as always

ALAN SUTTON™ and SUTTON™ are the
trade marks of Sutton Publishing Limited

Typeset in 10/13pt Sabon.
Typesetting and origination by
Sutton Publishing Limited.
Printed in Great Britain by
Bookcraft, Midsomer Norton

Contents

Acknowledgements   vii

Introduction   ix

CHAPTER 1   Wing Collars and Sea Boots   1

CHAPTER 2   Good Thinking and a Quintessential Chymist   12

CHAPTER 3   Inspiration from Above   18

CHAPTER 4   Not Going Like Clockwork   22

CHAPTER 5   Unhappy Day   24

CHAPTER 6   An Effort of Genius?   28

CHAPTER 7   Monsieur Fulton and Mr Francis   41

CHAPTER 8   On His Majesty's Secret Service   50

CHAPTER 9   Reaching for Reality   56

CHAPTER 10   Peripatetic Coffins   66

CHAPTER 11   The Curate's Eggs   81

CHAPTER 12   An Irish Invention   94

CHAPTER 13   The Salt Water Enterprise   99

CHAPTER 14   The Reason Why Not   107

CHAPTER 15   Misfits   113

CHAPTER 16   *Jamais . . . trop de sous-marins*   116

CHAPTER 17   Success in the States   123

CHAPTER 18   *Britannia* Takes the Plunge   137

CHAPTER 19   Setting up Shop   143

CHAPTER 20   Back to the Future   156

Notes   161

Select Bibliography   174

Index   177

Acknowledgements

I am especially grateful to Eve for cheerfully accepting chaos and confusion in our home during the lengthy preparation of this book, and for ensuring that successive drafts made some kind of sense; Michael W. Dash for allowing me to use his outstandingly clear and logical PhD thesis 'British submarine policy 1853–1918' (King's College, University of London, 1990) as a solid basis for my own research into that period of history: the work has saved me several journeys to the Public Record Office *et al.* besides helping to establish my own lines of thought; Dr Richard K. Morris, the undoubted doyen amongst chroniclers and interpreters of J.P. Holland's life and work, for friendship and generous help, including the provision of photographs from his own collection, over many years.

I am also especially grateful to Bill Garrett for generously giving me and the RN Submarine Museum, many years ago, a large number of source documents and photographs relating to his great grandfather George W. Garrett. I profoundly wish that my subsequent research had proved more positive, particularly with regard to the capabilities of *Resurgam*; Elizabeth Pugh for painstaking, accurate line drawings; the Director, Cdr Jeff Tall, OBE, and staff of the Royal Navy Submarine Museum (RNSM), Gosport, particularly Margaret Bidmead, for assistance with research, and Debbie Corner for the production of photographs from the Museum's extensive collection; the Red Dragon Press (Rhayader) and Charlie Collard for printing the author's own assembly of illustrations; Bill Hamilton, Managing Director of A.M. Heath & Co., Ltd (Authors' Agents) for his invariably sound advice and assistance, and to Conway Maritime for reverting all rights of *Submarine Boats* (1983) to me; Paddy O'Sullivan for advice on Irish affairs and for valued introductions; Tony and Ann Hampshire, the Revd Daniel Hurley, Maggi Llewellyn, Capt. John Moore, Bill Murphy and Geoff Ridyard for information on sundry subjects and for much appreciated help and encouragement in various ways.

Notwithstanding my sincere gratitude to those I have specifically acknowledged (and to others, over the years, for contributions too numerous to list), it will be apparent that I have sometimes arrived at conclusions which are markedly different from the beliefs of those who kindly provided me with opinions and data: such conclusions are, of course, entirely my own responsibility and in no way imply the agreement or assent of other people named or of authors cited in the Select Bibliography.

Introduction

The submarine pioneers included a generous share of oddballs in their company; but if, today, some of their projects seem wacky and others no better than middling weird, a goodly proportion were surely wonderful. In any event, long-gone inventors deserve to be remembered for sheer courage: each and every one that let the waters close darkly over him was perfectly aware that he might never see the light of day again.

The difficulty, when looking back through centuries of underwater exploration, is to separate sense from nonsense. In many cases records are scarce and sometimes deliberately misleading; certain words and descriptions have latterly taken on a different meaning; statements have more often than not been recorded at second or third hand, frequently after a considerable lapse of time, and behind a seemingly straightforward account there is apt to be a hidden agenda.

Historians have usually opted to accept traditional watery narratives more or less at face value. Romanticists, on the other hand, have let imagination run riot – understandably when a story cries out to be told and facts are few. Indeed it is sometimes impossible to avoid 'supposing if' when endeavouring to establish what really did happen in those early days beneath the waves.

However, the unashamed application of 20/20 hindsight, resulting from a user's knowledge of submarine principles and lengthy experience below the surface, is extremely helpful when it comes to deciding between what was probable or possible and what was unlikely or impossible. Thereby, although some conclusions will always depend to some extent upon conjecture, any guesswork can at least be well informed.

The submarine story is about secrets and brotherhoods, duplicity and deception, determination and despair, frequent failure and rare triumph: it would be all too easy to ridicule as well as admire. But this book in no way sets out to sell our ancestral submariners short – apart from a handful who emerge from the seas of time looking unmistakably like con artists. The chapters which follow aim, maybe for the first time, to discover what the underwater frontiersmen really accomplished, and how.

But anybody suffering from high blood pressure, who cherishes submarine mythology and believes that the archetypal submarine hailed from Connecticut and chased a British fleet out of New York Harbor in 1776, is advised to read no further. The real father of the modern submarine was a devoutly Catholic, unpretentious patriot from County Clare in Ireland.

RICHARD COMPTON-HALL
Rhayader, June 1999

HM Submarine Torpedo Boat No 1 ('Holland I') *at Portsmouth c.1903.* (RNSM)

CHAPTER 1

Wing Collars and Sea Boots

1901 launch of HM Submarine Torpedo Boat *No. 1*
1903 Orville Wright powered flight

The year was 1904. Society in the England of King Edward VII, amidst a swirl of gorgeous dresses and a good deal of adultery, was enjoying itself to the full after the last rather dull and dowdy years of Queen Victoria's long reign.

Britannia still ruled the waves, although she gazed warily across the Channel and the grey North Sea to where French, German and more distant Russian rivals were perennially building up their strengths. She could cope with threats she understood, given enough money and direction to update her navy, but lately something unthinkably nasty had been going on beneath her flowing draperies. The concealed commotion was caused by submarine torpedo boats, a considerable embarrassment to maritime pomp and circumstance. They were ensconcing themselves in otherwise respectable naval households around the world, and apparently breeding. At Portsmouth, the Royal Navy's principal base, a half-dozen stunted, ugly little craft contrasted crudely with stately battleships and cruisers.

But handsome is as handsome does. The big ships were superb for showing the flag but scarcely fit for war. Their long-range guns, accurate in themselves, were fired from rolling, pitching platforms: they stood little chance at present of hitting targets beyond three-quarters of a mile. Moreover, most potential opponents

The Irish-American John P. Holland, true father of the modern submarine, famously pictured emerging from his Holland VI *in April 1898, with the caption 'What me, afraid?'. (RNSM, USN Submarine Library and R.K. Morris: original probably taken by a New York newspaper photographer at Perth Amboy, NJ)*

were armour-plated from the waterline up and virtually impervious to shells striking their thick sides.

Hence the attraction of torpedoes. But fragile torpedo boats normally attacked under cover of darkness: otherwise they were liable to be blown out of the water by easily aimed light armament. Hence submarines – daylight torpedo boats.

That was all very well; but just before the Old Queen died, three years before, it was put about that submarines were unfair, underhand and damned un-English.[1] Moreover they threatened the very existence of the battle fleet. Now, quite suddenly, they were happily playing about in the Solent in increasing numbers. What had happened?

It was a contradictory situation for the world's greatest sea-power; and it arose largely from the ruthless ambitions of one man, Adm Sir John Arbuthnot 'Jacky' Fisher (1841–1920). A glimpse of the English scene while Jacky was C-in-C Portsmouth 1903–4 helps to unravel the Machiavellian planning that lay behind a burgeoning submarine service.

Edward VII was King and Emperor. Having waited a very long time, as Prince of Wales, to ascend the throne, he was dedicated to enjoying the opportunities that regal power and riches could command. His transparent appreciation of all things French, especially if feminine, had been noticeable since the 1880s when he was warmly greeted by ladies such as the lovely 'La Goulue' of the Moulin Rouge: 'Ullo Wales, *est-ce que tu va payer mon champagne?*' (which he did) and by the girls of the Chabanais (near the Bibliothèque Nationale) where furnishings

No. 1 *leaving Portsmouth Harbour for exercises in the Solent, April 1903. The two officers are Lt H.J.G. Good in command forward and Sub Lt H.G. Thursfield (second captain) centre. Petty Officer W.R. Waller, coxswain, is seated at the wheel and AB Banham is aft.* (RNSM).

No. 1 *in the Solent, c. 1904. Lt A. Quicke (CO) on the left, Sub Lt Adrian St V. Keyes on the right, Coxswain W.R. Waller, A.B. Wallace (with pipe), lost in* A1, *and A.B. Banham behind him.* (RNSM)

included a boat-shaped bath for twosomes and a custom-built couch-like contrivance which catered for gentlemen of majestic girth.[2]

Edward could take a measure of credit for renewing an *entente cordiale* with France, but the Navy could not drop its guard against a traditional enemy which had, incidentally, been trying out *les sous-marins* with hostile intent for decades. The British sailor's attitude to *entente* was tellingly instanced in front of the wardroom block of HMS *Excellent*, the gunnery school founded by Fisher at Whale Island. A company of seamen, dressed in white and arranged to form the words *VIVE LA FRANCE*, was viewed by French guests to the accompaniment of vociferous applause; but when it was all over a rating, rising from his knees, put the whole thing in perspective: 'I've been a steward, I've been a cook, I've been a signalman – but that's the first time I've been part of a bloody French letter.'[3]

The King, in his sixties, set a brisk pace which kept courtiers and doctors alike in a constant state of agitation while he travelled widely to conduct affairs of state and heart with equal vigour, undaunted by obesity and bronchial trouble due to smoking twelve large cigars and twenty cigarettes every day (but only one cigar and a few cigarettes before breakfast). An essentially happy marriage to the attractive Alexandra did not inhibit his appreciation of beautiful women. Miss Maude Walker, for example, would soon be offering to dance for the King at Marienbad where her speciality turned out to be a performance clad discreetly in two oyster shells and a 5-franc piece. Courtiers and hangers-on were also offered entertainment: when a Viennese beauty requested the honour of sleeping with His Majesty, who happened to be engaged elsewhere, she resignedly told Frederick Ponsonby (the King's assistant secretary) that 'if the worst came to the worst she would sleep with him instead.'[4]

'Join the navy and see the world!' promised the recruiting posters. Edward VII (first sovereign to head the *Navy List*) was able to see more of it than others; but although the young upper-deck officers of his navy were poorly paid they married late, and a modest outlay sufficed for them to share some deliciously upholstered pleasures of the Edwardian era. It was, for the privileged few, an idyllic lifestyle. But, almost as soon as soon as Edward was settled on the throne, Jacky Fisher (who was singularly unprivileged by birth) started to turn a class-ridden 'moth-eaten' navy upside down and recall ships from delightful foreign cruises before kicking the battle fleet into the twentieth century.[5]

Jacky could not count on corporate naval loyalty – not least because of a contrived and lasting quarrel with the popular and highly privileged Rear Adm Lord Charles William de la Poer Beresford (1846–1919) which split the Navy down the middle. Wardrooms were bound to resist changes to the very satisfactory, if hopelessly inefficient, *status quo*. Jacky had already befriended two powerful figures – Reginald Brett, later Lord Esher, the back room military manipulator, and the fiery journalist W.T. Stead, who later went down with the *Titanic*. Their keys opened heavy doors, but the backing of the King was wanted if

Admiral Sir John Fisher and King Edward VII, 1904. (RN Museum, Portsmouth)

naval reforms were to be so radical that there would also be a considerable impact on the Army, and on society itself at home and overseas, as well as personal triumph for Fisher.

Submariners were among those who fell on their feet in the shake-up. Fisher thoroughly approved the US Navy's integration of deck and engineering officers, and a submarine career implied just that: all submariners had to be technically literate. It may be, too, that he relished the general opinion of submarining as being 'no occupation for a gentleman'.[6] But his ostentatious support for submarines stemmed from a less obvious origin.

Fisher's basic intent was to scale down drastically the Army's defensive role and substitute a kind of local militia system, together with a small amphibious force for extraneous work, making the Army subordinate to the Navy.[7] This would purportedly save a huge amount of money and greatly reduce the rate of income tax: 'That will fetch the British Public', grinned Jacky.[8] Tax-saving is an unusual concern for admiralty. It may very well be that Fisher secretly had his eye on an important political position, perhaps ultimately the top job, in a Liberal government. After all, the Duke of Wellington had been Prime Minister from 1828 through 1830; and Jacky's arch-foe Beresford was intermittently a Conservative MP (permissable while on naval half-pay).[9] Certainly Jacky's views were Liberal, advocating freedom from alliances with continental powers and a reduction of colonial and imperial commitments; and his methods were more akin to a scruple-free politician than a properly apolitical admiral: use of the press to make points without attribution, crushing anyone who stood in his path and discussing with junior officers the faults of their seniors.

The French navy also had awe-inspiring but ineffective battleships. The Charles Martel, *pictured by Fred T. Jane in 1898, soon became a make-believe victim of submarine attacks.* (Illustrated London News, *29 October 1898)*

In 1903, while at Marienbad, Jacky had a 'new big scheme hatching' which aimed at restricting the Army Vote to £23 million while maintaining the Navy Estimates at £37 million.[10] An initial way of achieving savings (while doing down the Army) was to shift coastal defence responsibility from the Mining Engineers to the fledgling Submarine Service. Extravagant letters and recommendations followed, notably a picturesque paper 'Invasion and Submarines'. As it happened, soldiers did not enjoy administering 'aquatics', and the War Office did not fight for continuing control of minefields.[11] If submarines took the place of fixed coastal defences against invasion, public confidence ought to repose entirely in the Navy: another scare would not provoke demands for a large enough regular Army to repel boarders while depleting the naval budget to pay for it.[12] Jacky therefore portrayed the submarine as a sure guarantee against invasion, enabling the Army to be reduced by 300,000 men.[13]

There was, however, an arithmetical flaw in his reasoning. The Army's coast defences cost £550,000 annually, of which £125,000 was spent on mines. But one submarine cost about £40,000 and the quantity required to protect a thousand miles of eastern and southern coastline was very large. In fact, Jacky was understating the case in 1904 by calling for a further 125 boats.[14] Vast numbers were impractical: even the sixty-two coastal types laid down between 1902 and 1909 had to be so small, to keep costs within bounds, that they were unfit for independent 'oversea'

No 1 *diving in the Solent, c. 1904. As usual in the early days the boat was stopped when commencing the evolution and, when working with other ships, the Admiralty ruled that submarines 'be allowed from 15 to 20 minutes . . . to trim'. Boats had to 'surface at one hour before sunset at the latest so that their parent ship may collect them before dark'.* (RNSM)

offensives, though when war came some were despatched *faute de mieux*. Fisher's assertion that they could be towed at high speed in any weather to enemy ports[15] so that 'the Offensive will regain the ascendancy' was wishful thinking.[16]

A joint Army–Navy conference in December 1903 duly agreed to abandon Britain's mine defences in favour of submarines. But in truth, although his intuition was frequently inspired, Fisher knew little about submarine boats or their potential – nor did anybody else. For the moment, admirals afloat and politicians ashore dubbed them 'playthings': 'the money [to build more] had to be got by subterfuge.'[17] An important preliminary was to arrange for the King to come and stay for a weekend, in February 1904, at Admiralty House, Portsmouth. According to Lady Fisher, 'a bathroom, WC and lavatory' were hastily installed for the two best bedrooms, there being formerly 'nothing accessible of this sort without going up the back stairs' which only the servants used. The weekend went well: the royal visitor was 'so genial, so kind, and pleased with everything' that, later in the year, he appointed Fisher as principal Aide-de-Camp, a position 'giving access to the King at any time' – just what Jacky wanted![18]

Sales talk on the Saturday must have bored the monarch stiff. First, Fisher 'explained the principles on which a submarine worked'; then Reginald Bacon (first Inspecting Captain of Submarines) came to dinner and said it all over again, and finally, on board a submarine boat the following day, 'a very keen young officer gave a beautifully rehearsed repeat performance.' The King still managed to ask some pertinent questions: *Noblesse oblige*.[19]

In March Fisher consolidated the royal interest by asking if the Prince of Wales (future King George V) might take a trip to sea in HMS *A-1*. According to Esher, then

Admiral Fisher's vision of submarines being towed to invade an enemy port was amply fulfilled in September 1943 when X-craft were taken under tow by standard submarines from Scotland to Norway before being released to attack the German battleship Tirpitz *in her supposedly impregnable lair at the top of Kaa Fjord.* (RNSM)

Chairman of the War Office Reconstitution Committee, 'everyone was averse from the Prince's going down, but he *insisted* and I think he was right. It will give a lift to the submarines [crafty Jacky] and, being a sailor, why should he not take risks?'[20]

The Prince was greeted by officers correctly dressed in wing collars and sea boots. Three white mice were standing by in the engine room ready to die for King and Country: they would turn up their little toes if carbon monoxide (from the exhaust system) leaked into the interior without the crew noticing. The Princess of Wales cheerfully remarked that she would 'be very disappointed if George doesn't come up again' and they all had a good laugh, although Fisher himself was 'jolly glad when he saw the heir to the throne reappear' after a dip in the Solent.[21]

A few days later, on 18 March, *A-1*, while submerged, was accidentally rammed by SS *Berwick Castle*. The boat sank immediately, taking her two officers and nine men with her. Fisher hastily penned a positive letter to the Prince to put the tragedy in perspective: it was crucial to convince all concerned that submarines were not inherently dangerous. A month later he wrote to 'a High Official' (Lord Knollys, Private Secretary to the King):[22]

My Dear Friend,

I will begin with . . . our paucity of submarines. I consider it the most serious thing at present affecting the British Empire! That sounds big, but it's true . . .

It's astounding to me, perfectly astounding, how the very best amongst us absolutely fail to realise the vast impending revolution in naval warfare and naval strategy that the submarine will accomplish! (I have written a paper on this, but it's so violent I am keeping it!) Here, just to take a simple instance, is

Artist's impression of A1 *(wrongly shown as a 'Holland') and her loss.* (*Daily Telegraph*, March 1904)

the battleship *Empress of India*, engaged in manoeuvres and knowing of the proximity of Submarines, the Flagship of the Second Admiral of the Home Fleet nine miles beyond the Nab Light [i.e. in the open Channel], so self-confident of safety and so oblivious of the possibilities of modern warfare, that the Admiral is smoking his cigarette, the Captain is calmly seeing defaulters down on the half-deck, no-one caring an iota for what is going on, and suddenly they see a Whitehead torpedo miss their stern by a few feet! [Implying that it would have hit, if it had not been set to run deep, because its exhaust bubbles took a few seconds to reach the surface.] And how fired? From a submarine of the 'Pre-Adamite' period, small, slow, badly fitted, with no periscope at all – it had been carried away by a destroyer lying over her, fishing for her! – and yet this submarine followed that battleship for a solid two hours underwater, coming up gingerly about a mile off, every now and then, (like a beaver!), just to take a fresh compass bearing of her prey, and then down again!

. . . in all seriousness I don't think it is even *faintly* realised – *the immense impending revolution which the submarines will effect as offensive weapons of war . . .*

As things turned out 'the immense impending revolution' was not sparked until 1915, and then by single-mindedly offensive German U-boats. In the meantime, Britain's submariners pushed on as best they could. They were grossly hampered by tactical restrictions imposed after the loss of *A1* – the safety syndrome – and gloomy opinions in the press were not encouraging. The *Red Letter* journal told its readers on 10 September 1904 that, 30 feet below the waves, there was 'the silence of the tomb and an enshrouding dense-like darkness exceeding that of a thick London fog'. And the Army, in questionable taste, derided the usurping submariners in stanzas titled 'Reflections of a Garrison Gunner'[23]:

No 1 *alongside depot ship HMS* Forth *at Devonport, date uncertain. Another, unidentified,* 'Holland' *lies inboard.* (RNSM)

One of the 'large, new A-class' coming alongside at Fort Blockhouse, c. 1904. (RNSM)

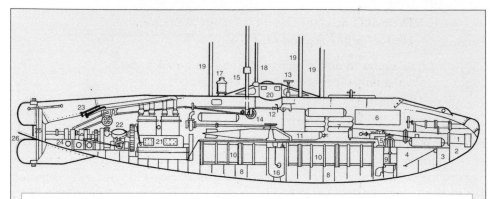

1. Torpedo tube with vertically raising bow cap
2. Fwd trimming tank
3. Torpedo compensating tank
4. Gasoline (fuel) tank
5. Hand-pumped porcelain WC (Doulton pattern no. 612)
6. Torpedo HP discharge cylinder
7. Some of approx. 50 HP air bottles
8. Main ballast tank: 9.16 tons
9. Main ballast tank Kingston valves (2)
10. Main battery (60 lead-acid cells)
11. Reload torpedo (designed for 2 but restricted to 1)
12. Steering linkage

HM Submarine Torpedo Boat No.1 salvaged in 1982 and now at the Royal Navy Submarine Museum, Gosport, Hampshire. Length overall 63ft 10in (or 'one yard shorter than a cricket pitch' as the Edwardian press had it). Displacement 113/122 tons.

Divin' down among the dead,
Goes the bloomin' submarine,
With the sunlight over'ead,
An' the ocean in between
An' I couldn't tell you w'en
She's a-comin' up again.

Ye may talk o' British valour wot is never know'd to fail,
But 'valour' as a word ain't gettin' near it,
For men as plays at Jony in the belly o' the w'ale,
An' knowin' of the danger – doesn't fear it.

Fer if this divin' man-o-war should get 'er works askew,
Wot ain't a rare occurrence in the Navy,

There ain't no gettin' out of it for any of 'er crew,
The lot 'as got to go to Mr Davy.

I'd prefer to do me dyin' with the men a-lookin' on,
An' a bullet in the 'ead to end me troubles,
To disappearin' sudden – no one knowin' that I'd gone,
Without they chanced to see a lot o' bubbles.

But the evolving submariners did not dwell on past disasters, and for the immediate future masters-at-arms, parade gunners, temperance societies and wayward women were enough cause for worry. All the same, a glance astern at what had happened during three centuries of trial and error underwater, might have helped to avoid a few expensive mistakes and maybe even sparked some good ideas.

CHAPTER 2

Good Thinking and a Quintessential Chymist

1588 Spanish Armada defeated
1605 Gunpowder Plot
1618 Thirty Years War begins in Europe

Naturally, it all started with divers – about 4500 BC – but they were not, in former times, a communicative race. However, they had one trick which may have got around. If a diver wanted to get to the bottom quickly, and make the most of his endurance, he took a small rock in one hand and breathed *out* before descending. Pressure at the bottom compressed the lungs to the point where he was in a state of neutral or slightly negative buoyancy; and the rock could be discarded. A few vigorous kicks were sufficient to regain the surface although a prudent soul might insist on a rope dangling nearby.

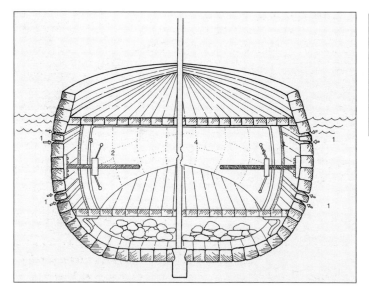

1. Inlet holes
2. Capstans for screwing sliding bulkheads in and out
3. Leather
4. Hollow mast with air holes

William Bourne's Invention, *1578.*

At some point it was realized that a whale dives or 'sounds' in the same way: it contracts its body, by means of a network of muscles, so that the volume of water it displaces becomes less. Its weight remains constant and now exceeds the weight of displaced water, so the whale can easily swim down to its desired depth. It reverses the process, expanding its volume, to swim upwards and refresh air at the surface. While consuming air at a given depth, the creature steadily contracts its body so that it constantly weighs about the same as the amount of water displaced – thus maintaining neutral buoyancy – but it cannot afford to hang about: it has to keep its flippers and tailfin moving to stay level.

Archimedes famously announced the buoyancy principle after a bath in the third century BC;[1] but it was not rediscovered for submarine purposes until the 1570s when William Bourne (1535–83), who had served as a 'poore gunner' under the Elizabethan Admiral Sir William Monson, apologized for producing a 'rude and barbarous volume' in his *Inuentions and Deuices*, 'the writer being most unlearned and simple'.[2] Modesty and self-deprecation are not characteristics normally associated with a gunnery officer then or now: Bourne must have intended a Very Important Person – perhaps the Queen herself – to take up his scheme for

. . . a Ship or Boate that may goe under the water unto the bottome, and so to come up againe at your pleasure, as this, as I haue declared . . . that anything that sinketh is heauier than the proportion of so much water, and if it bee lighter than the magnitude of so much water, then it swimmeth or appeareth aboue the water, according unto the proportion of weight, and then this being true . . . any magnitude or body that is in the water, if that the quantity in

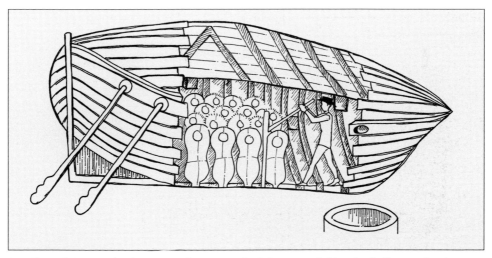

Borelli and Symons both suggested (1680 and 1747) animal skins for ballast tanks, forcing water out by leverage. (Sketch after illustration in Gentleman's Magazine, June 1749)

bignesse, hauing alwaies but one weight, may bee made bigger or lesser, then it shall swimme when you would, and sinke when you list: and for to make any thing doo so, then in the ioyntes or places that doo make the thing bigger and lesser, must be of leather, and in the inside to haue Skrewes to winde it in and also out againe: and for to have it sinke, they must winde it in to make the thing lesse, and then it sinketh unto the bottome: and to haue it swimme, then to winde the sides out againe, to make the thing bigger, and it will swimme . . .[2]

William Bourne had the right ideas. Presumably his 'deuice' was intended for plundering Spanish gold from hostile harbours with a little more discretion than usual; but piratical sea-captains like Francis Drake were doing very nicely on the surface. Nothing more was heard of Bourne's ballast tanks (which is what they were) until a rather more sophisticated proposal by the Italian Giovanni-Alfonso Borelli (1608–79) was published in 1680 and possibly tried out in the Thames by a Devonian, Nathaniel Symons, some seventy years later. Symons, covered a decked wooden boat with greased skins, leaving leather-sleeved holes for oars. Large bottle-shaped leather bags were fastened with their necks, throttled by ropes, protruding through openings in the bottom of the boat. The inverted bags were stowed below the water line: when the throttles were loosened, water flooded in until increasing air pressure inside halted the inflow.[3]

Neither Borelli nor Symons thought of introducing a vent at the top of each 'ballast tank' which could be opened or shut in the same way as the neck at the bottom. Submariners eventually came to flood main ballast tanks by simply opening 'main vents', often leaving holes at the bottom permanently open (if not installing Kingston valves for belt-and-braces safety), for very little water would enter such 'free-flood holes' while vents at the top were shut.

Bourne's book of 1578 was probably read by the Dutch artisan, philosopher (quasi-scientist) and 'chymist' Cornelis van Drebbel (1572–1634) who has time and again – wrongly – been styled the first submariner.

Drebbel's claim to fame arises, with hardly any other supporting evidence, from a letter written by Robert Boyle (of 'Boyle's Law') in 1662, twenty-eight years after Drebbel died:

I acquaint your Lordship with a conceit of that deservedly famous Mechanician and Chymist, Cornelius Drebbel who, amongst other strange things that he performed, is affirmed (by more than a few credible persons) to have contrived, for the late learned King James, a vessel to go under water, of which trial was made in Thames with admired success; the vessel carried twelve rowers besides passengers.

Having made particular enquiries amongst the relations of Drebbel concerning the grounds on which he conceived it feasible to make men, un-accustomed, to continue for so long underwater without suffocation or without inconvenience, I was answered that Drebbel conceived that it is not the whole body of the air, but a certain quintessence or spirituous part of it that makes it fit for respiration. . . . Beside the mechanical contrivance for expelling air, he had a chymicall liquor which . . . [would] speedily restore to the troubled air such a proportion of vitall parts as would make it againse for a good while fit for respiration . . .[4]

Drebbel, of good parentage and said to be 'a very fair and handsome man of gentle manners altogether different from other suchlike characters', was from Alkmaar in Holland.[5] He came to England at the age of thirty-two to pursue inventive work, specializing in perpetual motion which intrigued King James I (1566–1625). He also built 'machines for producing rain, lightning, thunder or extreme cold at any time' which he demonstrated before the King at Westminster Hall one fine summer's day, 'driving all the audience hastily out of the building'.[6] He was that sort of man.

The Thirty Years War was under way in 1618 and Drebbel perceived a market for a weapon system that could secretly attack 'enemy ships lying safely at anchor

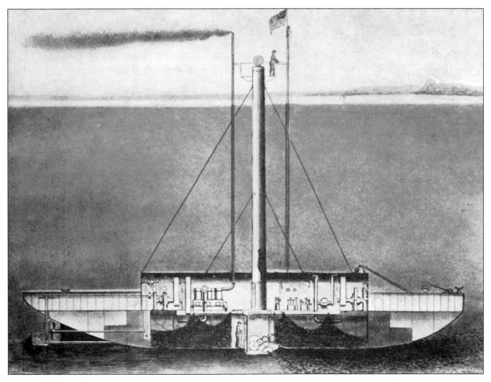

Bourne's idea for a hollow mast taken to its limit and beyond by Simon Lake in 1900. The schnorkel (snorkel or snort) did not start to become fully operational until early 1944.

. . . by means of a battering ram' by which he meant a petard at the end of a pole
– a spar torpedo in fact[7] – mounted on a submarine of sorts.

No drawing or detailed description has come to light of the boat which he
demonstrated in the early 1620s; but (following a metallic box-like first
endeavour) a wooden tub-like craft, looking rather like a huge garden watering-
can and reportedly constructed on Drebbel lines, was built by Denis Papin
(1647–1712) for Prince Charles Landgrave of Hesse-Cassel in 1689. This was
weighted down by solid ballast until low in the water when water was dribbled in
through a cock until only a touch of positive buoyancy remained. Oars then drove
the contraption right under. An ejector pump, together with more work at the oars,
brought it up again. However, Drebbel's boat, which may well have had a whale-
head sloping bow, was supposed to submerge by forward motion: a friend of the
inventor, George Harsdorffer, said that the Dutchman had watched a fisherman

*Cornelius (or Cornelis) Drebbel
(1572–1633), variously called
'Mechanician and Chymist', 'strange
Monstar', or 'braggart and
windmaker'.*

towing baskets of fish on the way up to London and
noticed that while the strain was on the towing line
the baskets were more immersed than when it was
slack.[8] It followed (he thought) that a twelve-oar
rowing boat, wholly covered by leather and rowed in
the awash condition, would slip beneath the surface.
It was obvious, however, that the air inside the boat
would have to be refreshed for the crew to breathe –
hence the reported 'chymicall liquor'.

Too many questions are begged about Drebbel's
invention. None the less there is little doubt that the
King watched the boat from some vantage point
while it made its way down the Thames, assisted by
the stream, from Westminster to Greenwich; but it
would have been entirely against the hesitant nature
of James I to venture (as related) inside.

If the oar-blades were below the surface, as implied,
skilful coordination was needed to feather them for
each return stroke. But it was much more likely that
the craft was never intended to submerge completely:
with its upper decking just clear of the water and the
oars passing through leather sleeves, the rowers could
have adopted a circular sort of stroke. Anyway, it is
unthinkable that the craft descended 12 or 15 feet into the river (as often claimed)
because there was absolutely no way of controlling the depth line. And, if the boat
was wholly sealed, how did the steersman see where he was going?

Boyle's letter has prompted a few authors to interpret 'quintessence' as meaning
'one-fifth' and to credit Drebbel with the discovery and means of producing
oxygen – but the element was not even isolated until 1771 (by K.W. Steele and

possibly by Joseph Priestley in the same year). Many people came to conclude that the fifth essence was alcohol;[9] but the Abbé de Hautefeuille (a keen commentator on matters of this kind) assured readers: 'The secret of Drebbel was in the apparatus, which consisted of bellows with two valves and two pipes coming on to the surface of the water, one bringing the pure air down and the other conveying the foul air away.'[10]

A fair guess is that magic liquor was indeed involved, but it was a strong smelling compound for overcoming the stench of a dozen sweating London labourers – which makes Drebbel an originator of the air-freshener rather than the submarine.

CHAPTER 3

Inspiration from Above

1647 Christmas abolished by the Puritan Parliament
1648 Execution of Charles I
1660 Restoration

D reams of slipping beneath the waves captivated a number of Christian churchmen from the time that blind faith started giving ground to inquisitive reasoning in the early seventeenth century. Clerics were generally better educated than lay folk, and also better placed to hear the latest ideas from universities and intellectual religious communities, especially the Jesuit College of Rome. It was anyway safer to enquire into the watery depths (where praise was promised by the psalmist) than to offer dubious opinions about God's domain in the heavens above: the Inquisition's heavy tap on Galileo Galilei's shoulder in 1633 reminded all concerned where the upper limits lay.

A number of thoughts about sub-surface activities had been voiced before the Reformation although Leonardo da Vinci (1452–1519) declined to divulge his method of remaining underwater 'on account of the evil nature of men, who would practise assassinations at the bottom of the seas by breaking the ships in their lowest parts and sinking them together with the crews who are in them'.[1]

Unfortunately, evil mankind did not go on to read the ubiquitous Leonardo's broad hint about pressure: 'If all the bed of the sea were covered with men lying down these men would sustain the whole of the element of water, consequently each man would find that he had a column of water a mile long on his back.'[2]

When the French clerics Marin Mersenne (1588–1648)[3] (Order of Minims) and Georges Fournier (1595–1652)[4] (Jesuit) teamed up to publish an all-encompassing educational survey in 1634, Mersenne included a reverie on submarine design although no allowance was made for the immense force exerted by the sea at depth. For the rest, his ingenuity was equal to the sorry standard anticipated by Leonardo. As well as facilities for recovering goods lost on the bottom (by block and tackle and a means of exit and re-entry for divers), there was to be a gimlet for piercing enemy hulls from beneath, and heavy guns for fighting seabed battles would have arrangements for preventing the ingress of water on recoil. Propulsion by oars (like Drebbel the clerics gave no thought to feathering submerged) would be no more difficult going astern than ahead because the boat was spindle shaped. Phosphorescent lighting, glass scuttles and a compass would help to find the way, and air was to be refreshed through tubes leading to the surface.

Mersenne's formula was borrowed from a daydream patented by the Englishman Richard Norwood in April 1632;[5] but no one, anywhere, bothered about plagiarism until the end of the eighteenth century.[6] Fournier's contribution was research into the exploits of Polish Cossacks who went privateering (mainly against Turkish galleys) in 40-rower longboats, with watertight leather decking and sealed apertures for oars, which could temporarily submerge in the marshlands. Breathing through long reeds until nightfall, the pirates were able to escape retaliation.

It can be assumed that the Jesuit Fournier was working more on behalf of the Papacy than his native France, led on the anti-Habsburg side by the pragmatic Cardinal Richelieu during the complicated Thirty Years War. Perhaps Fournier foresaw the need for defending Rome against seaborne invasion and co-opted Marin Mersenne for the vegan friar's extraordinarily wide intellectual connections.[7] Mersenne garnered and spread ideas very widely, but nothing practical transpired.

In England nobody perceived the advantage of life below the waves more clearly than the great divine Dr John Wilkins DD (1614–72), brother-in-law of Oliver Cromwell, Freemason, founder member of the Royal Society (whose patron was King Charles II) in 1660, and Bishop of Chester from 1668. In a very busy, not to say adroit, career rivalling the famously flexible Vicar of Bray, he found time to publish, in 1648, a prescient dissertation 'Concerning the possibility of framing an Ark for Submarine navigation', in Chapter 5 of his book *Mathematical Magick*.[8]

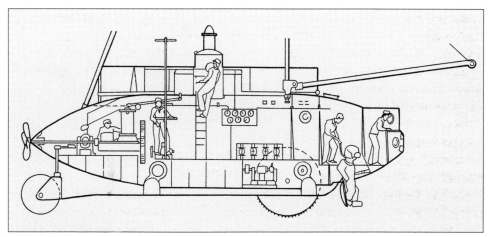

Simon Lake's bottom-crawler, Argonaut, *finally completed in 1900 and a logical outcome of suggestions by Mersenne and Wilkins.*

Dr John Wilkins DD (1614–72), a founder of the Royal Society, Freemason and early submarine proponent.

John Wilkins acknowledged a debt to Mersenne but looked further forward and attended to details which others neglected. For example, oars should be 'like the fins of a fish to contract and dilate' (which dealt with feathering) and he was about right in noting that 'eight cubic feet of air will not serve a diver for respiration above one quarter of an hour.' He was way off target in saying 'it is not altogether improbable' that the mere circulation of air round a lamp or fire would purify the atmosphere and, contrariwise, that purification could also be achieved by 'refrigeration . . . helped by bellows which would cool it [the air] by motion'. However, he was correct to reassure potential undersea explorers that if there were a leak at the bottom of the Ark 'very little water would get in, because no air could get out' – a point that escaped Borelli and Symons. And his list of 'advantages and conveniences' of a submersible Ark were generally right:

1. 'Tis private; a man may thus go to any coast of the world invisibly, without being discovered or prevented on his journey.
2. 'Tis safe; from the uncertainty of *Tides* and the violence of *Tempests*, which do never move the sea above five or six paces deep; from *Pirates* and *Robbers* which do so infest other voyages; from ice and great frosts, which do so much endanger the passages towards the Poles.
3. It may be of very great advantage against a Navy of enemies, who by this means may be undermined in the water and blown up.
4. It may be of special use for the relief of any place that is besieged by water, to convey unto them invisible supplies, and so likewise for the surprisal of any place that is accessible by water.
5. It may be of unspeakable benefit for submarine experiments and discoveries . . . But above all, the discovery of submarine treasures . . .

Furthermore the Bishop understood the crucial necessity of dealing with 'many noisome and offensive things that must be thrust out . . . and yet the water doth not rush into it with such violence as it doth usually in the leak of a Ship.' The answer was to install:

. . . certain leatheren bags made of several bignesses . . . long and open at both ends. Answerable to these let there be divers windows . . . round the sides of

From the late 1950s submarines did indeed reach the Pole and operate in the frozen Arctic ocean as foreseen by Wilkins. (RNSM)

which one end of these bags may be fixed, the other end coming within the ship to open and shut as a purse. Now if we suppose this bag thus fastened to be tyed close about towards the window, then anything that is to be sent out may be safely put into the end and within the ship which being again close shut, and the other end loosened, the thing may be safely sent out without the admission of water. . . .

The bags anticipated submarine garbage disposal units and – most important of all for submariners – the 'heads', naval parlance for WCs or toilets. If the good Bishop is remembered for nothing else he should be immortalized for pointing the way to undersea plumbing.

CHAPTER 4

Not Going Like Clockwork

1652–4 First Anglo-Dutch War
1653–8 Oliver Cromwell Protector
1656 Huygens invents pendulum clock

The greatest concern for prospective submariners used to be a deficiency of air although it turned out to be the least of their worries. Respiration was not fully understood in the time of John Wilkins, but he did appreciate that a man working hard needed to breathe more than a man resting. (The difference is between 100 litres and 8 litres per minute.) Therefore, muscle-power propulsion for a submarine compounded the problem. A Frenchman named de Son, 'one of the most Excellent Mechanics in the World',[1] thought he had the answer in 1653: accordingly, he went to the great port and shipbuilding centre of Rotterdam to oversee the construction of a mechanical semi-submersible.

As usual, the European states and nations were jockeying for position. The current conflict, the First Anglo-Dutch War (1652–4), was between England and the Dutch Republic over trade and colonies, with action focused on the East Indies. Warring would seriously deplete Dutch coffers over the next twenty years, but for the moment there was plenty of money about. Sheer speculation was not so wild as it had been in the 1620s and '30s when a rare tulip bulb fetched 20,000 stuivers (£60,000 today);[2] but Rotterdam was still a good place for an entrepreneur to find capital, although labour was more expensive than in France. A skilled carpenter earned 8,000 stuivers per annum (£24,000 today) and de Son needed to employ several craftsmen to build a 72-ft wooden craft strengthened by iron girders. However, he was reportedly 'encouraged' by the State.[3]

De Son saw no need to go completely underwater to avoid the enemy: it was enough to protect watertight cabins forward and aft by putting them below the waterline when the boat was ballasted down. A long, stout beam ran through the boat and, pointed and iron-tipped for ramming, projected from each end; and a star-shaped paddle wheel, about 8 ft in diameter, was mounted inside the craft's

De Son's clockwork racer, 1653

free-flooding area amidships with its axle at water level. This was rotated by a clockwork mechanism which worked encouragingly well while the novel warship was still on the stocks. The plan was for two crewmen to rewind the spring every eight hours at sea, and de Son confidently expected this propulsion to drive the craft 'at unbelievable speed'. He assured Adm Opdam, the Dutch Commander-in-Chief, that, if he cared to accompany him just across the Channel, he could watch the ram destroying English men-of-war. Alternatively they could simply take a trip to Dieppe, have lunch there, and return to Rotterdam that same evening. If, on the other hand, the Republic had in mind venturing a little further afield, the craft could go to London and back in a day (and send a hundred ships to the bottom in the same time)[4] or, still better:

> . . . in 6 Weekes to goe to the East Indiens, and to run as Swift as a bird can flye no fire, nor Storme, or Bullets, can hinder her, unlesse it please God, Although the Ships meane to bee safe in their hauens, it is in vaine, for shee shall come to them in any place, it is impossible for her to bee taken, unlesse by treacherie, and then can not bee governed by any but himselfe.[5]

It was just what the Dutch wanted. Notabilities from all over Holland, and some foreigners as well, were invited to view the boat on 14 October 1653; but then a delay was announced. The launch was eventually rescheduled for Monday, 6 July 1654;[6] and de Son must have tried the mechanism soon afterwards – because, alas, he found that the clockwork spring was not strong enough to rotate the paddlewheel in the River Meuse. Like the vast majority of his contemporaries Monsieur de Son was not well acquainted, in any way, with the properties of water.

CHAPTER 5

Unhappy Day

1759 Guinness brewed in Dublin
1773 'Boston Tea Party'

Finally, someone put theory into practice: on 20 June 1774 John Day, an English millwright and sometime ship's carpenter from Suffolk, went down and stayed down.

Day was an odd, solitary individual, addicted to dark waters. In the summer of 1773 he had to be rescued from a potholing expedition in Peak Cavern, Derbyshire when he:

> . . . attempted to swim under this Rock: after being gone for some Time and the By Standers supposing he was drowned, they heard a Voice, and then a plunging: upon which R. Daykin, our Guide, ventured as far as he dared, & very happily put his Hand down & caught hold of Mr. Day's arms, & a Man behind Daykin caught hold of him & saved the drowning Man; but Mr. Day was speechless for some Time: but no sooner had his Senses returned, but he said, he would take another Plunge: but those present, finding him disorder'd, prevented him.

> This Mr. Day was a Projector [inventor] & perhaps not of the soundest Mind; for, some Time after, he undertook to sink a Vessel at Plimouth, to sink himself with it & to live under Water for some Time; he made the Attempt; the Vessel was sunk with him, but neither however rose again.[1]

Day converted a small market boat into a diving machine by installing a watertight chamber. Some accounts speak of him deliberately sinking to a depth of 30 ft in a Suffolk Broad and surfacing unharmed twenty-four hours later; but the version which has him simply allowing the tide to cover and uncover the beached contrivance is a lot more credible. External pressure at 30 ft (9 m) would have been more than 13 lbs per sq. in.

The experiment was the first step towards a major money-making venture, for Day was inspired by the passion for gambling in England under the Hanovarian monarchs, and he hit on a way of making himself rich. Having acquainted the East Anglian sporting gentry with his supposed initial success, he reckoned on considerable wagers being laid on the feasibility (or otherwise) of sending a full-size ship to the bottom – a depth of 100 yards was mentioned – and bringing it up again with the crewman still alive.

A patron was necessary to fund the project, and in November 1773 Day got wind of a likely punter, a Mr Christopher Blake. Day wrote to him straight away:

Sir,

I found out an affair by which many thousands may be won; it is a very paradoxical nature that can be performed with ease; therefore, sir, if you chuse to be informed of it, and give me one hundred pounds out of every thousand you shall win by it, I will very readily wait upon you and inform you of it. I am myself but a poor mechanic and not able to make anything by it without your assistance.

Yours etc.,

J. Day[2]

Mr Blake was hooked, and he offered to pay Day's expenses for a trip to London. Meanwhile, Blake independently gathered (unlike Day himself, it seems) some idea of the colossal force that would be exerted on a watertight container 300 ft below the surface. He urged Day 'at any expense to fortify the chamber . . . against the weight of such a body of water' and insisted that the depth should not exceed 20 fathoms (120 ft or 36 m) while the total time below was to be reduced from 24 hours to twelve. That agreed, Blake was willing to finance the project.

Day thereupon purchased the *Maria*, a sloop of 50 tons burden, for £340 (around £15,000 today). The little vessel was 31 ft long and 16 ft broad with a hold 9 ft deep. *Maria* was taken in hand for refit at Plymouth in March 1774, the principal addition being a stoutly constructed chamber about 12 ft long, 9 ft broad and 8 ft deep, 'containing 75 hogsheads of air' built into the hold and projecting around 2 ft above main-deck level. It was reinforced by strong timbers on the inside and entered by a square opening at the top sealed by a heavy bevelled hatch.

Three differently coloured signal buoys were fastened above with catches which could be released from inside to signify that Day was 'very well' (white), 'indifferent' (red) or 'very ill' (black) when they floated up to the surface.

Maria carried ballast such that she would sink when water was admitted to the open hull through two plugged holes in the bottom. When Day was ready to surface, he could release (by turning iron rods which passed through watertight tubes into the chamber) some 20 tons of boulders held in nets below the keel.[3]

At 2 o'clock on the afternoon of 20 June, 1774 the *Maria* was towed out from the Pool of Plymouth (Sutton Harbour) to a spot about equidistant between the north foreshore of Drake's Island and Firestone Bay, a little to the east of the normal shipping route in Plymouth Sound and some 300 yards from either shore.

The position was given as 'Cross bearings: St Nicholas Sd due South; Fire Stone Bay N 1° W'. The depth of water was later recorded as 22 fathoms (132 ft or 40 m) presumably measured, as customary, at Mean Low Water Springs. The pressure on the diving chamber at the bottom was therefore at least 58 lb on every square inch of a shoe-box shape that was far from ideal for resistance.

The intrepid adventurer 'appeared more than ordinarily cheerful' and was 'confident that his enterprize would be crowned with success and universal acclamation'. He took with him 'a hammock, a watch, a small wax taper, a bottle of water, and a couple of biscuits' and 'watched the hour with the greatest impatience' while Mr Blake settled himself on a barge nearby.[4] The frigate HMS *Orpheus*, whose captain had been ordered to render assistance if required, was also anchored nearby. Quite by chance Lord Sandwich (1718–92), First Lord of the Admiralty, was in Plymouth at the time. (It was he, an inveterate gambler, who had ordered some slivers of meat between two slices of bread that he might not be distracted from his club's gaming table: Sandwich very probably wagered a large amount of money on the outcome of Day's venture.

When all was ready, Day walked to the forecastle to pull up ropes for withdrawing the plugs in *Maria*'s bilges; and then, as the vessel was on the point of going under, stripped off his coat and waistcoat. Bidding his well-wishers goodbye, he climbed down into the chamber 'with the greatest composure' and shut the hatch. *Maria* 'sunk gradually down with her stern somewhat foremost' while his patron 'beheld the spot from whence he vanished, with a pensiveness that seemed to forebode to his mind an evil omen, and a solemn silence seized all the witnesses of the extraordinary and awful sight.'

About a quarter of an hour after *Maria* had vanished the surface of the sea was suddenly agitated, as if boiling (the description anticipating the result of a submarine sinking in wartime). Clearly the air chamber had collapsed. None of the three buoys came to the surface, and nor did the body of John Day. However, large sums of money were literally at stake, and Lord Sandwich was doubtless as anxious as Christopher Blake to find John Day still alive. The First Lord ordered the Dockyard to help and two hundred dockyard workers, with lighters and lifting cables, worked non-stop for three days to raise the sunken *Maria* – to no avail.

All hope was abandoned, save by a Dr N.D. Falck, MD who believed that the wreck could be brought up and that Day could yet be resuscitated. There was:

. . . a Philosophical probability of restoring life to a man whose death I presumed not to be real, but a mere cessation of the animal functions, and whose congealed mass of blood would remain a considerable time, in so cold a region, before a chance of putrefaction could take place . . .[5]

Dr Falck was referred to Blake who wrote to him on 17 July:

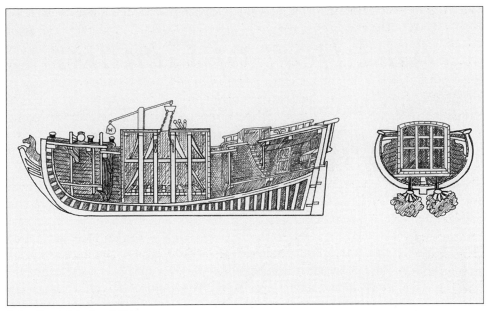

John Day's Maria, *1774.*

SIR,
In consequence of a letter you wrote . . . offering your service to get up the ship, . . . [if it] proves successful, you shall have her for your reward, . . .[6]

Dr Falck then solicited more Admiralty assistance, but Lord Sandwich declined on 20 July:

SIR,
I must beg to be excused from concerning myself in any shape about the vessel that was sunk at Plymouth; while there were any hopes of saving the life of the unfortunate man [subject of the wager] who sunk in her, I was ready to lend any assistance in my power, but as soon as that became desperate [despaired of] my interference ended.[7]

Nevertheless, Dr Falck organized a thoroughly efficient search and salvage operation but, due to continuing gales, only succeeded in heaving the wreck a hundred yards closer to Drake's Island. Subsequent spasmodic attempts to rediscover *Maria* have been unsuccessful. She is probably silted over; and searchers (who are known to have focused on the given position of the original dive) may not have looked a hundred yards southwards towards the island, where the wreck was finally abandoned. Poor John Day became the first of 65,000 submariners who rest on the deep sea bed.

CHAPTER 6

An Effort of Genius?

1770 Edmund Burke, *Thoughts on Present Discontents*
1776 Declaration of Independence

The American War of Independence (1775–83) nurtured the most enduring of all submarine legends. Exaggerated in its own time (for good reason) it has improved in the telling ever since. The story of a wooden one-man submarine pitted against England's mighty men-of-war is not entirely mythical; but, even examined from a sympathetic submariner's viewpoint with specific experience of military mini-subs, it abounds with physical impossibilities.[1]

The saga, which most historians and schoolteachers accept, begins (accurately enough) with David Bushnell being born to a 'hard scrabble' farming family on 13 August 1740 in the western parish of Saybrook, known today as Westbrook.[2] Three sisters and brother Ezra followed him into the world. David was not strong but his thirst for knowledge was insatiable and he was fascinated by things mechanical. Unfortunately, there was no money to spare for a proper education until, after his father's death, his mother remarried, leaving the farm to her two grown boys.

Ezra was delighted to continue farming and gladly purchased David's share of the property, and, in 1771 at the age of 31, David entered Yale College (which became Yale University in 1887).[3] By now David was acquainted, thanks to the local Congregational minister, with some of the finest minds in colonial America. One was Jared Eliot (Yale '06), pastor, physician and member of the Royal Society in London, and another was the doctor-cum-politician Benjamin Gale to whom we owe the more cogent descriptions of Bushnell's engineering and its consequences.[4]. Eliot was a close friend of the renowned Benjamin Franklin, a connection which was to afford Bushnell credibility.

David was nearly twice as old as his classmates but he settled easily into Yale society and was proposed by Nathan Hale for the prestigious Linonia Fraternity. He may have been initiated into the Craft – Freemasonry – at about the same time. He pursued a broad course of studies but his extra-curricular interest lay in demonstrating that a gunpowder charge exploded with greater effect underwater than in air. His purpose was obviously warlike, and the only enemy in sight was the British fleet whose warships sailed up and down the coastline, arrogantly prepared to impose King George's will. Someone – or more likely several people encouraged by Gale – must have helped to finance Bushnell's endeavours from now on, for hitherto unasked questions already begin to arise. Was the money which Ezra paid David for a few acres of poor land sufficient to pay the fees at Yale for four years together with subsistence, travel, material for private studies, subscriptions to the fraternity and library – and, soon, the investment needed for a very substantial boat-building enterprise?

A speculative answer is that the Craft charitably helped Bushnell with his expenses from about 1772, and from 1775 supplemented meagre government grants with help in kind and organisation for a promising patriotic endeavour. After all, Brother George Washington himself had been a Mason since 1752 and the dollar bill bears not only Washington's likeness but also symbols of Freemasonry: several signatories to the Declaration of Independence (Franklin among them) were declared Masons and others have since been claimed by the Brotherhood.[5] One of the strengths of a Freemason was (is) the ability to keep a secret – a factor to consider as the Bushnell narrative unfolds.

On 19 April 1775, the bloody engagements between British and American forces at Lexington and Concord signified that the Revolutionary War had formally commenced. Some of the Yale students marched straight off to the Colonial lines at Cambridge, but at the end of the semester David returned to Saybrook where he asked brother Ezra to help construct a watertight oaken magazine for holding 150 lb of powder and a 'water machine' to carry it covertly to the enemy. No contemporary drawings survive; but an imaginary, and maybe deliberately light-hearted, sketch by Lt F.M. Barber USN in 1875 depicts what came to be called the *American Turtle* as a coconut-shaped craft with vertical and horizontal Archimedian screw propellers rotated by a gentleman in late Victorian business suiting.[6] The drawing has been used as source material by numerous earnest authors (including the present one) ever since. In fact, neither Barber's design nor the specifications given by Bushnell and associates would have been workable in practice. All the same, Ezra Styles, President of Yale, wrote in his diary (in Latin) on 15 August 1775:

This man is the inventor of a machine which is now made and almost perfected for the destruction of the fleet in the harbor of Boston [New York in the event] by the explosion of gunpowder. The machine is so constructed that it can move rapidly for 20 or more feet underwater, and can carry and attach to the hull of a ship 2000 pounds [*sic*] of gunpowder. A clock work will ignite the whole mass either immediately or in 10 minutes or in half an hour, according to the will of the operator.

Believers in Bushnell's boat-building ability make light of constructing an unprecedented submersible, capable of withstanding pressure down to at least 20 ft (9 lb per sq. in. at 6.1 m) with muscle-powered propulsion in two planes, a rudder, a compass and depth gauge, a brass conning tower with glass ports and a hatch, a delayed action charge (that is an archetypal limpet mine) carried piggyback and tied to a wood-piercing auger (worked from inside the *Turtle*, the whole weapon system detaching when fixed). The craft supposedly employed a Kingston valve for admitting water into its bilges, and a forcing pump to eject it; a heavy weight that could be dropped and hauled up again, from inside, like an anchor; a mass of fixed lead ballast; two ballcock-equipped intake and exhaust devices mounted on short pipes (primitive snorkels) for air; and, finally, a bench for the lone pilot to sit on while he turned the up–down and forward–aft propulsion cranks, navigated, steered, adjusted buoyancy, and screwed an auger into the target.

The navigator would have had to be a multi-limbed superman, but the craft itself must be more closely questioned before looking at operational problems. The pump and clockwork firing mechanism were credited to Isaac Doolittle of New Haven (who also made the first American printing press in 1769) and Phineas Pratt Sr (1747–1813) of Saybrook.[7] However, it can be deduced that although plans for the *Turtle* were drawn up over a year or so, from about mid-1774, building did not commence until the Yale vacation of May 1775.[8] Meanwhile Ezra Bushnell had become a Sergeant in 3 Company, 7th Connecticut Regt (Company Commander Lt Nathan Hale) and could only help when given leave of absence.[9] It is not known who tended the farm; but it is hard to swallow the implication that David and Ezra had completed and tested the complex craft by 9 November 1775 when Dr Gale advised Silas Deane, representative to the Continental Congress:

> . . . by the time this reaches you the machine will be in the camp . . . [Bushnell] has conducted matters . . . with the greatest secrecy, both for the greatest safety of the navigator, and the greater astonishment against those to whom it is designed. . . . I have seen the machine while in embryo and every addition made to it fills me with fresh astonishment and surprise . . .[10]

Two weeks later, Gale wrote again to say that the 'machine' was still undergoing trials in the Connecticut River because the pump 'did not answer'. Gale reported yet another delay on 7 December: the foxfire, required for phosphorescent illumination of the instruments, which was derived from rotting wood, had been killed off by frost. Bushnell had already been 'detained near two months for want of money, and before he could obtain it the season was [too] far advanced.' Gale begged Deane not to think he had imposed upon him an idle story and asked that he 'inquire of Dr Franklin whether he knows of any kind of phosphorus which will give light in the dark and not consume the air . . . otherwise the execution must be omitted till next spring. . . . I am therefore requested to ask your strictest silence in that matter.' Gale sent a reminder a few weeks later on 1 February 1776, secretively concluding 'you will well understand my meaning, if I am not more explicit'; but the subject of his note would have been perfectly obvious to anybody who had wind of it.[11]

Gale had in fact particularized the 'Tortoise' (as he then called it) in his letter of 9 November to Deane following a visitation from Dr Franklin *en route* to Boston. Franklin had supposedly accompanied Gale to Ayers Point, the secluded building location on the Connecticut River close to Poverty Island where trials were said to be conducted. Franklin reportedly witnessed Ezra Bushnell diving the machine but left no record of his impressions. Gale's description of the craft has frequently been copied or paraphrased and sometimes altered:

The Body when standing upright in the position in which it is navigated, has the nearest resemblance to the two upper shells of a Tortoise joined together. In length, it doth not exceed 7½ feet from the stem to the higher part of the rudder: the height not exceeding 6 feet [scarcely like an upright coconut]. The person who navigates it enters at the top. It has a brass top or cover, which receives the

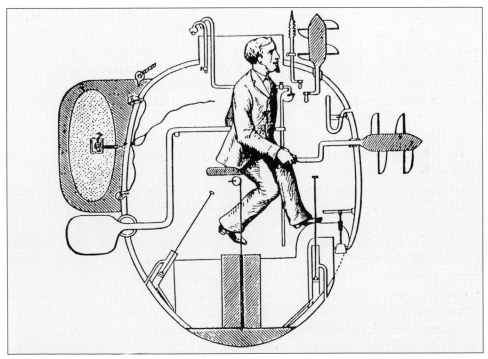

The imaginative and anachronistic sketch of The American Turtle *by Lt F.M. Barber USN in 1875 – a foundation of much mythology.*

Model of Turtle, *as popularly but impossibly supposed to be, following Barber's sketch, by Major M.C. Gray for the RN Submarine Museum.*

person's head as he sits on a seat, and is fastened on the inside by screws. In this brass head is fixed 6 glasses, viz. 2 before, 2 on each side, 1 behind, and 1 to look out upward. In the same brass head are fixed 2 brass tubes, to admit fresh air when requisite, and a ventilator at the side to free the Machine from air rendered unfit for respiration. On the inside is fixed a Barometer, by which he can tell the depth he is underwater; a Compass, by which he knows the course he steers. In the Barometer and on the needles of the Compass is fixed fox-fire ie wood that gives light in the dark. His ballast consists of about 900 wt. of lead which he carries at the bottom of the machine, part of which [200 lb] is so fixed as he can let run down to the bottom and serves as an anchor, by which he can ride *ad libitum*. He has a sounding lead fixed at the bow, by which he can take the depth of water under him; and to bring the machine into a perfect equilibrium with the water, he can admit so much water as is necessary, and has a forcing pump, by which he can free the Machine at his pleasure, and can rise above water, and again immerge, as occasion requires.

In the bow, he has a pair of oars, fixed like the two opposite arms of a windmill, with which he can row forward, and turning them the opposite way, row the machine backward; another pair fixed upon the same model with which he can row the machine round, either to the right or left; and a third, by which he can row the machine either up or down; all which are turned by foot, like a spinning wheel. The rudder by which he steers, he manages by hand, within board. All the shafts which pass through the machine are so curiously fixed as not to admit any water to incommode the machine. The magazine for powder is carried on the hinder part of the machine, without board, and so contrived that, when he comes under the side of the ship, he rubs down the side until he comes to the keel, and a hook so fixed as that when it touches the keel it raises a spring which frees the magazine from the machine, and fastens it to the side of the ship; at the same time, it draws a pin, which sets the watch-work a going which, at a given time, springs the lock and explosion ensues.

Three magazines are prepared; the first, the explosion takes place in twelve, the second in eight the third in six hours after being fixed to the ship. He proposes to fix these three before the first explosion takes place.[12]

Can this have been the work of two men, neither of them a shipwright, over less than seven months of intermittent working time using the tools of the period?

A tour of a small family boatyard on, say, a Greek island where electrical drills, circular saws and so forth are available should persuade even the most ardent Bushnell fan that David and Ezra simply could not have done the job with eighteenth-century tools on an isolated beach. Incidentally, what lifting gear was used for a boat that must have weighed about three-quarters of a ton? And how was it secured against the current in a deep enough part of the river for a test dive?

On 14 November 1775, the British Governor of New York, William Tryon, sarcastically informed Vice Adm Molineux Shuldham, Commander-in-Chief of the Royal Navy's North American Squadron: 'The great news of the day with us is now, to Destroy the Navy, a certain Mr Bushnell, has completed his Machine . . . you may expect to see the Ships in smoke.'[13] Undoubtedly Tryon had been apprised of Gale's letter dated 9 November; this was to be expected because the postmaster at Killingworth, Gale's home town, was a man named Sheader and a notorious Tory spy.[14] It begins to look as if Gale was intent on passing disinformation to the British: he must have been sorely irritated to hear (if he did hear) that he was not being taken seriously.

In June and July 1776 a large British fleet, under Vice-Adm Sir Richard 'Black Dick' Howe (1726–99),[15] flying his flag in the 64-gun HMS *Eagle*, anchored in the approaches to New York City. Twenty frigates and four hundred transports comprised the largest expeditionary force ever assembled by Great Britain: The Army C-in-C was Black Dick's younger brother Gen Sir William Howe (1729–1814).[16] British strategy aimed to possess New York, take command of the Hudson River, open communication with Canada and thus separate the eastern from the middle American states, enabling war to be carried into the interior.

George Washington had correctly anticipated the Howe brothers' intentions and transferred his headquarters from Boston (whence the British had withdrawn) to New York in April. There he could at last see his dentist whose surgery was four doors down from the theatre, towards St Paul's Church. Washington had suffered appallingly from toothache during the battles around Boston, and by now he retained but one tooth of his own – a pre-molar which lasted him, solitarily, till the age of sixty-four. For $15 a set, Mr Greenwood, dental practitioner, provided him with false teeth: an elk furnished the upper set, but the lower teeth were human. The dentures were connected and spring-loaded, like a rat-trap in reverse: positive effort was required to shut the mouth – hence the clenched expression on much of his portraiture.[17] Washington had a lot more on his mind than history relates.

Initial encounters with Sir William's force, moving northwards across Long Island, were disastrous. By the end of August, the weakened Colonial lines guarding the city were directly opposed by some 15,000 of the King's men. The Americans strung makeshift barriers across the waterways to prevent British ships sailing up the Hudson and East River on either side of Manhattan but no one thought they would delay ingress for long, and so it proved. The entire ragtag Colonial navy was no match for even a couple of British frigates; of the 28,000 patriot troops in the area, 10,000 were unfit for combat: disease was rife and desertion not uncommon. The Howes had between them 32,000 regular soldiers, 8,000 Hessian mercenaries and about 10,000 sailors.

It was the sort of desperate situation that the *American Turtle* was intended to remedy. Patriot morale was low: good news of any kind – the destruction of an enemy ship, for example – would be exceedingly welcome. And if a covert attack were to fail, mere rumours about an invisible sea-monster abroad in New York Harbor might deter Black Dick from coming any closer, and perhaps even frighten him away.

The Bushnells are said to have shipped the *Turtle* down Long Island Sound to the Colonial-held Battery on the southern tip of New York Island. The assigned target was the *Eagle*, believed to be anchored off Staten Island, four or five miles across the Bay, at the head of a line of transports. At this juncture, Ezra Bushnell, exclusively trained to pilot the submarine, succumbed to the prevalent fever. Thereupon 'a sergeant [Ezra Lee, 1749–1821] of a Connecticut regiment was selected for the business who, for want of time, could not be properly instructed.'[18]

At 11 p.m. on 6 September 1776 (to continue with the received version), Sergeant Lee lowered himself down into the *Turtle* to be towed by a whale-boat as close to the flagship as seemed prudent. According to his only surviving account (presented nearly forty years later), the tow-rope was then cast off and he, 'rowed about' for two-and-a-half hours until the ebb tide slackened, when he 'rowed under the stern of the ship, could see the men on the deck & hear them talk' before he 'shut down all doors', sank down, and 'came under the bottom of the ship'. But the woodscrew would not bite. He 'pulled along to try another place, but deviated a little one side and immediately rose with great velocity and came above the surface 2 or 3 feet between the ship and the daylight – then sunk again like a porpoise.'[19] With dawn approaching, Lee decided to call it a night. Bushnell complained (eleven years afterwards) that the Sergeant had probably struck an iron rudder-bar and that if he had but moved a few inches 'which he might have done without rowing [implying he was on the surface and could push with his hands], there is no doubt he might have found wood where he might have fixed the screw.'[20] Lee went on to say that he returned on the flood tide, but his compass failed and he 'was obliged to rise up every few minutes' to see if he was going the right way. Observing a boat from Governor's Island (then occupied by British troops) pulling towards him, he let loose the magazine which in due course exploded, exciting Gen Israel Putnam, watching from the Battery, to exclaim 'God curse 'em, that'll do it for them!'[21]

Sadly there are manifold objections to all this. First of all, the peculiar windmill-like 'oars', measuring 12 in by 4 in[22] could not have coped with a lengthy wandering, even tide-assisted, whether turned by hand (exhausting) or foot-pedalled, to say nothing of water entering through the shaft penetration, which had a close-fitting iron sleeve but no packing. The vertical oars were irrelevant because it is inconceivable that such a craft could hover: neutral buoyancy was not sustainable (as continually rediscovered over the next hundred years). Second, HMS *Eagle* was not at Staten Island. She was moored off Bedloes Island (1776 cartographer's spelling), close to where the Statue of Liberty now stands. To reach her, Lee would have had to progress a little across, rather than with, the tidal streams. In addition, discipline on board *Eagle* was enforced by floggings. Unambiguous orders for Marines keeping continuous watch around the ship were such that something scrabbling under the stern could not pass undetected.[23]

Three comprehensive official diaries were kept on board HMS *Eagle*: the Ship's Log written by Lt P. Browne; the Master's Log; and Capt Henry Duncan's *Journal of the Proceedings of His Majesty's Ship* EAGLE. There are references to sounds of cannon ashore, the activities of 'Flatt boats', flags of truce being sent to New York, parole signals, and minor ship movements. But nowhere is there any entry associated with a suspected attack on any vessel nor an unexplained explosion off Governor's Island. The noteworthy items in Browne's Log for 6/7 September were that Samuel Kingston, Seaman, was punished with twelve lashes for drunkenness at 5 p.m. and, at 1 a.m. on the following day, 'several muskets were fir'd at the Guard Boats'.[24]

Finally, even if Lee miraculously opened the Kingston valve for the right length of time to admit just enough water to dive the *Turtle*, then immediately pumped out exactly the amount necessary to achieve neutral buoyancy, then revolved the 'propellers' to position himself precisely under the target, and then tried to screw the auger into the oaken hull above, the law of equal and opposite reaction would merely push the submarine *down* while the woodscrew was pushing *up*. Result nothing! (The rounded hull would not have helped either, as Second World War midget submarine and human-torpedo operators became aware when attaching limpet mines.)

In any event, Adm Howe was not in the least deterred or frightened. On Sunday 15 September HMS *Renown*, *Repulse* and *Pearl* proceeded up-river past the Battery whose fire had little effect. Continual assertions, voiced as recently as 1998, to the effect that 'one submarine, with one magazine, crewed by one soldier actually forced a fleet of more than 200 ships to retreat several miles to a safe anchorage' are nonsense.[25] The other frequent canard is that Lee's auger would not penetrate *Eagle*'s copper sheathing; but the ship was not coppered until 1782.[26]

On 12 September Washington moved his headquarters to the heights of Harlem and British troops landed at Bloomingdale, only two miles from the American camp. The *Turtle* is said to have paddled off on two more missions from a new base at Fort Lee on the west side of the Hudson River, a little above Harlem, whither the craft had again been transported by schooner. Ezra Lee was apparently pilot for one attempt and Phineas Pratt (clockmaker) for the other.[27] Again, there were no results and no corroborative evidence.

By this time Bushnell was 'very unwell' and despairing of adequate assistance from the American Government. He also knew that operators for the *Turtle* needed more training than circumstances permitted (similar to the situation facing the German *Kleinkampfmittel-Verband* crews when attempting to sink units of the Normandy Invasion fleet in 1944). He 'therefore gave over the pursuit for that time, and waited for a more favourable opportunity, which never arrived'. Anyway, 'the enemy went up the [Hudson] river and pursued the boat which had the sub-marine vessel on board – and sunk it with their shot.'[28] No casualties were recorded and no remains of the *Turtle* were salvaged.

Bushnell now turned his attention to a deadly variation of the *Turtle*'s weapon system. His first device comprised a pair of magazines connected by a long length of rope supported by wooden floats at regular intervals. Each magazine was equipped with a spiked wheel which triggered the firing mechanism when, drifting downstream, the connecting rope caught on a ship's anchor cable and drew the magazines towards either side of the victim.[29]

The Connecticut Council of Safety thoroughly approved of floating mines when Bushnell presented his scheme on 23 April 1777. He was voted whatever assistance he required;[30] but an assault on HMS *Cerberus* off New London on the night of 13/14 August was frustrated. The buoyed rope was spotted by sailors in a small sailing boat recently captured by the British and now anchored up-river of the warship. The sailors thought they had found a fishing line and hauled it on board whereupon the magazine detonated, killing three men, blowing the other overboard and sinking the boat. Cdre Symons, on board *Cerberus*, was not much alarmed; but he remarked on Colonial 'villains' with 'singular ingenuity' for 'secret modes of mischief' and warned his ships to watch out for what he dubbed 'infernals'.[31]

The next attack was (literally) launched in the Delaware River upstream of Philadelphia, where a sizeable part of Howe's fleet was moored over Christmas 1777. By the New Year, Bushnell had assembled numerous pairs of floating mines consisting of small kegs with integral spring-locks which detonated instantly on contact with any object.[32]

Unfortunately the 'infernals' were let loose so far up-river, at Bordentown, that they took days to drift down on a sluggish winter current and many were held up by the ice which had already prompted most of the British ships to shift berth.

When kegs eventually started to appear, in daylight on Monday 5 January 1778, the crews of British vessels still at Philadelphia effectively tackled them with musket-fire. The ships suffered no damage, but the affair prompted Francis Hopkinson (a signatory to the Declaration of Independence) to write a ribald rhyme entitled *The Battle of the Kegs*. It ridiculed the British musketry; and Verse 9 took a personal shot at Gen Howe, who was enjoying an ongoing affair with the outstandingly beautiful Elizabeth Loring, wife of a prominent Boston Tory:

Sir William he, snug as a flea,
Lay all the time a-snoring,
Nor dreamed of harm, as he lay warm,
In bed with Mrs Loring.[33]

Hopkinson's PR exercise was about par for the Colonial course.

The 'Battle of the Kegs' concluded Bushnell's direct involvement with submarine and mine warfare, although his expertise in these fields was sought, and copied, elsewhere. Needful of a regular salary he joined the US Army Corps of Engineers (Sappers and Miners) and was commissioned with the rank of Captain-Lieutenant on 2 August 1779. When the fighting had finished he was mustered out of service in November 1783, accepting a commutation of five years' pay and 400 acres of land in lieu of half-pay for life.[34]

Soon after leaving the Army, Bushnell fell seriously ill. He never married, and the death of his close younger brother Ezra in 1786 doubtless affected him deeply. News of David thereafter is spasmodic and, for long periods, entirely lacking.

On 17 July 1785, Thomas Jefferson, US Minister in Paris from 1785 to 1789, asked Washington (in a postscript to his regular despatch):

The USN (although having excellent 'Swimmer Delivery Vehicles' for SEAL units) has only once seriously attempted a midget submarine in the Turtle *tradition; and unfortunately X-1, launched at Oyster Bay, Long Island, on 7 September 1955 with a sophisticated propulsion plant, was a failure. Richard Boyle, then her Engineer and Officer-in-Charge (now submarine historian), very sensibly concluded '. . . high concentration unstabilized hydrogen peroxide has no place in a fighting ship.' David Bushnell would surely have sympathized. (US Navy)*

. . . be so kind as to communicate to me what you can recollect of Bushnell's experiments in submarine navigation during the late war, and whether you think his method capable of being used successfully for the destruction of vessels of war. *As not having been actually used for this purpose by us, who were so peculiarly in want of such an agent, seems to prove it did not promise success.* [emphasis added][31]

Washington responded on 26 September:

. . . I am sorry that I cannot give you full information respecting Bushnell's project for the destruction of ships. No interesting experiments having been made, and my memory being bad, I may in some measure be mistaken in what I am about to relate. Bushnell is a man of great mechanical powers, fertile in inventions, and master in execution. He came to me in 1776, recommended by Governor Trumbull [of Connecticut] and other respectable characters who were converts to his plans. Although I wanted faith myself, I furnished him myself with money and other aids to carry his plan into execution. He labored for some time ineffectually; and although the advocates for his schemes continued sanguine, he never did succeed. One accident or another always intervened. I then thought, and still think, that it was an effort of genius,[36] but that too many things were necessary to be combined to expect much from the issue against an enemy who are always upon guard.

That he had a machine so contrived as to carry him underwater at any depth he chose, and for a considerable time and distance, with an appendage charged with powder, which he could fasten to a ship and give fire to it in time sufficient for his returning, and by means thereof destroy it, are facts, I believe, which admit of little doubt. But then, where it was to operate against an enemy, it was no easy matter to get a person hardy enough to encounter the variety of dangers to which he would be exposed; first, from the novelty; second, from the difficulty of conducting the machine, and governing it underwater, on account of the current; and thirdly, from the consequent uncertainty of hitting the object devoted to destruction, without rising frequently above water for fresh observations, which when near the vessel, would expose the adventurer to discovery and to almost certain death. To these causes I have always ascribed the failure of his plan, as he wanted nothing that I could furnish to insure the success of it . . .[37]

This reply was obviously worded with care and loyal to all concerned. But a lapse of nine years was enough by itself to excuse an imprecise recollection, and Washington had, after all, been mightily distracted, not least by elk-tooth dentistry. Nevertheless, if the *Turtle* had actually been able to dive into the sea it would have been one of the most exciting developments of the century and quite unforgettable.

The French were very interested in submarine navigation, and were doubtless stimulated thereto by Benjamin Franklin who sailed for France, soon after signing the Declaration of Independence, to be an intractably unfashionable US Minister there until 1785. He was joined in Paris by Silas Deane who had also been closely involved with Bushnell's ambitions at the outset;[38] it is reasonable to suppose that so-called submarine secrets were slid across to the French in part exchange for the physical and financial assistance to America's cause which Franklin was negotiating. There was certainly no call to underrate Bushnell's inventive powers, and it could well be that in the course of time hyperbole proved a profound embarrassment to the inventor. However, Franklin achieved his objective and France allied herself with America in the spring of 1778: it is debatable whether the United States could have emerged victorious, five years later, without the Bourbon navy's help.

On 13 October 1787, David Bushnell himself wrote to Jefferson, explaining that illness had prevented him from corresponding earlier and emphasizing that he had 'carefully concealed' his 'Principles & Experiments, as much as the nature allowed, from all but my chosen Friends. . . .'[39]; but he enclosed details of the *Turtle* and its armament which repeated, pretty much parrot fashion, the 'particular description' which James Thacher had 'obtained' for his *Military Journal* dated 10 February 1778.[40] Bushnell was not about to deviate from the script; but, fearing that the package to France might be lost in transit, he sent a duplicate of the details to President Ezra Styles at Yale with a covering letter saying, *inter alia*: '. . . I could wish that what I have written should not come to the knowledge of the public, for the same reason, as I have written to the Governor [Jefferson], that I had ever wished to be silent upon the subject. . . .'[41]

It is possible that Bushnell was next lured to Paris for a while under an assumed name, but the evidence is tenuous.[42] His next accredited appearance was in the late 1780s at the Georgia home of Abraham Baldwin, Class of '72 at Yale. Here he became known as Dr David Bush, finally settling at Warrenton in December 1803. The town annals showed him as a practising physician in 1818 although nothing is known about his credentials. Early in 1826 he died, leaving an estate valued at around $10,000 (around $250,000 today), at which time it became known that the reticent Dr David Bush of Georgia and David Bushnell of Connecticut were one and the same person.[43]

Why the move South? Why the false name? The most rational supposition, lacking any better, was that Bushnell became sick and tired of the entire *Turtle* episode, knowing full well that it was largely fraudulent – albeit concocted for patriotic reasons. Alternatively, it may be that post-war administrations under George Washington until 1797, John Adams (1797–1801) and Thomas Jefferson (1801–9) preferred Bushnell to disappear with his secrets, and paid him to do so.

But was there not *something* real about the story? It would have been unnecessary to introduce Ezra Lee into the tale unless there was a degree of truth in it. Certainly David Bushnell demonstrated, possibly before anybody else, that an explosion underwater is more powerful than in air; and he invented ways of 'annoying' an enemy thereby. And he devised plans for a 'sub-marine' vessel that embodied some good ideas, although the 'propeller' concept was not original. (It had been mooted by Robert Hook (1653–1703) among others.) He might have put together the rudiments of a submersible (perhaps by upturning one cockleshell boat on another) even if the product was never complete as advertised.

Whatever, it is at least conceivable that Sgt Lee was put into some kind of skiff with muffled sculls and sent out to do what damage he could. The powder charge, line and auger would have been concealed beneath tarpaulins together with a uniform jacket – for he could not risk being executed as a spy like Nathan Hale. The tide could take him down to a worthwhile target off Staten Island – not, of course, HMS *Eagle*, but one of the transports guarded by no more than a couple of ship-keepers.

Lee's account, dated 20 February 1815, smacks of an honest man trying not to spoil the game nearly forty years after the event.[44] Given generous latitude, his version can just be reconciled with working his way under, say, the stern overhang of a largish vessel, getting temporarily snagged, and making off before he was caught.

David Bushnell's widely publicized 'effort of genius' inspired any number of followers. The pity is that they believed Bushnell's tale, for their own endeavours were misled thereby.

CHAPTER 7

Monsieur Fulton and Mr Francis

1783 Manned flight in a French balloon
1792–99 French Revolutionary Wars
1799–1815 Napoleonic Wars

Robert Fulton (1765–1815), albeit far from gullible, was among the first to take Bushnell's legendary submarine legacy on board. He was born in Lancaster County, Pennsylvania on 14 November 1765, to a Scottish-Irish family farming 394 acres at Little Britain even less successfully than the Bushnells cultivated their hillside in Connecticut: in the winter of 1791–2 the Fultons had to sell up and move back to their origins in the city of Lancaster where Robert's father died soon afterwards.

With scant money at home to support three sisters and a young brother besides himself, young Robert went to Philadelphia where he obtained a precarious living, first as a jeweller's apprentice and then as a landscape and miniature portrait painter. When, in 1786, he had saved enough for the fare, he emigrated to England to study art under Benjamin West with whom he stayed until 1793. A personable, persuasive young man with more than his half-share of Irish charm, not to say blarney, Robert made friends easily. He was soon engaged in canal schemes for improving inland navigation, inventing and patenting devices for flax-spinning, sawing marble, twisting ropes and dredging. Ultimately, his fame was to rest on the steamboat which he made a commercial success in America, but he always said that his submarine proposals were more important.

Fulton was undeniably brilliant. He was also bumptious and egocentric; but it was his dramatic shifts of allegiance as a would-be arms supplier – to France, to Great Britain, to the United States – that earned him odium.

He professed paramount concern for freedom of the seas and free trade, arguing that the world's problems were caused by armies and navies, especially the latter which demanded heavy taxation and enforced recruitment.[1] The thing to do, he said, was to get rid of navies altogether. The great attraction of this policy was that it would save America, where ships were decidedly in short supply, from having to pay for a proper fleet. Equally it would save France from having to face a persistently more powerful Royal Navy. To achieve these desirable ends, Fulton was devoting his whole attention to finding out 'means of destroying such [naval] engines of oppression.'[2]

A worldly-wise observer might suspect that Robert Fulton had a hidden agenda when advocating international disarmament on the one hand, while offering for sale (to successively opposing markets) 'plunging boats' and 'torpedoes' on the other. But despite the caveat about his motives (which, after all, only anticipated twentieth-century arms dealers), his resourcefulness and sheer engineering ability were exceptional. So were his selling techniques. But it was artistic merit that first led him to the world of underwater warfare.

In 1797, with France governed by the Directory after the Revolution, Fulton was invited to paint a colossal panorama of Paris. Here, his thoughts continually returning to maritime affairs, he witnessed the effects of the Royal Navy's blockading strategy which the French Navy was unable to break. Fulton thought he might be able to help.

He was familiar with Bushnell's ideas which had been proclaimed in Paris by Franklin and Jefferson. It is likely, too, that Bushnell's former chief in the Engineer Corps, Brig Louis Duportail (imported from France in 1778 to improve Colonial engineering skills) took back details of Colonial weapon systems when he returned to France. Another American connection was the notorious land speculator and businessman Joel Barlow with whom Fulton lodged in Paris: Barlow was the brother-in-law of Abraham Baldwin who first sheltered Bushnell in Georgia. In other words, Fulton had a head-start when turning his mind to covert warfare on behalf of the French Navy.

His first device for attaining freedom of the seas was a self-propelled explosive 'carcass'[3] or 'submarine bomb' built with Barlow's help. It failed to attract backers, but on 13 December 1797 he wrote to the governing Directory of the First Republic:

Citizen Directors,
Having taken great interest in all that would diminish the power of the English Fleet, I have planned the construction of a mechanical engine, in which I have the greatest confidence, for the annihilation of this Navy. . . . The grandeur of the project has excited in me an ardor to share in a demonstration of this engine. To this end, in order to save you more trouble, I have formed a Company which will undertake the expense and carry out the work on the following terms . . . .

His terms were steep. The French Government would have to pay the Company of the 'Nautulus' (as he spelled the submarine he proposed) 4,000 francs per gun for every English ship above forty guns destroyed and 2,000 francs per gun for every ship below forty guns. English merchant ships or war vessels captured were to become the property of the Company 'without any hindrance on the part of the government agents to prove they are English property'.[4]

The implied success rate is reminiscent of De Son, and, in the event, *Nautilus* achieved no more sinkings than the clockwork craft of 1653; but at least Fulton's boat was capable of (very slow) movement under its own power.

As a sop to patriotism, Fulton stipulated that the *Nautilus* (or anything similar) would not be used by the French against the United States 'or, at least, the Americans must use them first against France before this stipulation is annulled'.

He was well aware that 'in the case of . . . contrivances . . . which are considered to be against the Laws of War, the people who take part in these enterprises are hung. . . .' He therefore demanded a naval commission for all crew members so that, if taken prisoner during 'one of the Company's expeditions', they would be treated properly as prisoners of war. He concluded in his usual vein of trusting that 'this engine will give liberty of the sea' and that 'the Terror [British fleet] will be scattered before the invasion of England, and the boat can be employed in assisting this invasion'.[5]

The French Directory was inclined to accept the proposition in principle, although the rewards were drastically reduced and a commission to the submarine's crew was briskly refused: such a method of waging war at sea was unworthy of French uniform.

Then, on 5 February 1798, the project was turned down altogether after the Minister of Marine, Adm Pléville le Pelley (1726–1805) declared that his conscience would not allow him recourse to so terrible a weapon. However, le Pelley was replaced on 28 April by the younger Adm Eustache Bruix (1759–1805) who reopened the matter and appointed an advisory commission which included the naval architect Pierre Forfait. Forfait, who had himself suggested a submarine for like purposes in 1783, championed Fulton but the scheme was rebuffed because it too openly implied French naval inferiority. However, when Citoyen Marc-Antoine Bourdon de Vatry (1761–1828) succeeded Bruix on 1 July 1799, Fulton submitted a fresh proposal.[6] On 9 November, Napoleon seized power as First Consul and Forfait was promoted to Minister: no obstacles now remained.

The copper-skinned *Nautilus*, 6.48 m long and 1.94 m broad, was laid down in the Perrier Brothers' works on the River Seine at Paris. The firm would soon be associated with steam navigation; but the submersible was propelled by a two-bladed hand-cranked propeller (similar to Bushnell's 'oar', but Fulton called it his 'flyer'). A collapsible sailing rig was provided for use on the surface.

Launched in May 1800, *Nautilus* made her debut in the Seine off the Hôtel des Invalides. Fulton, like Drebbel, used the current to advantage so that, running awash, he was able to make it appear that the submarine was quite fast. Onlookers crowding the banks cheered wildly although *Nautilus* never submerged

The Nautilus, *as envisaged by Wills for a cigarette card.* (Author's collection)

fully. However, Fulton may have managed to dip momentarily, having judiciously flooded his three ballast tanks to a pre-determined level. The 30-degree up, level, or 30-degree down horizontal rudders aft (an undeniable first) cannot have had much effect when maximum speed through the water was no more than one or two knots – for so long as musclemen Sergeant and Fleuret held out.[7] Monsieur St Aubin, a Member of the *Tribunale*, informed the *Naval Chronicle* that the boat 'made way at the rate of half-a-league an hour' (a league equalled three miles) – which sounds reasonable – and that, during later experiments at Le Havre, 'Mr Fulton not only remained a whole hour underwater with three of his companions, but held his boat parallel to the horizon at any given depth' – which sounds entirely wrong. The spin-doctoring St Aubin went on to wonder:

> Who can see all the circumstances of this discovery or the improvements of which it is susceptible? Mr Fulton has already added to his boat a machine, by means of which he blew up a large boat in the port of Brest; and if by future experiments, the same effect could be produced on frigates or ships of the line, what will become of maritime wars . . . ?[8]

Trials at Brest were more hazardous than they had been in the Seine, where the depth of water had been at most 25 ft. Fulton claimed his boat went down to between 25 and 30 ft and held her depth. Corroboration is lacking and he could not possibly have kept control submerged for any meaningful length of time. He himself confessed that *Nautilus* was 'extremely difficult to manage'. The weapon system was never demonstrated: this (cribbed from Bushnell, as were other features) comprised a copper magazine attached to a barbed spike which could be driven home from inside the helmet-shaped conning tower which had thick glass scuttles at the top and sides. Estimated safe depth was 9 m (30 ft); and on 3 June 1801, at Brest, the boat was bottomed at 7 m (23 ft) and remained one hour, which is believable. Then the crew pumped out water to bring her up again. The money actually paid to Fulton is uncertain although sums of 10,000 and 6,000 francs (from Forfait) have been mentioned against building costs reckoned at 28,000 francs.[9]

Nautilus ventured to sea several times from 12 to 15 September 1800 in the area between Le Havre and La Hogue – all credit to Fulton for taking her so far. But the submarine was too slow to approach a target, and Capt Samuel Linzee of the potential British victim *L'Oiseau*, on patrol off Le Havre, was warned by an Admiralty message on 14 September.[10]

Fulton changed his plan of attack from spike and magazine to towed 'carcass' (knowing that he would never drive the spike into a moving vessel), but this unilateral alteration upset Forfait, as did the submarine's continuing inability to conclude an attack. When Forfait was replaced by the hardnosed, seamanlike Adm Decrès on 1 October 1801, the date on which preliminaries for a short-lived peace were agreed with England, Napoleon's advisers lost interest in the submarine. Fulton had, in fact, already sold it for scrap.

So much for Fulton's own faith in *Nautilus*! As for the French Navy, Decrès finally dismissed the inventor with: 'Go, Sir, your invention may be good for Algerians or pirates, but be advised that France has not yet abandoned the oceans.'[11] Fulton next tried (unsuccessfully) to sell his plans to the Dutch; but, after due consideration unimpeded by probity, he decided that England was a better bet.

Receiving his *congé* from Paris in a letter, dated 5 February 1804, which confirmed that all his propositions were rejected, he left the French capital on 29 April and arrived unabashed in London on 19 May.[12] Fulton was nothing if not adaptable – like the good Bishop Wilkins – but he continued to preach freedom of the seas as his sole interest.

The British Intelligence Service was efficient; and, although there was scepticism about *Nautilus*, there was markedly less doubt about explosions beneath the surface. It was known that one of Fulton's 'torpedoes' had been towed against a shallop, which sank immediately. (Fulton was the first to adopt the word 'torpedo', taken from the North Atlantic species of ray *Torpedo nobiliana* which produces strong shocks to stun its prey.) Mr Francis (Fulton's alias in England) was worth wooing.

There was some naval huffing and puffing about ignoble principles; but British politicians were by no means averse to using cheap weapons which could destroy enemy ships, including invasion barges, without imperilling significant elements of the Fleet. Economy was an important factor: Prime Minister Pitt had been forced to introduce Income Tax in 1798 to finance the war, and it was not popular at 2 shillings in the pound on incomes above £60 per annum.

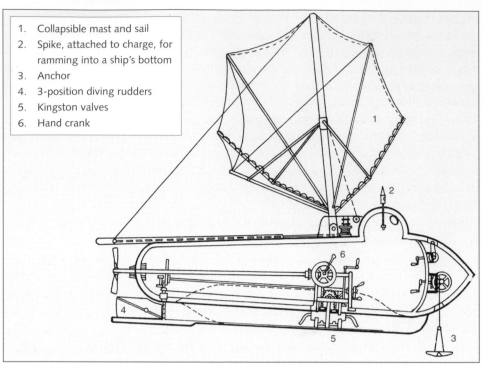

1. Collapsible mast and sail
2. Spike, attached to charge, for
   ramming into a ship's bottom
3. Anchor
4. 3-position diving rudders
5. Kingston valves
6. Hand crank

Fulton's Nautilus, *1801; length 6.5m, max beam 2.1m.*

There was also a strategic reason for adopting irregular weaponry. Adm Horatio Nelson, no less, had been charged with defeating French invasion plans in the summer of 1801. His hope was to encounter Bonaparte at sea and make him 'feel the bottom of the Goodwins'; but in the event he had to be content with bombarding Boulogne for sixteen hours on 4 August. He returned, with a force of fifty-seven boats, eleven nights later, with the object of capturing the invasion barges assembled at Boulogne and towing them back to England. French shore batteries and gunboats moored off the port, together with strong tidal streams inshore, defeated the noble admiral's purpose. Nelson uncharacteristically comforted himself by concluding that natural conditions in the Channel were so adverse that a crossing and landing by French invasion craft would be impractical in any case; but Parliament's fears were not eased. Pitt turned to Fulton.

A Commission duly debated Fulton's 'Nautilus' plan which was paralleled by a suggested one-man submersible, only 9 ft long, which he named 'The Messenger'. The larger craft would be 35 ft long, 10 ft wide and 8 ft deep, capable of accommodating a crew of six for twenty days at sea. It could, the American added, anchor while submerged.

Fulton's designs did not impress. Before a verdict was announced he learned of the Commission's unfavourable reaction and wrote directly to William Pitt: '. . .

Robert Fulton, known by the name of Francis, Author of Submarine Navigation
. . . I beg 20 minuets [*sic*] conversation with you as soon as possible.'[13] Pitt invited
Fulton and the Commission's Chairman to breakfast at his country house and
here, on 20 July 1804, a contract was signed with Fulton who would receive £200
a month for explaining how to attack an enemy fleet with 'submarine Bombs' and
supervising consequent operations. He would also be paid up to £7,000 for his
'mechanical preparations'. The Royal Dockyards and Arsenals would provide
materials; and the Government would pay £40,000 for every decked French
vessel sunk.[14]

On 2 October 1804, Adm Keith, flying his flag in HMS *Monarch* and with Mr
Francis on board, led an expedition to Boulogne where, ironically, Adm Bruix was
in command of the invasion fleet. Although historians have referred to Fulton's
torpedo-mines as catamarans, they were no more than casks in pairs connected by
a rope – the Battle of the Kegs restaged.

The operation commenced at 9.15 p.m. and lasted seven hours. Clockwork
delay mechanisms were set for ten minutes, so the point of release was about 100
yards to seaward on the flood tide. Most of the connected mines, which the
French christened 'fireship chains', were driven onshore where they either
exploded or fell into inquiring enemy hands.[15] Only one French ship was lost.
When the attackers started to withdraw, at 4.15 the following morning, an officer
from HMS *Leopard* confided his hope to 'return the remainder of the machines to
store from which, as a true friend of the service, I heartily wish we had never
taken them.'[16]

The results were greeted in London with more warmth than they deserved, and
the performance was repeated a year later on 1 October 1805. Nothing significant
was achieved: Napoleon described the raid as 'breaking the windows of the good
citizens of Boulogne with English guineas'.[17]

Fulton hastened to restore his reputation. On the afternoon of 15 October
1805, he organized a test against the redundant brig *Dorothea* anchored in
Walmer Roads not far from Pitt's country estate near Dover. Naval officers were
scornful: a Capt Kingston vowed that if a 'torpedo' were set off under his cabin
while he was at dinner he would not be worried. None the less the brig was
deserted by the afternoon of 15 October when a couple of eight-man galleys
snared two pairs of mines across the anchor cable. Calculating that previous
'torpedoes' had been too heavy and hence too deep to rub against a hull (which of
course curved inwards towards the keel), Fulton arranged for these mines to be
held up by buoyant cork. The resulting explosion broke the vessel in half: it
disappeared in less than a minute.

Fulton was ecstatic and an unusually prompt Chancellor of the Exchequer
agreed to advance him £10,000, one-quarter the sum promised for complete proof
of success. The Admiralty immediately planned to send 'Mr Francis' to assault
French and Spanish warships gathered at Cadiz; and on 27 October Lord

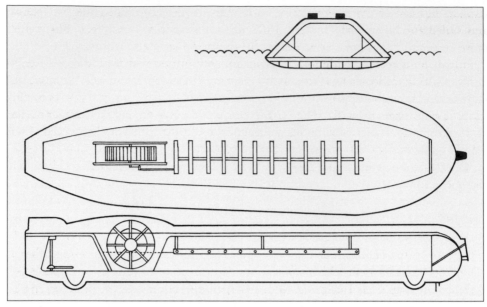

Fulton's unfulfilled 85ft semi-submersible bullet-proof Mute, *1814, with handcranks linked to a paddlewheel and seven underwater guns, intended for silently sneaking up to the King's ships on Lake Ontario.*

Castlereigh, Secretary for War, wrote to tell Adm Lord Nelson of the intention.[18] But Nelson had already done what was necessary, and lost his life, at the Battle of Trafalgar six days earlier.

There was therefore no more need for Fulton's type of warfare, which British sea-officers professed to abhor as unmanly and assassin-like, comparing it to the midnight attack of a burglar. Vice Adm Sir George Berkeley thought that 'The Author or rather projector . . . tried his hand upon John Bull's credulity . . . and after a very expensive Trial the scheme was scouted not perhaps so much from its Failure as from the Baseness & Cowardice of this species of Warfare.'[19] Anonymous 'F.F.F.' writing to the *Naval Chronicle* agreed (at length): 'How base! How horrible! . . . when we see men openly stooping from their lofty station to superintend the construction of such detestable machines, what are we to infer . . . ?'[20]

More to the point Adm Lord St Vincent told Fulton to his face that 'Pitt was the greatest fool that ever existed to encourage a mode of warfare which those who commanded the seas did not want, and which, if successful, would deprive them of it.'[21]

When Fulton perceived, after Trafalgar, that his chances in England were at an end he endeavoured, fruitlessly, to extract a massive sum from the Treasury, primarily, as he put it, to ensure that he 'would remain tranquil', meaning that he would not sell his 'torpedoes' elsewhere.[22] In November 1806, with a severely reduced but not unfair settlement in hand, Mr Francis reverted to Robert Fulton and sailed for New York. In July 1807 he conducted, in New York Bay, three more demonstrations (two of which failed) similar to the *Dorothea* trial.

Fulton badgered President Jefferson and recommended that the US Navy develop his 'torpedo' tactics with weapons that he had improved in various ways. Jefferson, strongly opposed to the expense of a large navy, was broadly supportive: he had been alarmed by the encounter between USS *Chesapeake* and HMS *Leopard* off Virginia on 22 June (whereat the American ship acceded to Adm Berkeley's demand to return British deserters) and feared a blockade, or even an attack, against ships in Hampton Roads. The President wrote (spelling 'as was') on 16 August:

Sir,

Your letter of July 28 . . . it has not been sooner in my power to acknolege it. I consider your torpedoes as very valuable means of defence of harbors, & have not doubt that we should adopt them to a considerable degree. Not that I go the whole length (as I believe you do) of considering them as solely to be relied on . . . If, indeed, the mode of attaching them to the cable of a ship may be the only one proposed, modes of prevention cannot be difficult. But I have ever looked to the submarine boat as most to be depended on for attaching them, & tho' I see no mention of it in your letter, or your publications, I am in hopes it is not abandoned as impracticable. I should wish to see a corps of young men trained to this service. It would belong to the engineers if at land, but being nautical, I suppose we must have a corps of naval engineers, to practise & use them . . .

I salute you with great respect & esteem.[23]

In 1810 Fulton was permitted to test his latest 'torpedoes' against the US Frigate *Argus* whose captain, Cdre Rogers, protected his vessel so comprehensively that the assaults were wholly defeated. Bushnell-type weapons were employed without results during the War of 1812 although an attempt to pin one on HMS *Ramillies* off New London irritated the late Lord Nelson's friend Capt Hardy.

Meanwhile Jefferson's hopes for Fulton's submarine boat were in vain. It had indeed been abandoned as impracticable; and unconsummated plans for the semi-submerged armoured gunship *Mute*, formulated in 1814, bore no relation to a true submarine. Fulton's story had much in common with David Bushnell's, together with the fulsome hype that sent false signals to successors.

CHAPTER 8

On His Majesty's Secret Service

1801 Trevithick's steam locomotive
1807 Fulton's paddle-steamer
1815 Battle of Waterloo (18 June)

Robert Fulton attracted influential persons while in England, but they were not all in the upper or middle classes: one was in a class of his own. Tom Johnson (or Johnstone or Johnston) (1772–1839) aka 'The Famous Smuggler' was a Channel pilot and a spy as well as the designer of at least one submarine which had characteristics explained to him by Fulton.

Tom was the son of a Hampshire fisherman-cum-smuggler: he went to sea at the age of nine. His early life is recorded only in *The Historical Gallery of Criminal Portraitures*;[1] this somewhat inhibits a ready belief in doings which in any case are blurred by his mischievous sense of humour and a gift for mimicry. Nevertheless, the noted biographer Tom Pocock trusts 'it is possible to put together a life story that is maybe somewhere near the truth and is certainly exciting.'[2]

So, with due caution, we find Tom, at the age of twenty-one, a tall handsome man with blue eyes and a mop of dark hair, joining the crew of the privateer *Three Friends* at Gosport, Hampshire in 1793. Essentially, privateering was legalized piracy and war with Revolutionary France was offering splendid opportunities for little ships working 'on the account' (a euphemism for piracy) while nominally on Government service in the Channel. Unfortunately the *Three Friends* was captured by the French and Tom, young though he was, was immediately recognized as a prominent smuggler – one of several supplying brandy to English country gentlemen in exchange for gold which in turn paid for French army boots and other military necessities. Smugglers were inherently trustworthy, so the French authorities had no hesitation in asking Johnson to spy for them. There are two versions of his response. One is: 'A smuggler I am, a traitor I am not!' and the other has him accepting the offer but reporting it to the English Admiralty and becoming a double agent. Either way his value to France as a source of gold would have ensured quick release.

He now took up Channel pilotage professionally, although this was not entirely compatible with smuggling and espionage. He was repeatedly in trouble of one kind or another, made worse by debts resulting from an affair with 'a wild-natured young redhead married to a 60-year-old colonel and yearning for excitement' living in Berkeley Square.[3] He was confined in the New and Fleet Prisons for debt but escaped from the latter to take refuge in France where he first met Fulton. Meanwhile, wartime travel between France and England was not difficult for a smuggler who knew the way.

Tom may have helped to pilot British expeditions to Boulogne in 1804 and 1805 (see Chapter 7), and a similar pass made at Calais in 1804;[4] he was pardoned for any outstanding transgressions after piloting British landing craft to Walcheren in 1809. He was also at sea off Brest for some mysterious reason in 1806: Adm Lord St Vincent complained that: 'The vigilance of the enemy alone prevented Tom Johnstone from doing what he professed.'[5] Then, despite pride in his title of 'The Famous Smuggler' along the south coast of England, he promised to mend his ways and was awarded command of the Revenue cutter *Fox*. Temptations to smuggle abounded when a small vessel could charge £30,000 (about £510,000 today – inflation was rampant during the Revolutionary and Napoleonic Wars) to bring a cargo from Calais to London in 1801;[6] and there was constant illicit (or discreetly ignored) trade and passenger traffic between England and the Continent during the Wars.

In 1812, the Famous Reformed Smuggler demonstrated a clockwork model of a submarine and (reportedly) the Cabinet offered him £100,000 if he could construct

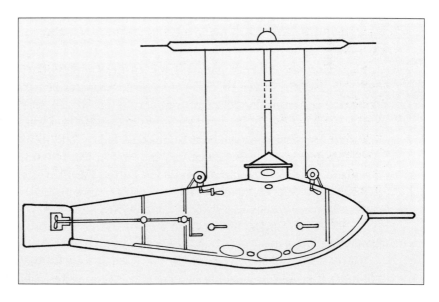

Monsieur Castera, a potential rival to Johnson in 1810, proposed this submarine suspended from a float with breathing tube thereto, drop weights for even more safety, a horizontal rudder forward, and leather sleeves in its lower part for its operator to work with infernal machines.

the real thing '. . . capable of being steered, elevated and depressed at pleasure underwater, and at the same time affix the torpedo on bottoms of ships'.[7] Civil engineers in High Holborn undertook to build the boat at Wallingford on the Thames, in sheet iron, 'her figure that of a salmon swimming, her length about 20 ft; and her space in the inner chamber about 6 ft sq. . . . formed of cork and wood'.[8]

By 1813, Johnson was moving in high society; and in October, having been granted Letters of Security from the Admiralty, the Army and the Home Office, following an interview with the Duke of York, Army C-in-C, he became formally employed 'on His Majesty's Secret Service on submarine, and other useful experiments by Order'.[9] The country was then at war with the United States (until 1814) where Fulton was marketing torpedo warfare, as well as with France (until 1815) where native inventors had been hard at work regardless of the American's activities. The Army's chief, ultimately responsible for defence, doubtless wanted to determine how effective a submarine might be and, if necessary, find a countermeasure – hence the welcome to Tom's submarine boat. But in July 1815, at peace with America and a month after Waterloo, the severely practical (not to say cash-strapped) Lordships of the Admiralty 'could not agree with the proposal' and 'they would not give Mr Johnson any further trouble upon the business'. He was reminded that he had 'no authority from their Lordships for carrying out experiments . . . or for incurring any expense thereon'.[10]

Their Lordships were too late. The boat was 'ready for experiment' that very month; and Tom's notification to the effect, coupled with a request for £20,000 down payment, had prompted the Admiralty's niggardly reaction.[11] In law, Tom had a case, arising from employment (at the Army's initiative) on His Majesty's Secret Service. Very likely the Navy assumed the Army would meet the costs, and vice versa. But it was indisputably a maritime matter, and the Admiralty eventually paid the bare, indeed close-shaven, costs of £4,735 11s 6d – a far cry from the £100,000 Tom had asked for – and not until two months after a committee had examined the boat in January 1820.[12]

Like *Nautilus*, the craft had sails for surface running, but rather than a 'flyer' propeller she was driven by oars submerged. Air pipes penetrated a wrought-iron carapace, optimistically believed to be 'proof against 12-pounders at point-blank range', which strongly implies that Johnson harked back to Drebbel and had no intention of submerging the boat completely. Fulton had probably tipped Johnson the wink that semi-submergence was the best he could bank on. However, Tom installed cylinders of compressed air (as Fulton had) sufficient for two men for twelve hours while the hatch was shut.[13]

The weapon system comprised a gunpowder coffer which could be nailed to a target's bottom (copying Bushnell and Fulton) but the boxed charge could alternately be mounted on a projecting spar – another forerunner of the spar torpedo.

It was put about that trials run in the Thames were so successful that (echoing Fulton) 'there may reasonably be expected a final termination of naval combats

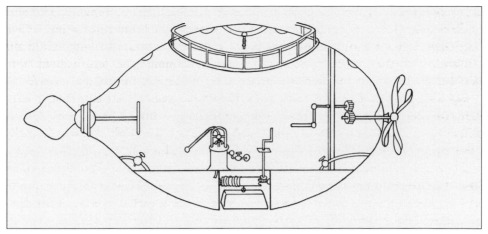

Submarine dreamed up in 1854 by a young convict in Ajaccio prison, doubtless inspired by Fulton, Johnson et al., but with a different kind of recessed anchor and a propeller forward.

between fleets of men-of-war and frigates, for no vessel can be secured by any vigilance which lies afloat in any water, against sub-marine assaults'.[14] Naturally, French agents made a bid for the boat, and this came to the ears of the Under-Secretary of State, Mr Becket: Johnson was arrested but released after questioning. There was American interest as well: John Quincy Adams, US Minister in London 1815–17 (and sixth President 1825–29) was purportedly asked how such a mode of warfare could even be considered. Adams defended the use of submarines and reminded his questioner about 'the Congreve rockets, fired from a British fleet into a crowded and almost defenceless metropolis' (Copenhagen in 1806) and observed that the more destructive the instruments, the shorter the wars. He went on to anticipate, rather bleakly, that whenever the Republic of the United States and the Monarchy of Great Britain should be next at war 'this tremendous instrument of destruction, as well as steam batteries [cannon mounted on steam-propelled vessels] would be brought into action'.[15]

Comparable sentiments had been evident in France for a couple of decades and, besides sheer dreamers, there were more than a dozen serious would-be submariners busy with their schemes in Europe, mostly in France, around the time of Fulton and Johnson. None was successful, but the brothers Coëssin deserve a mention for their *Nautile* of 1809 with hydroplanes forward and aft – an advantage for control which the brothers correctly appreciated although they could not give their boat enough speed for the planes to be effective.[16] Frankly, the Coëssins produced a notably better design, for a real submarine, than either Fulton or Johnson.

It is not clear what happened to Johnson's boat but one reputable historian believed that the Admiralty did witness trials;[17] and others aver that a test of the 'coffer' charge was involved:

. . . the boat . . . got foul, while submerged [awash] with a ship's cable, and stuck fast. [Johnson] said to his assistant: 'we have but two minutes and a half to live, lest we can clear of that cable.' The assistant, who had only been married for a few days, started to sob, crying out piteously, 'Poor Nancy! Poor Nancy!' To which Johnson's response was 'What good are these jeremiads? Take off your shirt and get ready to block our hawsepipe!' Then, taking an axe, he cut their own cable and set the submarine free.

They did get clear, 'owing to Johnson's coolness and presence of mind'.[18]

The incident sounds like one of several tall stories surrounding Johnson but, in light of the Admiralty's grudging financial obligations towards the Famous Smuggler, and the unavoidable secretiveness in dealing with a double-agent, it is quite possible that one or more Navy-sanctioned trials did take place. On the other hand, rumours that Tom built a submarine for the King of Denmark and another to salvage a treasure ship wrecked in the Caribbean, and that in the spring of 1822 he took a submarine built for Spain down the Thames to Blackwall with the ultimate intention of helping to lift the blockade of Cadiz, must be taken with a spoonful of sea-salt.

It was also said that in 1820 Johnson was offered £40,000 for a submarine and a still greater sum for success if he succeeded in rescuing Napoleon from his rocky prison on St Helena in the South Atlantic 4,000 miles from England.[19] The plan envisaged sailing a 100-ft submersible to within a few miles of the island coastline, evading the loose cordon of British guardships (diving if necessary), and embarking Napoleon at a quiet cove to which friends would spirit him at the appropriate time. The submarine was then to make its return submerged until

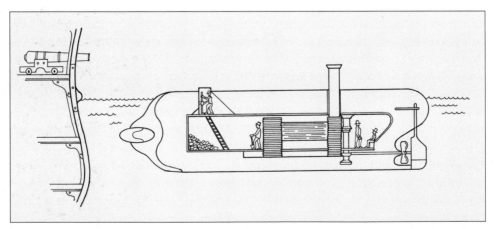

James Nasmyth's 'floating mortar' or 'steam-hammer', 1855, with a gigantic bomb in the bow – no less vague or impractical than anything 'The Famous Smuggler' had offered several decades earlier.

clear of the guardships, and rendezvous with a French frigate. The Emperor's death on 5 May 1821 halted the hare-brained project.

The Famous Smuggler's sub-aqueous activities did not end there, and there are strong indications that Johnson returned to his old trade for which a submarine would have been ideal (as it is today). Allegedly, 'one dark night in November' in 1821, Tom was intercepted as he attempted to run the boat (supposedly the one intended for Napoleon) down the Thames at the bidding of his French masters: '. . . she managed to get below London Bridge, the [Revenue] officers boarding her, Capt. Johnson in the meantime threatening to shoot them. But they paid no attention to his threats, seized her, and taking her to Blackwall, burned her.'[20]

Some of the stories were probably spread by Johnson himself to strengthen belief in his invention. In 1828 he tried the Fulton trick of blackmailing the Admiralty, informing Their Lordships that two other Powers had shown strong interest in his submarines, and that his poverty would compel him to negotiate with them if British authorities continued to ignore him.[21] They did ignore him.

Tom Johnson died in 1839, peacefully in his sleep at home in the Vauxhall Bridge Road, at the age of sixty-seven, happily married but scantily rewarded for his submarine work which, really, was outdated and outclassed. Already the fruits of the Industrial Revolution were beginning to allow submarine inventors a glimpse of what might be truly practicable.

CHAPTER 9

Reaching for Reality

1832 Morse invents code
1837 Electric telegraph
1854–56 Crimean War

apitaine de frégate Jacques-Philippe M. de Montgéry had a brilliant idea
in 1823. He propounded (but did not build) the all-iron submarine
L'Invisible, 28 or 29 m long, and 7.6 m broad with ninety-six men on
board;[1] and, uniquely so far, it was to be mechanically propelled, both on the
surface and submerged.

The propulsion systems devolved on a curious type of thruster known as a
Martenote (after its invention in 1704 by M Martenote who had probably
watched a coxswain surreptitiously waggling his tiller while 'in irons'). This was a
deep quarter-cylinder (picture a generous slice cut from a thick cake), recessed in a
semi-cylindrical cavity with its rounded side inboard at the stern of a vessel,
pivoted at its sharp outboard point so that the two flat surfaces could rotate a
quarter-turn from side to side. The pivot was twisted back and forth by a crossbar
connected to an engine.

On the surface a geared water-turbine powered by steam from a coal-fired
boiler would be the prime mover; but for submerged propulsion the ingenious de
Montgéry designed a gas engine energized by continually exploding small
quantities of gunpowder. The powder was poured into cups and ignited, by the
action of a hammer on an adjacent primer, when each cup was successively
positioned under a piston, the piston being driven upwards by pressure from the
resulting gas. Speed could be regulated by adjusting the frequency of cups arriving
in place. Horizontal and vertical rudders were positioned respectively above and
on either side of the *Martenote*.

The vessel was to have heavy underwater cannon (*columbiades*[2]) besides a
hundred underwater rockets, as many *torpilles* (floating mines) and a flame-
thrower – *formidable*! Two short retractable towers facilitated conning on the
surface but there was of course no periscope. The intention was probably to duck
briefly, to avoid shelling, rather than dive properly. Montgéry was going to have

ready for erection a bowsprit and two masts to supplement the steam plant – a prudent precaution.[3]

Meanwhile depth-keeping was the most intractable requirement for submarine navigation, and it was closely linked with a higher speed than muscle-power could offer for any length of time. Horizontal rudders (hydroplanes) were commonly being fitted from the early 1800s; but it took a long time to realize that their effect at very slow speeds was minimal and too tardy to check violent pitching when a boat's delicate longitudinal balance was upset. Machinery for propulsion submerged was demonstrably essential when at last it became apparent that a sustained 2.5 knots submerged was the very least speed for control by reasonably proportioned planes worked continually: a diving helmsman could not afford to lash his wheel or take a stand-easy.

Captain Bacon (First Inspecting Captain of (RN) Submarines 1900–1904, and first encountered in Chapter 1) pointed out in the 1900s:

Anything of any sort whatever that is heavier than water will sink when placed in water, and will continue to sink until it arrives at the bottom of the ocean. There is no half-way house. Either it floats on the surface or it rests on the

Reginald Bacon, first RN Inspecting Captain of Submarines and pictured here second from right at the launch of HM Submarine A1 at Barrow on 9 July 1902, was probably also the first to formulate and publish basic submarine principles – although J.P. Holland clearly understood them by the 1870s.

bottom of the sea. In order, therefore, to keep a submarine boat floating at the desired depth below the surface it must be kept moving, in an exactly analogous manner to which an aeroplane is kept from falling to earth. If an aeroplane stops it will immediately tend to come down to the ground. Nor is the principle of gliding available to a submarine, for gliding is only possible by making use of ascensional currents of air, and there are no ascensional sea currents at all comparable with those met in the air. We see, therefore, that a submarine must have some form of motive power and be able to steer itself in a vertical plane in order to keep or vary its depth. If the motive power fails the submarine will sink to the bottom unless sufficient water is expelled from its water-tanks to make it once more buoyant in the water.[4]

(However, certain submarines nowadays, with sophisticated modern equipment, are capable of hovering; and Second World War midget craft were usually able to regulate their depth while stopped.)

Achieving and maintaining neutral buoyancy (important even when under way) is tricky because a boat's weight is continually altered by minor leaks and the discharge of weapons or wastes, while changes of sea density make a boat apparently light or heavy. Compression of the hull is another factor: sea-pressure causes a submarine to displace less as it goes deeper (like a diver) and compensating water has to be pumped out of an internal tank. It is hardly surprising that all this was not appreciated in pioneering days. (Indeed, submariners have been known to neglect the basic facts of underwater life in recent times – with dire or even tragic consequences.)

Projectors like Fulton actually spent their time either on the bottom with slight negative buoyancy or awash where a low profile was often enough for concealment in the days before binoculars. And, to be fair, an awash state with hatches shut seemed like being underwater to men inside the boat.

As usual, witnesses believed what they wanted to believe. When Monsieur Brutus de Villeroi showed off his tiny submersible, 10 ft long and 3 ft wide, in the broad Basin at Noirmoutiers on 12 August 1832, there was room for him to get out of sight without going completely below the surface. A drawing, made after the event, shows a propeller on the craft, but it was almost certainly pushed along by sculling.

Another demonstration was arranged at Saint-Ouen in 1835 in the presence of Rear Adm Bergeret, Gen Juchereau and the English Adm Sir Sydney Smith who had, said a French writer, been 'one of our most desperate enemies'. (Smith had torched the Toulon fleet in 1794 and defeated Napoleon, on land, at Acre in 1799; but he settled in Paris after Waterloo where he was admired for being 'a true romantic hero, French-like in his arrogance' while, as a womanizer, 'he felt more at home in France.')[5] Sir Sydney's attendance should have ensured approval of de Villeroi's project; but when a less rarefied team, including de Montgéry and the

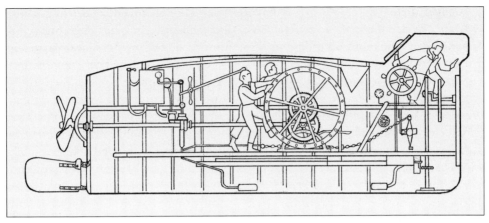

Bauer's Brandtaucher, *1850. Length 8.07m; displacement 27.5/30.5 tons.*

naval architect Gustave Zédé (a submarine enthusiast on his own account: see Chapter 16), examined the little craft their report was far from favourable. Disgruntled, Villeroi took his plans to America at the beginning of the Civil War.

Alas, there were two fatalities in the 1830s. A Spaniard named Cervo built a submarine in the shape of a sphere – ideal for strength – and announced that he could descend in it to a great depth. At the first attempt he failed to surface. The sphere was made entirely of wood: memories of unhappy Day. Three years later, in 1834, Dr Jean-Baptiste Petit of Amiens constructed a small metallic cigar-shaped boat 4 m long. The inventor sat on a seat in the entry hatch and paddled the craft like a canoe, pulling a watertight cover over himself before diving. On 15 August 1834, more than a thousand people surrounded the large natural basin at the mouth of the great River Somme at Saint-Valery while Dr Petit paddled around and saluted his public before drawing alongside the quay to fetch some heavy weights, from a butcher's shop, for ballast. When the weights were duly stowed he shouted out 'Adieu!' and pulled down the hatch. The water closed over him and the onlookers waited for him to reappear. Some twenty minutes after he had vanished several corks, attached to strings, rose to the surface. Nobody knew what they signified but their appearance boded ill. In any event there was nothing to be done because neither divers nor lifting apparatus were at hand. The crowd dispersed but returned at low tide the following day to find the boat exposed and intact: inside was slumped the body of the poor doctor, asphyxiated. His death certificate registers his demise as occurring at 8 o'clock on the preceding evening. He was thirty-one years old.[6]

The luckless Cervo and de Petit brought the number of early submarine martyrs to three. The next notable inventor, spanning most of his work over the period of the Crimean War, very nearly became a fourth.

Wilhelm Bauer (1822–75) was a Bavarian non-commissioned officer of artillery in the Duke of Holstein's army. His talent and ingenuity took him high above his humble beginnings and, according to one authority, he became 'the most persistent inventor to be found in the whole history of submarine navigation'.[7] In January 1850 he submitted plans for a submarine boat to break the blockade imposed by Schleswig-Holstein; and he persuaded the Minister of Marine to allocate him thirty Prussian thalers from the naval budget. This was enough to construct a 70 x 18 x 29 cm clockwork model which, demonstrated in Kiel Harbour to an assemblage of notables, led to construction of a full-sized submarine at Kiel funded – inadequately – by voluntary contributions from army personnel and local civilians. The structure of the boat, which he called Der Brandtaucher ('Diving Incendiary'), had to be degraded in order to economize. Bauer cautioned that diving depth would consequently be reduced from 30 m to 9.5 m, but the warning was not heeded.

Der Brandtaucher was completed on 18 December 1850 at the iron foundry of Schweffel and Howaldt and towed, on rails, into the water. The craft was 8.07 m long, 2.012 m at maximum beam and drew 2.63 m. Displacement submerged was 30.5 tons with a 3-ton margin of buoyancy – that is, displacement on the surface was 27.5 tons. A crew of three navigated and propelled the boat by means of a treadwheel with two gears which revolved a three-bladed propeller at 60–115 rpm according to the gear selected. The treadwheel, hideously reminiscent of contemporary penal punishments, could be turned at up to 20 rpm which generated a speed of 3 knots, although that pace could not be maintained for long. Space between the keel and interior decking served for ballast and compensating water. Water, admitted through a hull valve and a regulating valve, was expelled by two hand-operated piston pumps. External water pressure, indicating diving depth, was measured by a spring gauge; and fore-and-aft trim was corrected by a hand-wheel in the steering compartment which moved a 500 kg cast-iron weight to and fro along rails under the deck planking – an excellent idea.[8] There was the usual steering rudder but no diving rudders because Bauer reasoned that pitch, for changing depth, could just as well be achieved by the sliding weight.

During the initial trial an undeclared fault caused Brandtaucher, unmanned, to sink at her berth, but she was raised and ready for further trials on 1 February 1851. At 9 a.m., Bauer, together with a blacksmith and a carpenter named Thomsen and Witt, climbed down through the hatch with the intention of proving to the navy that the boat could dive to a depth of 1 atmosphere (10 m or 33 ft), a touch beyond the inventor's calculated limit. The crew had no practical experience and no safety precautions were taken.

Passing 9.4 m, and still going down fast, the slab-sided submarine creaked and groaned alarmingly while the hull plating started to distort. The bottom at 16.3 m was reached in 54 seconds with a stern-down angle of 34 degrees, the treadwheel having broken adrift. The pumps could not cope and water poured in through popped rivets.

Observers quickly realized that something had gone wrong; but attempts to raise the boat by grappling were ineffectual and nearly blocked the crew's eventual escape. There are two versions of what happened inside the submarine which was not itself salvaged until 5 July 1887.[9]

The official story is that Bauer waited six-and-a-half hours until internal and external pressures had become equal (by reason of leaks), at which point he opened the hatch, allowing the crew to float to the surface in a bubble of air. (Equalizing air pressure has always been the single most important aspect of submarine escape, but it requires a trapped crew to do what instinct forbids: open valves to admit yet more water from the insistent sea outside.) The alternative account – entirely credible – has Bauer, worried about foul air, threatening his two companions with a spanner in order to persuade them that the boat had to be *deliberately* flooded, as quickly as possible, so that the hatch could be opened.[10]

Submarine activities at Kiel came to an end when Schleswig-Holstein was restored to Denmark. Bauer took his plans elsewhere, eventually leaving Germany for Austria and then travelling on to Great Britain. In the summer of 1853, the Bavarian projector demonstrated a model submarine to the Royal Family at Osborne, and Prince Albert (top Freemason and technological enthusiast) was enthralled.[11]

The German-speaking Prince Consort decided to help Bauer, who spoke no English, and eventually told Prime Minister Palmerston: 'it is *a priori* impossible that so important and new a fact as submarine navigation should be useless in the hands of men of genius.'[12] With such influential support,[13] Bauer was sure of a hearing in high places. In spite of rejections at the outset the Admiralty Surveyor's Department undertook, on 26 August 1854, to re-examine Bauer's proposal and arrange an interview with the distinguished professor Michael Faraday. Prince Albert also arranged an introduction to the renowned naval architect John Scott Russell who owned a shipyard bordering the Thames on the Isle of Dogs. Bauer thereupon moved to nearby Greenwich where he drew up a new design.

Russell's role (to please Albert) was to assist Bauer in presenting his plans, through an interpreter, to the British Admiralty Surveyor (later the Controller). Misunderstandings were inevitable: Bauer became convinced that his ideas were being plagiarized and that the contract offered in due course by the Admiralty was crooked.

Distrust was mutual; and, with war in the Crimea looming, the paranoid Bauer hurriedly took himself to Russia where he was brought before Russia's Navy Minister, the Grand Duke Constantine. Meanwhile, Scott Russell's yard finished Bauer's boat and tested it in the Thames. It sank.

There was no need to cajole Imperial Russia into playing an active role in the development of underwater warfare. Between 1720 and 1724, half a century before David Bushnell's *Turtle*, Peter the Great sponsored Efim Nikonov's efforts to construct two secret submersibles for defending the shallow Baltic approaches to the capital; and experiments with mines were initiated between 1807 and 1810 by Ivan Ivanovitch Fitstum (c. 1765–1829), an Army engineer who had gleaned Western whispers about such matters. The Committee on Underwater Experiments, formed in 1839 within the Engineering Section of the Army, researched the feasibility of using mines for harbour defence, and it was expertise acquired in the 1840s that enabled Russia to employ sophisticated, albeit poorly managed, defensive mining systems in the Black and Baltic seas during the Crimean War.

Thus it was in a receptive atmosphere that Bauer, in May 1855, accepted a commission to build his third submarine at the Duke of Leuchtenberg's machine factory, St Petersburg. The *Seeteufel* (Sea Devil) was completed within six months, to stringent specifications, on 1 November. She was twice the size of *Brandtaucher*, 16.132 m long and 3.45 m broad; the propeller was again powered by treadmill. Bauer calculated the safe diving depth as 47 m.[14]

It took an additional six months for the Russian Navy to transport the boat from St Petersburg to Kronstadt, the principal Baltic naval base which the Grand Duke was anxious to protect against marauding British men-of-war. Here, a four-piece band was embarked to play on the harbour bottom to celebrate Tsar Alexander II's coronation day: the music was much enjoyed from the surface.

Bauer conducted no less that 134 diving trials; but, tantalizingly, there is no record of what they comprised – very likely bumping on the bottom in the main. On 2 October 1856, the submarine's screw tangled with an obstruction on the seabed – tending to confirm an assumption that *Seeteufel* performed either on the bottom or on the surface, but not much in between. Pumping out water brought the bow up, but no more, whereupon a Russian lieutenant on board opened the hatch before it was fully clear of the water (a stupidity frequently to be repeated in submarine history) and the boat sank swiftly back again.

Everybody escaped and the boat was salvaged but not refitted. The Navy Ministry informed Bauer: '. . . your ideas on underwater travel are basically correct . . . if your boat is perfected more satisfactory results can be achieved.'[15]

The inventor's expenses were paid and he started modelling a 24-gun submersible corvette propelled by steam. The boat was to approach an enemy vessel underwater, surface, fire her guns and then submerge to reload. The concept did not find favour. (However, it was seen again in the Royal Navy's M-Class monitor submarines towards the end of the First World War, but they had to reload their single 12-in guns on the surface.)

Bauer, still disappointed, left Russia in the spring of 1858. He did not return to the submarine world until the end of 1864, during the German–Danish War, when he volunteered for Prussian service and embarked on his final but uncompleted submarine project, the *Küstenbrander* ('Coastal Incendiary'). On 18 December he wrote perceptively to the Royal Prussian War and Naval Ministry:

... the future for ... ironclads ... is limited because ... they are unlikely to keep pace with the development of artillery, and in the event of an accident the State may well lose millions ... I submit wholeheartedly my plans for an underwater fighting ship to the German State of Prussia without reserve, because I am convinced that in them are the best means for war and peace without a heavy expenditure in men and money.[16]

Admiral Dönitz would proclaim similar sentiments before the onset of the Second World War. Significantly, the thickness of the hull for Bauer's boat above the waterline was 25 mm but only 12.7 mm below, implying that, in common with practically all submersible designs, the boat was expected to spend its time on the surface in the presence of an enemy, diving only when it had to. The principal weapon was a huge mortar mounted on the bow for firing a shell directly upwards into an enemy ship. If that did not do the trick, the captain had recourse to a battery of horizontal underwater guns with arrangements (unexplained) to minimize the effects of recoil on stability – an advance on *colombiads*.

Two propositions for *Küstenbrander* were eminently sensible. The ten-man crew would have sufficient air for twenty-four hours, but a remarkably advanced air purification system, providing oxygen for breathing and caustic potash for absorbing exhaled carbon dioxide, would increase the time shut down for a further full day. And Bauer's internal combustion engine pre-dated Dr Walter's air-independent hydrogen peroxide plant for U-boats by some eighty years. Paraffin mixed with oxygen (generated by manganese dioxide) would be ignited by an electric spark to create high-pressure gas to force water out of cylinders on to turbine blades (it was not yet feasible to use steam directly for a turbine).

Nothing came of Bauer's dedication to submarine development – other than encouragement for others: ill-tempered outbursts and mistrust distanced him from backers. He inevitably suffered from low social standing in a class-ridden society and carried a sizeable chip on his shoulder.

Engineers and inventors in the United States, often immigrants from humble backgrounds in Europe, were not so prone to encounter class barriers – at least, not if they showed a way to making money – and technology prospered accordingly. But, for the time being, America, a world away from Crimean battles, produced only one submariner, and he confined himself to the Great Lakes.

According to a contemporary magazine, the *Marine Cigar* was built in 1851 on Lake Michigan by Lodner Philips (a shoemaker by trade) and patented in 1852. It had two double hatches, two observation domes, and 'four interrupted keels to prevent it turning over when submerged'. Lights with reflectors were placed opposite some of the bulls' eyes on the sides ... [enabling] those within to see their way in the water.' If the boat ran foul of a wreck, it could 'be extricated without injury, having on its point or bow a thimble or outer case' which would detach itself and be left behind when the boat was backed. It sounded great; but

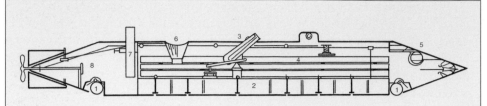

1. Anchor-weights (fwd and aft)
2. Ballast tanks with Kingston valves
3. Cannon
4. Compressed air cylinders
5. 'Torpedo' (mine) and fuse mechanism placed by diver using double-hatch 6 (impossible without grossly upsetting the trim unless special arrangements were made as in a Second World War X-craft
7. Air tube for use awash
8. Hand-cranked propeller

Phillips' (spelling variable) submarine of 1851 as the inventor wished it could be.

Philip's mistake, and the ultimate cause of his death, was to believe that the submarine could 'be kept stationery at any required depth of water from 1 inch to 200 feet, and in this lies the secret which makes the boat effective'.[17]

Imagination ran riot in the article, and the *Cigar* embodied any number of other secrets which Mr Philips was happy to divulge. It could be propelled by electro-magnetism with a screw (of Mr Philip's own invention) fitted to a shaft with a universal joint, thereby dispensing with a rudder, and it could carry up to thirty men.

As journalistically described, the *Marine Cigar* was a chimera; sadly, the sensibly simple boat (or possibly pair of boats) which Philips actually did make, with handraulic propulsion for pearl-fishing and wrecking and with Fulton-style weaponry on the side, did not impress the British Admiralty Surveyor. An official in that hard-pressed department wearily minuted: '. . . it does not appear that there is any great novelty in the plan nor any advantage in it over the numerous propositions in regard to the construction of boats for similar purposes.'[18]

That, in 1859, said it all. But Philips was long dead. He had been so sure that his boat was safe, that he took his wife and two children to explore the shallows of Lake Michigan with no mishap. But then he took a trip by himself in Lake Erie.[19]

His procedure (it seems) was to open a fine-adjustment valve, when already ballasted, until the boat was a trifle negatively buoyant. In shallow water, it would gently settle down on to the bottom a few feet below. Provided the lake-bed was level he could rotate the propeller (propellers were reasonably efficient by now)

Bauer's version of an underwater gun on his proposed 'Coastal Incendiary' submarine, 1864. (Burgoyne)

and slither across the mud. But the spot he chose in Lake Erie was not shallow: he was way out of his depth. It is impossible to believe that any boat of the period could withstand much pressure – certainly nothing like the 90 lb per sq in at 200 ft which he boasted about. Either his boat collapsed on the way down or, becoming more and more negatively buoyant under compression, it hit the bottom with a devastating crash.

De Montgéry, Bauer, Philips were reaching for reality. But poor Philips, last of a relatively practical trio, was another victim of self-advertisement, like Cervo and de Petit before him: he overstretched himself.

CHAPTER 10

Peripatetic Coffins

1861–65 American Civil War
1830–60 Widespread development of railways
1865 Lewis Carroll: *Alice's Adventures in
Wonderland*

The American Civil War was entering its third bitter year in 1864 and the Confederate States were weakening from lack of trade and imports. Off Charleston, a commercial port crucial to Southern interests, a Northern Squadron under Rear Adm John A. Dahlgren USN (1809–70) was maintaining a crippling blockade. An occasional blockade runner evaded the net, usually by coast-crawling; but two 'stone fleets', thirty old stone-laden whaling vessels scuttled by the Federal government across the main shipping channels, narrowed the sea-area to be guarded by ironclads and roaming patrol boats inshore and other vessels keeping watch from the outer anchorage three or four miles from the coast.

Downtown Charleston itself seemed safe despite a lot of noise due to spasmodic bombardments from seaward and extravagant carousing by (mainly English) sailors from a scatter of richly rewarded blockade runners who had reached their haven. But everyday necessities, let alone war materials, were in short supply. The Confederate Navy had no regular warships to challenge the Federal squadron. Somehow, though, the blockade had to be broken, and much Confederate debate had been devoted to solving the problem for the past two or three years.

Underwater warfare seemed promising: USS *Cairo* succumbed to rebel mines in the Yazoo River, Mississippi on 12 December 1862, barely two months after the Confederate Congress authorized a torpedo bureau within the Army and a 'submarine battery service' for the Navy.[1] But 'torpedo' (mine) ordnance could not help beleaguered Charleston unless it was taken out and placed alongside an alert enemy – as Bushnell realized ninety years before. So a small pack of torpedo boats – Davids by biblical contrast with Goliath-sized adversaries – had been hastily contrived under the direction of Capt Francis D. Lee, an Army engineer.[2]

The blockaders were keeping a sharp look-out after a worrying attack on the USS *New Ironsides* in the previous October. Something queer had suddenly emerged out of the darkness looking like a cigar-box with a pole sticking out of it

The Confederate Pioneer *of 1862 at Louisiana State Museum, New Orleans.* (RNSM)

like a bowsprit – in reality a tiny steam launch, very low in the water, bearing a lance-like 20-ft spar torpedo tipped with 134 lb of gunpowder in a 32-in copper case. The 3,486-ton *Ironsides* was damaged, albeit not fatally, when, at 9.15 p.m. on 5 October 1863, the torpedo detonated against the hull.

The tiny launch's captain, Lt Glassel CSN, and his fireman were captured when the explosion's backwash poured down the funnel, extinguishing the fire; but the other two crewmen managed to relight the boiler and take the torpedo boat back to Charleston where thirteen bullet holes were found in the superstructure: none were below the waterline. The idea of reducing buoyancy until the vitals of a boat were underwater – Drebbel's scheme reinvented many times since – was proving sound in action: it was not absolutely necessary to submerge completely for self-protection. On the other hand, a boat with very low freeboard going into attack with a spar torpedo was at serious risk of flooding unless sealed off.

Dahlgren mouthed the expected complaints: '. . . this base style of rebel warfare . . . it savors to me of murder'; and threatened to hang the launch's crew; but he was soon writing to Secretary of War Gideon Welles: 'It is evident . . . that the enemy intends to prosecute this mode of warfare, and I therefore urge reprisals in kind.' Welles replied blandly that 'the Department concurs.'[3]

In fact 'the Department' had endeavoured to procure a submarine boat at the beginning of the war, having a particular eye on undermining the Confederate floating battery *Virginia* (formerly USS *Merrimack*) at Norfolk.[4] Details of underwater devices were freely available to both sides in the War of Secession. It was not difficult to strike secret deals with itinerant European vendors, or to plagiarize foreign designs.

While Northerners sought French advice, two Confederate technicians convinced themselves that a real submersible – not a mere David – was essential for disrupting a blockade, and that they could design and build one themselves. James McClintock (a disenchanted American with English leanings) and Baxter Watson Jr, owners of a small machine shop, found a wealthy patron in Horace L. Hunley, Deputy Collector of Customs, lawyer, planter and merchant of New Orleans. He well understood the consequences of unremitting blockade. In June 1861 he had led an expedition to Cuba to buy arms and munitions for the Confederate States and arrange a safe route to and from Louisiana; but blockade breaking on a broader scale was his top patriotic priority, and he was attracted by submarine proposals.

With Hunley's backing a 34-ft 'Submarine Propeller' christened *Pioneer* was ready by February 1862. She was tested in Lake Pontchartrain under the command of John K. Scott, a Customs House colleague of Hunley, and a Letter of Marque was granted on 31 March for a privateering commission.[5] It is not known if she ever dived before Adm David G. Farragut USN ('Damn the torpedoes!') captured New Orleans on 25 April 1862, when the boat was scuttled.[6]

McClintock, Watson and Hunley retreated to Mobile where they set up shop at the Park & Lyons' well-equipped factory and started on a rather larger submarine which was to have an 'electro-magnetic engine'. The brave and very early attempt at electric propulsion failed, and so did a replacement steam plant. A four-man hand-crank served little better; and Adm Franklin Buchanan CSN, in charge of the city's naval defences, 'considered the whole affair as impracticable from the commencement'.[7] The *American Diver*, afterwards called *Pioneer II*, was nevertheless towed out of harbour in the first week of February 1863 to savage the blockading fleet, but Providence mercifully ordained she should be swamped and sunk before the crew could board. Salvage was not attempted. (A competing Confederate engineer named Alstitt devised an even more advanced propulsion system with steam on the surface and electricity submerged, but the craft was stillborn.)

Horace Hunley had lost a lot of money by now, but Mr E.C. Singer (nephew of the sewing machine trailblazer) stepped in to incorporate the Singer Submarine Corporation and fund a third vessel which was expected to cost $15,000 (around £400,000 today). Singer took a one-third share for $5,000 and Hunley acquired another third. The new 'diving machine', to be named CSS *Hunley*, started taking shape forthwith. A 30-ft cylindrical boiler, with a 42-in diameter that increased to 4 ft in height by the insertion of longitudinal iron strips, formed the pressure hull to which wedge-shaped fairings were bolted forward and aft, extending the length to about 40 ft. A ballast-cum-compensating tank was formed at each end with a Kingston flood valve and a pump; but the tanks had no tops – a fatal omission. Iron castings, fastened below the shell for stability, could be released by turning bolts inside the boat.

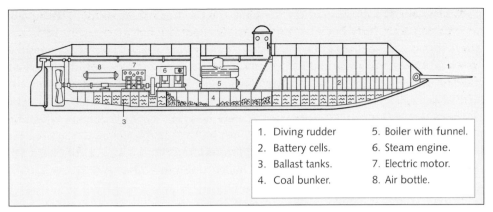

1. Diving rudder
2. Battery cells.
3. Ballast tanks.
4. Coal bunker.
5. Boiler with funnel.
6. Steam engine.
7. Electric motor.
8. Air bottle.

Alstitt's too technically advanced steam/electric submersible, 1863.

An eight-man crank passing longitudinally through a stuffing-box rotated a three-bladed propeller. When the crewmen took their places, on a narrow bench on the port side, there was no room for anyone to pass from forward to aft or vice versa. Two hatches were positioned forward and aft on 8-in coamings pierced with glass scuttles. A 4-ft hollow pipe, with an elbow joint to an air inlet in the top of the hull and a stop-cock, could be raised or lowered like a crude snorkel.

The *Hunley* was launched in July 1863 at the Theater Street Dock, Mobile. On 31 July, she demonstrated her prowess by trailing a powder charge under a flat-bottomed old coaling boat and blowing it skywards. Adm Buchanan promptly recommended the boat for Charleston, where it would obviously be most welcome; and on the morning of 12 August the submarine arrived there by rail, stretching over two flat cars. The crew made haste to put her in the water and recommence practice drills.[8]

In very calm waters it would be feasible for the *Hunley*'s captain to glide the boat down to about 20 ft and, with an eye on the mercury (depth) gauge, gently reverse the balanced 'side fins' to plane her up again – so long as the 'engineers' kept her going at close to 2.5 knots. Given that there were no diving rudders at the stern, the hydroplanes were quite well positioned a quarter-length – 10 ft – abaft the bow and, with effective watertight glands (stuffing boxes) for all hull penetrations, there should have been no significant leaks to add unwanted weight. A swoop down and up again was, in fact, all that was required for the torpedo-towing tactics envisaged.

The first disaster occurred in the afternoon of 29 August 1863 with Lt John A. Payne in command. After making a number of practice dips in the harbour, the boat was approaching its berth at Fort Johnson. Payne, peering out of the open hatch forward, inadvertently stepped on the hand-lever controlling the adjacent lateral fins, and depressed them. According to Charles Hasker, a crewman who survived, Payne had just ordered the crew to go ahead. In that case, there would have been enough movement on the boat for the horizontal rudders (relatively large at 5 ft long by 8 in wide) to have some effect if Payne had rashly, or lazily, failed to have the ballast tanks pumped dry to restore full surface buoyancy; the very act of Payne leaning out of the hatch to grab a berthing rope could have tilted the lips of both hatches below water. Payne pushed himself clear of the forward hatchway and two crewmen managed to climb out of the after hatch before the boat slid downwards in 42 ft of water. Hasker was following the captain when the forward hatch slammed down on his leg, but he struggled free before the boat hit bottom. Five men were drowned; their decomposed bodies were extracted with difficulty through the 16-in by 12-in hatchways when the submarine was raised on 14 September. On 28 September Horace Hunley requisitioned from army stores 'Half box of soap . . . and six brushes for scrubbing . . .'.

On 1 October Lt George E. Dixon was detached from A Company, 21st Regiment Alabama Infantry (for an optimistically brief thirty days) to take over a command becoming known as 'The Murdering Machine', 'The Diver' or, more pointedly, 'The Peripatetic Coffin'.

Dixon, promoted from the ranks, learned to handle the *Hunley* in a bare ten days – which says something about the simplicity of manoeuvres. Towing a simulated torpedo at the end of a 150-ft line, the *Hunley* plunged repeatedly beneath the CSS *Indian Chief* anchored, as a dummy target, in Cooper River.

It has generally been assumed that the boat could reach a speed of 4 knots, which is what McClintock claimed at the outset, but there is good reason to think that his *Hunley* never in practice attained as much as 3 knots, and that submerged control was not assured. This is established (leaping ahead in time) by an assessment of the *Hunley* by McClintock himself when he was making a sales-pitch to the British and endeavouring to paint a rosy yet realistic picture in October 1872.[9] This was more than eight years after events at Charleston, the sort of interval which (as suggested in relation to the Bushnell legend) leads to distortion of the facts. But such distortion always tends to *improve* on historical actualities, which is why a delayed account is suspect. However McClintock, when confronted by highly professional naval officers on board HMS *Royal Arthur*, flagship of the North America and West Indies Station, actually *downgraded* the capabilities he had presented to Confederate backers in the 1860s. Anxious to do business with the British, he made a number of points which are entirely credible and go a long way towards explaining what the *Hunley* was, and was not, capable of doing. McClintock's written statement for Flag Capt Nicholson and Chief Engineer Josiah Ellis admits that 'the Power was too uncertain to admit of her venturing far from shore'; that twelve miles in a night was the most the crew could manage; and that 'Could an Artificial Power have been obtained to have made a speed of even 3 miles an hour the Sub Marine Boat as Built by me in the Confederate States would have been the most Formidable Engine war ever yet invented as no Port can Blockade it by ships against the Sub Marine Boat.'

Mr Ellis was a practical engineer. He carefully appraised the characteristics of *Hunley* concluding, in his report to Admiralty officials (on whom depended his reputation and career), 'that the attempts to obtain a proper motive power resulted in failure, only about two knots being accomplished. . . .'

Then, after calculating how long air would last in a submarine, came a particularly telling aside although Ellis and the Flag Captain evidently did not appreciate its significance at the time. Having agreed that the mercury in a U-shaped tube with one end open to the sea would register depth, and that overcoming the vagaries of a magnetic compass in an iron hull did not present insuperable difficulties, they saw a need for perfecting 'some simple machine' to indicate speed through the water:

> . . . when underweigh [*sic*] beneath the surface, it is quite impossible to ascertain whether the vessel is progressing as there are no passing objects by which to recognise the fact of motion: *on several occasions when experimenting with his boat they* [the crew] *continued working the crank while all the time the boat was hard and fast in the mud.* [Emphasis added].

In other words the boat was, very likely, on the bottom during periods when the captain blissfully thought he was engaged in submarine navigation.

McClintock provided three references from notables who had observed his work at New Orleans; but their letters of commendation were curiously lacking in quantitative confirmation that *Hunley* dived and steered beneath the surface.[10] Capt Matthew Maury CSA, the foremost contemporary underwater explosives expert, said simply that:

> . . . attempts to construct such boats have been made over and over again, the idea is an old one and I am not aware of any attempt which has been *so near success* as that of your boat . . . *there are so many difficulties in the way of navigating and managing a boat under water that I think nothing short of actual and practical demonstration will convince me that it can be done* . . . [Emphasis added][11]

Before returning to the tragic but inspiring story of the *Hunley* in operations, what could McClintock's boat really do in light of reasonably well-substantiated evidence? Witnesses testified that the little submarine could dive some 200 yd short of *Indian Chief* and come up again the other side – a manoeuvre which would have been accomplished in about six minutes: the depth of water here was 9 fathoms (54 ft).[12] Assuming almost perfect neutral buoyancy at the moment of diving – not impossible to achieve by trial and error over a number of test dives – depression of the 'side wings' followed by levelling and then elevation after a judiciously timed interval could have resulted in a predictable catenary. This would have had the desired effect of towing the torpedo, at the end of its 150-ft line, under the target's keel in such a way that, with a live charge, it would have detonated on contact. We know that such an attack was rehearsed several times, because the torpedo's towing rope became frayed and had to be renewed. However, although this weapon system worked satisfactorily, it became increasingly plain that dragging an explosive package through a confined and busy harbour was bound, sooner rather than later, to result in the sensitive detonators blowing the torpedo up prematurely; the likelihood was increased when *Hunley* was herself towed from place to place, by the original steam David, to rest the hand-cranking crew. Thus the authorities insisted on reversion to a spar torpedo, which would not, incidentally, require the submarine to submerge. However, the *Hunley* could dive for a few minutes if required, and circumstantial evidence implies that she could dip to 60 ft. But her longitudinal stability was tender: a crewman complained that merely leaning his body forward or aft caused the boat to take an angle.

Horace Hunley – now respectfully termed 'Captain' Hunley – had little or no personal experience of handling the craft named after him; but on 15 October 1863 he took the commander's post on a step below the forward hatch with the steering control, side-wing lever, forward ballast tank flooding valve and forward pump close to hand. There was an improved compass, which he had demanded five days before together with a fresh tow-rope, on the bulkhead in front of him. Thomas Park, First Officer (son of Thomas W. Park of Park & Lyons machine shop), sat at the aftermost propulsion crank ready to tend the after seacock and pump. Hunley would have passed the word back to Park to fill the stern ballast tank (up to a set level) as soon as the submarine shoved off from the jetty: the customary diving position was only 500 yd away. Park would certainly have shut and secured his hatch before opening the flood valve and Hunley would have been prudent to shut and bolt the forward hatch as soon as he had let go the last mooring rope.

At 9.25 a.m. the boat left her berth, and at 9.35 she was seen to dive. In other words Hunley only allowed himself ten minutes to work the boat into position and perform a number of unaccustomed tasks. Doubtless he took the helm on that day to prove his own faith in the submarine and thereby stiffen the crew's morale after the recent tragic accident. There is every likelihood, however, that while endeavouring to appear totally calm and collected he fumbled the drill. The submarine took a sharp bow down angle and buried itself, up to the side fins, in the clinging mud of the Cooper River 50 ft below the surface.

A little more than three weeks later, on 7 November, the iron hull was raised. Gen P.G.T. Beauregard CSA, military commander of Charleston, was one of the first to peer inside:

> The spectacle was indescribably ghastly; the unfortunate men were distorted into all kinds of horrible attitudes, some clutching candles, evidently

endeavouring to force open the man-holes; others lying in the bottom, tightly grappled together, and the blackened faces of all presented the expression of their despair and agony [13]

The body of Capt Hunley was under the forward hatchway: his right hand lay on top of his head as if he had been trying to raise the hatch. His left hand grasped a candle which had never been lit, and the boat, which was found at an angle of 35 degrees bow down, had obviously been plunged into darkness. The forward flooding valve was wide open and the wrench which turned it was lying in the bilges. The forward ballast tank had therefore over-filled – under increasing pressure as the boat went down – thereby flooding the boat itself until the air inside was sufficiently compressed to equalize the pressure. Efforts by the crew to release the iron ballast had only partly rotated the securing bolts which were either too stiff or too difficult to operate in darkness. The after ballast tank was dry: First Officer Park, able to breathe air under pressure at one-and-a-half atmospheres (until carbon dioxide poisoning combined with lack of oxygen killed him), had vigorously worked the hand pump, but he could not open his hatch against four-and-a-half tons of water.

This time it took ten black slaves to clean up the boat with five scrubbing brushes, one barrel of lime, and a box of soap. The horrible task, finished by the end of the month, was supervised by George Dixon.

A man of quite extraordinary determination, Dixon now had the considerable problem of recruiting a third crew; but the rewards offered by Charleston firms and businessmen for destroying Union blockade vessels were so great that they overcame fear and superstition. John Fraser & Co., for example, guaranteed $100,000 (around $2.5 million today) for putting an end to the USS *Ironsides* and the same for sinking the *Warbash*. By now cargoes of arms and ammunition from Europe were beyond price in the South. Confederate finances, which might have been assured if the government had seized all the cotton in the country before the blockade had become fully established, and sent it to England for storage and trickle sales, were in a deplorable state which could only be alleviated by trading. Somehow, the blockade just *had* to be broken.

George Dixon was the city's last hope. Undeniably he was blessed with courage in full measure, and leadership too. Better still, he was lucky: it was said that the bullet which had wounded him at the Battle of Shiloh would have lost him a leg, and maybe his life, had it not been stopped by a $20 gold piece given him for good fortune by his sweetheart Queenie Bennett. It struck the gold piece in his pocket and carried it into the flesh of his thigh. When removed the coin was found to be doubled up around the ball: Dixon never failed to carry the bell-shaped charm thereafter.

Charleston needed luck like that, but Dixon was not a man to take unnecessary chances. He planned and prepared for the forthcoming operation with exacting care.

With five sailors who had volunteered from the *Indian Chief* and three men who had been associated with the project from its concept in Mobile, Dixon exercised the *Hunley* day and night, often conferring with Engineer Tomb whose David of *Ironsides* fame was always ready to give a tow past Fort Sumter to the open sea.

The directive issued to Dixon on 14 December 1863 was commendably succinct: 'Proceed to the mouth of the harbor and sink any vessel of the enemy which comes in conflict.' Unfortunately, Adm Dahlgren had ordered the closest ironclads to defend themselves against another attack by surrounding their hulls with chained booms: these would defeat both spar and towed torpedoes. Worse, on the night of 5 January 1864 Seamen Shipp and Belton, from the *Indian Chief*, purloined a small rowing boat and deserted to the Union fleet: they supplied full details of the HL *Hunley*, prompting Dahlgren to warn his ironclads to anchor only in shallow water where a submarine could not pass under them, and to suspend netting, weighted with shot, around each vessel. However, these orders were not directed to the wooden warships further out from shore, although they were warned to be alert.

The moon rose early over Charleston on the evening of 17 February 1864. The skies were clear and a light north-westerly wind barely ruffled the sea. At about 7.30 p.m., two hours before low water, the submarine stealthily emerged from her forward base at Breach Inlet, Sullivan's Island, and set course for the wooden steam sloop-of-war *Housatonic*, anchored in 28 ft of water south of Rattlesnake Shoals, two-and-a-half miles distant. The ebb tide assisted although Dixon, needing to make good a south-easterly course, had to allow for the stream tending to set him a little west of his intended track. If the attack was not delayed, the crew could look forward to help from the flood tide coming back.

It is fair to suppose that Dixon promised his crew that he would not submerge unless that was the only way to get out of trouble. The men knew all about the catastrophes and would scarcely have agreed to a deliberate submerged attack. (Adm Dahlgren's intelligence had reported three accidents so far, killing seventeen men: some historians have quoted four, but the number – bad enough in all conscience – was actually two, killing thirteen men.) Moreover, the Fulton-harpoon type of spar torpedo which is likely to have been adopted was hinged and could be tilted downwards if desired, so that the warhead was 8 ft below the waterline, making it less necessary than ever to approach beneath the surface. A steel thimble was fitted over the end of a 10-ft spar and the submarine rammed this into the target's hull where it was retained by barbs when the boat backed and the thimble slipped off. The latter was connected to a copper canister of powder triggered by a 150-ft line attached to a point on *Hunley* close to the forward hatch.[14]

It did not make sense for Dixon to shut the forward hatch and stay below: it was difficult to see through the glass bull's-eyes and, to ensure success, he had to stand with head and shoulders in the night air. There would be time enough to duck down, shut and dog the hatch – if he moved smartly – while backing away

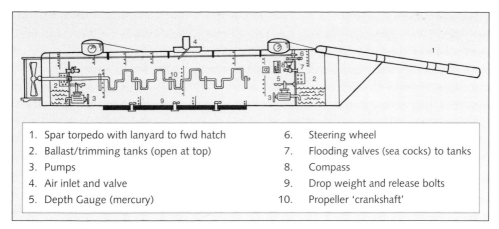

1. Spar torpedo with lanyard to fwd hatch
2. Ballast/trimming tanks (open at top)
3. Pumps
4. Air inlet and valve
5. Depth Gauge (mercury)
6. Steering wheel
7. Flooding valves (sea cocks) to tanks
8. Compass
9. Drop weight and release bolts
10. Propeller 'crankshaft'

Confederate Hunley, *1863.*

before the attached line triggered the explosion. If things went a little wrong (he might not embed the harpoon, for example), he could pull the line and fire the charge himself – albeit more at risk from the blast.

On board the *Housatonic* that evening, Capt Charles Pickering USN wrote in his Night Orders that the Officer of the Deck, Officer of the Forecastle and Quartermaster were to keep glasses (actually telescopes, and far less effective for searching than twentieth-century binoculars) in constant use, and there were to be six look-outs besides. The anchor-cable was to be slipped immediately at any alarm and the engines reversed. Powder and shot were to be kept ready at all guns.

At about 8.45 p.m., the lookout sighted an object on the starboard beam. Acting Master and Officer of the Deck Lieutenant F.K. Crosby looked from the bridge and saw 'something on the water . . . like a porpoise, coming to the surface to blow' (which is how the *Hunley*'s slender upperworks would have appeared; the description does not imply that the submarine was surfacing).

Crosby beat to quarters. There was a glimmer of light coming from the intruder (fairly obviously from the open forward hatch) and sentries opened fire with muskets. Capt Pickering raced on deck with his own double-barrelled shotgun and fired downwards at 'two projections or knobs about one third away from the bows' (the 'wing fins'), a discharge which may have wounded Dixon. Meanwhile, three bells were struck and the engine was duly backed, but the propeller had made no more than three or four revolutions before there was a violent explosion accompanied by the sound of rushing water and crashing timbers. Just before the blast, it was seen that the attacker stopped and then appeared to move off slowly.[15] The *Housatonic* sank quickly and settled on the bottom, with mast and spars above the surface, five or six minutes after the spar torpedo had been triggered.

Nothing more was seen of the submarine until successive searches culminated, in 1995, with confirmation that the hull of HL *Hunley*, the tomb of nine brave men, had been discovered close to where the attack had taken place. Both hatches were shut, indicating that Dixon had indeed endeavoured to draw away from his victim before the torpedo did its deadly work. But some water probably washed down before the forward hatch was dogged, and perhaps entered through one of the glass scuttles (found broken, maybe by blast) as well. The exact cause of *Hunley*'s loss is not important; Dixon and his men had finished the job which, with great gallantry, they set out to do.

The fact that the attack was not made submerged in no way robs *Hunley* of title to the first wartime sinking by a submarine. The majority of submarine and U-boat attacks during both world wars were conducted on the surface.

The *Hunley*'s success was such that it eclipsed Federal attempts to undertake submarine business although two or three relatively sophisticated submersibles were produced in the industrialized North. They deserve a mention, but none saw action in the war.

On 17 May 1861 the *Philadelphia Evening Bulletin* reported that the harbour police had stumbled on a 'submarine monster' at the lower end of Smith's Island in the Delaware River. At first the sinister object was attributed to a devilish Confederate conspiracy:

> Never since the first flush of the news of the bombardment of Fort Sumter, has there been an excitement in the city equal to that which was caused . . . by the capture of a mysterious vessel which was said . . . to be used for all sorts of treasonable purposes, including the trifling pastime of scuttling and blowing up government men-of-war. . . . Two tiers of glass bull's eyes along each side of the submarine monster . . . gave it a particularly wide-awake appearance.

Police towed the stranger to Noble Street Wharf where a large crowd gathered, eager to see inside; but, presumably with some financial advantage to the lawmen, only the *Bulletin*'s investigative reporter was permitted to enter:

> . . . divesting ourselves of our coat and hat, we squeezed into the machine . . . [and we] found ourselves squatting inside of a cigar-shaped vessel, about 4 ft. in diameter. There was a crank for . . . the propeller . . . [and] apparatus . . . connected with fins outside . . . which had something to do with steadying and sinking the craft. There were . . . pumps, brass faucets, pigs of ballast lead and numerous other things, which might be intended for infernal or humane purposes for aught we know . . .

Enquiries determined that the work (which bore a marked resemblance to McClintock's design or, of course, vice versa) was that of the ubiquitous Brutus de Villeroi, now well past middle age: he had been endeavouring to peddle underwater wares for thirty years or more. Capt Samuel F. Du Pont USN,

Commandant of the Philadelphia Navy Yard, ordered an examination of the craft by three officers who were impressed. A French journal described one of de Villeroi's trial trips:

> ... M. Villeroi was in his machine and it was pushed offshore. The submarine ran awash for about half an hour after which it descended into from 5 to 6 metres of water, when it descended to the bottom and gathered some sea shells. [Journalistic imagination or was there a diver?] He cruised in various directions during his submersion to deceive a party of boats which had followed him since the beginning of his experiment, M Villeroi coming to the surface of the water in different directions. After this experiment had lasted an hour and a quarter, he opened his hatch and was received with lively interest.[16]

Sceptical inference is that the submersible could dip-chick (or dive to the bottom) but could not hold a steady depth. None the less on 4 September 1861, the inventor addressed the highest authority, President Lincoln:

> To the grave circumstances which threaten the unity of this glorious country ... no means whatever, defensive or offensive, should be neglected. . . . the best system is that one which . . . can present great effects with little means. . . . Submarine navigation . . . , is now a problematical thing no more. The last experiments made . . . in the Delaware River have demonstrated positively that with a submarine boat like mine, well constructed and properly equipped, it becomes an easy matter to reconnaissance the enemy's coast, to land men, ammunition, etc., at any given point, to enter harbours, to keep up intelligence, and to carry explosive bombs under the very keels of vessels, and that without being seen. With a few such boats manoeuvred each one by about a dozen men and the most formidable fleet can be annihilated in a short time. . . .
> I have the honor to be with distinguished consideration,
> Your Excellency's most obedient servant,
> De Villeroy, [as de Villeroi spelled his name in the US]
> Civil Engineer
> 1325 Pine Street, Philadelphia.[17]

De Villeroi's assurances were taken at face value, and the rather ingenuous Navy Department contracted for a larger 'Submarine Propeller', which was launched on 30 April 1862 at Neafic and Levy's shipyard, Philadelphia.[18]

An armchair warrior's opinion was that if the *Alligator* (as christened) had been in service at Fort Munroe (Hampton Roads), the heavily-armed, much-feared Confederate ironclad *Virginia*, constructed Phoenix-like from the burned-out wooden Union *Merrimack* and renamed, would have been 'destroyed or at least rendered harmless' at her moorings.[19] There would have been no need to send the

The Intelligent Whale. (Author's collection)

'cheesebox on a raft' *Monitor* into battle on 8 March 1862. This was despite the *Alligator*'s propulsion – sixteen men pulling at oars which, for stroke and feather, flapped open and shut like the pages of a book – to which de Villeroi had reverted, presumably believing it to be more efficient than a contemporary propeller. (He may even have been right.)

Another boat, nicknamed *Intelligent Whale*, became better known. Built by Oliver Halstead the sensibly whale-shaped boat caused, according to unsubstantiated reports, more deaths than the Confederate *Hunley*: thirty-nine men (but more likely thirteen) were supposed to have drowned during excursions in the broad-waisted 26-ft iron craft hand-cranked by six burly seamen.[20]

There was plenty of industrial and military espionage going on during the 1860s and 1870s; one senior officer, who should emphatically not have been involved in clandestine activities (at least, not with the admitted knowledge of his Ambassador) was the British Naval Attaché in Washington, Rear-Admiral E.A. Inglefield. A letter, to an unknown official in the Admiralty, postmarked New York and dated 4 March 1872, is an interesting example of how a Victorian officer and gentleman engaged in spying:

PRIVATE
Sir,
Having obtained permission from Sir Edward Thornton to communicate to you privately the information contained in this letter . . .
I have heard from officers who had served in the Confederate Services that, what had been thought was a huge fish, had been observed by the people on board their vessels [after the war] on more than one occasion, crossing the river

[Hudson?], just below the surface of the water at nights [awash], . . . and it was at first supposed that it might be some monster of the deep.

I afterwards heard accidentally that there existed in one of the Navy Yards a torpedo boat that had been nicknamed the 'Intelligent Whale', that the Gov'mt had faced a large sum for . . . its construction and that it was only known to the Gov'mt officials and the vessel was concealed and secured by a Gov'mt deal. All the enquiries I cautiously made failed to afford any further information.

At my last visit to Brooklyn Yard, I was shown by the Chief Constructor and his assistant all the vessels built or under construction and amongst them the 'David' and the new gun-torpedo boat. He and his assistant told me these were all of the sort they had there. When these gentlemen went to their luncheon I found means to get to a remote part of the ordnance wharf, which had been avoided during any previous visits, where I had reason to believe the craft might be found.

By a process it is unnecessary to describe I not only found this vessel but after a while got inside her and noted all the peculiarities of her construction, making myself as much master of the secret as those who have paid for it.

I quite believed what I heard rumoured (and which the messenger who assisted me in the examination declared) being that the inventor and his wife and two daughters had remained hours under the water – he occasionally leaving the boat and coming to the surface – and that, since, the Government had purchased the secret and men had remained for 24 hours without inconvenience and moving about at pleasure underwater. I fancy the seal [on the hatch] must have broken for the purpose of cleansing the machinery and I was fortunate to visit the spot at that moment. [How very fortunate!]

I made ample notes and a sketch on my return to the hotel but these would hardly convey to the whole of the information I acquired . . .[21]

A final product of the Civil War was the *Spuyten Duyvil* (archaic Dutch for 'Devil with a Syringe') built at Fairhaven, Connecticut, in 1865 to the designs of a local naval architect, in the remarkably short time of three months. With a length of 84 ft and a beam of 19 ft she rode very low in the water with a 3 ft conning tower, stubby funnels and a whale-back deck armoured with 1-in iron which lapped down over the sides to well below the waterline. The conning tower was sloped and protected overall by 12 in of armour. Steam-driven pumps could fill or empty huge ballast tanks in minutes, varying the draught between 7 ft 6 in when attacking to 4 ft when cruising. A 20-ft tubular iron spar torpedo improved on the weapon system carried by previous Davids: it could be retracted into the hull for reloading and, when extended, it could be depressed (from within the craft) to strike a vulnerable part of the target's hull; no significant compartments in the *Duyvil* were liable to be flooded by the backwash.

Spuyten Duyvil was too late to fight, but her design indicates that the principle of total submersion was being abandoned, for the time being, in light of wartime

The Spuyten Devil *at full buoyancy.* (Burgoyne)

experience. Fast spar torpedo boats, with tiny superstructures, would suffice for coastal defence until outstanding questions of underwater control and propulsion (inextricably linked) could be answered satisfactorily. The British Admiralty took this view while keeping an open mind and not spending money on experiments.

However, there was still guarded enthusiasm for real submarine projects in Russia and Germany; and France always gave quiet encouragement to underwater projects, doubtless noting that Confederate achievements had included the mining of no less than thirty-three Union ships.[22]

CHAPTER 11

The Curate's Eggs

1876 4-stroke gas engine: Otto
1883 Petrol engine: Diesel
1885 Motor car: Benz

The Church militant was represented beneath Britannia's waves by a Manchester curate. He came to style himself Cdr the Revd George W. Garrett, Pasha, BA; and the wildly improbable title for an Anglican curate was more or less legitimate.[1]

Exploring the career of George Garrett (1852–1902) is like stepping into a Bunyan-esque allegory: strange figures and surreal scenarios appear and disappear along a winding downward path. But, alas, the trumpets were not heard to sound for him.[2]

Garrett possessed diverse personal qualities of flair, erratic brilliance, theatricality, plausibility, duplicity and gullibility. He was born on 4 July 1852 in Lambeth, the third son of John Garrett, a clergyman who came from Ballymote, Co. Sligo, and was then in high standing due to a Masonic connection with Prince Albert, who admired a modest book he had written on education. The Garrett name was highly respected by the Brotherhood; and the Craft would, in due course, assist young George in the furtherance of his submarine projects although, as events turned out, it might have been better if he had not been given this helping hand.

George enjoyed a good education and did well at Rossall School and Manchester Grammar School (French, English, mathematics, physics) which he left in June 1869. He taught at Seighford village school, near Stafford, for two terms and at Owen's College for twelve months while doing the first year's degree course of Trinity College, Dublin, as a permitted 'pensioner' (absentee) student. Research on human respiration at Kensington Museum followed, and then headmastership (at age twenty-one) of Pocock College, Co. Kilkenny for eighteen months during which time he met, and later married, Jane Parker, daughter of a wealthy Irish lawyer. In 1874–5, he actually took up residence at Trinity for long enough to qualify both for an honours degree and the award of a special medal for being the first lightweight boxer to win a heavyweight championship.

By way of celebration he cajoled his fiancée's parents into paying for a year in Fiji and New Zealand 'teaching and practising navigation in all its branches'.

Subsequent events indicate that he never mastered the art; but he returned in the summer of 1876, married Jane, and enrolled for Theological Studies at Trinity College, Cambridge. This deflection towards the Church was urged by his father who was now the impoverished vicar of Moss Side, Manchester and much in need of a low-paid curate. On 17 May 1877, the Bishop of Manchester ordained George a Deacon and duly appointed him to the curacy of Moss Side.

Almost immediately Garrett turned his gaze from dull parochial duties towards the Russo–Turkish War of 1877. On 10 June, Lt Zinovi Rozhdestvensky, commanding a spar-torpedo boat, led an attack against the 2,266-ton *Idjalalieh* of the Turkish Danube Flotilla. The flotilla was so well protected that Rozhdestvensky bent the bows of his boat without being able to thrust the spar through steel-chain curtains. Two weeks later, two more boats were launched against a Turkish monitor up the Danube at Nikopol, and these were also defeated by anti-torpedo nets around the gunship. How much better, thought Garrett, if the attacks had been made under the water, below the defences.

However, Garrett's first interest lay in enabling a man to survive in a suit, independent of the atmosphere, below the water or in a coal-mine disaster. For these purposes he invented a self-contained breathing apparatus, quite unlike the common air-supplied 'hard hat' diving dress, which he called the 'Pneumataphore'. He demonstrated it in the River Seine in 1877, and again in 1880 when he remained on the bottom, with no air hose, for 37 minutes. The French Government was more interested in sub-surface possibilities than the British, and Garrett never allowed patriotism to interfere with commerce.

In the spring of 1878 he registered Patent No. 1838, dated 8 May of that year, for 'Improvements in and Appertaining to Submarine or Subaqueous Boats or Vessels for Removing, Destroying, Laying or Placing Torpedoes in Channels and other Situations, and for other Purposes'. The 'torpedoes' were still mines, and the other purposes were underwater surveying and diving tasks. At the same time he incorporated the Garrett Submarine Navigation and Pneumataphore Co Ltd at 56 Deansgate, Manchester with a capital of £10,000 in £1 shares. Five Mancunian businessmen took stock in the enterprise encouraged by the reputation, in Freemasonry and the Church, of the Chairman, George's father, the Revd Dr John Garrett, DD.

Garrett forthwith built a tiny experimental one-man submersible. It was 14 ft long, 5 ft in diameter and weighed four-and-a-half tons. Displacement was varied by sliding a sea-connected piston in or out as suggested by Fournier in 1634. A hand-crank turned the propeller and, when not otherwise occupied, the crewman – Garrett himself – could thrust his hands through greased leather sleeves to create mischief with explosives. The ovoid shape has naturally resulted in it being called 'the Curate's egg' after the famous *Punch* cartoon, but it would be over-generous to imply thereby that parts of it were excellent.[3]

Warlike schemes for 'subaqueous vessels' included, according to Garrett's patent, using several of them tied together to tow an enemy vessel away from its moorings, by 'connecting powerful cables, first taking the precaution (with a steam vessel) to disable the propeller and rudder.'

Dr Garrett at Moss Side justified his son's extra-clerical activities in prolix correspondence with the press. In a letter to the *Manchester Courier* dated Monday 15 December 1879, he fully appreciated that 'clergymen ought to have nothing to do with war or its destructive appliances'; but all would be well with 'our National religion', and 'all the labours of life in our country would derive increased stability and energy if clergymen as a body could earn public confidence in their skill and power to develop a healthy example of all that is good and practicable in the life of Englishmen . . .'

After passing references to 'our unseen Friend' he continued (for a total of 36 column inches) in the same vein, with a sound explanation of his son's invention for purifying air underwater, concluding that submarines would alleviate the need for 'vast fortifications to defend harbours and

George Garrett, young and confident. (Garrett family)

towns round our coasts' and become 'a means which a few brave coastguard men can easily keep ready to effectively prevent any enemies . . . from attacking our Island home . . . no large iron-clad or troopship will dare to approach a coast upon which a few Garrett submersibles will be maintained.'

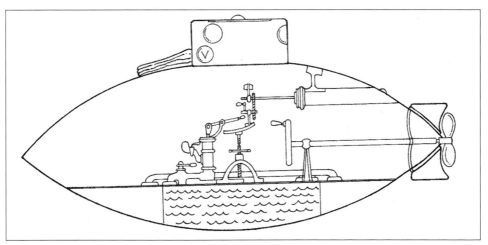

Garrett's 'egg', 1878, with ballast tank, piston-tube for adjusting displacement, pump and armholes (v) for leather gauntlets.

The prospectus of the Garrett Submarine Company began: 'As to the inventions being for murdering people – this is all nonsense. Every contribution made by science to improve instruments of war makes war shorter and, in the end, less terrible to human life and to human progress.' This assurance was given by no less a divine than the Revd Norman McLeod, Chaplain to Her Majesty and a former editor of *Good Words*. Churchmen were quick to close ranks in the face of possible public opposition.

Although evidence of the 'egg' diving is scant, initial experiments were sufficiently encouraging to build a larger vessel powered by steam: it was to be trustingly christened *Resurgam* – 'I shall rise again'. Garrett, following tradition, designed the engine on the back of an envelope bearing a small Victorian halfpenny stamp.[4] A letter was despatched to Messrs Cochran and Company, new and dynamic owners of the Britannia Engine Works and Foundry at Birkenhead, requesting an estimate of building costs 'not wanting the immediate price to be such as will frighten potential backers and perhaps stopping the *proper* carrying out of my plans'.

The letter was posted in Manchester on 31 March 1879, arriving at Birkenhead the following day, and the estimate of £1,538 was ready a week later on 7 April. Business, including postal services, moved briskly in those days. The estimate included £53 for the cost of launching but omitted (an indicative afterthought in pencil) £60 for 'centre rudders' (hydroplanes). *Resurgam* weighed 30 tons and had spindle-ends as advocated by Father Mersenne. Power was provided on the Lamm fireless locomotive principle, patented by Eugene Lamm in 1872; it was devised for San Francisco streetcars and used (to avoid smoke pollution) on the London Underground Railway's Central Line as well as in Royal Dockyards. A coal furnace heated water in a boiler to a temperature corresponding (in *Resurgam*'s plant) to 130 lb per sq in. The very hot water was then transferred to an insulated reservoir where it became a source of latent energy. When a throttle valve to the engine was opened, about 15 per cent of the water flashed into steam at 30–40 lb per sq in to drive the pistons.

The furnace was shut down and sealed as soon as steam had been raised so that no oxygen was consumed when the boat itself was shut down – although residual heat was another matter altogether. Endurance was expected to be 4 hours at 2 or 3 knots. On the surface, the furnace was stoked for the boiler to feed the engine directly. In due course, two locomotive Whitehead torpedoes were to be fastened externally to the boat's heavy oaken sheathing: they would be discharged 'by means of the usual telescope and spring which are used in the Admiralty'.[5]

At the beginning of December 1879, 'photographic views' were shown of 'The New 30-ton Submarine Torpedo Boat and its Crew' at a sale of work held at Christ Church School, Moss Side, for church and school expenses. The well-informed *Manchester Courier* attended and afterwards took its readers to task for presuming wrong tactics:

An idea has prevailed that the natural position of the boat is underwater and that it comes to the surface at a given time. But the real fact is that its proper position is what the inventor calls on the surface, with the tower just out of the water. When the boat has to go under the water, it is made to do so by means of side rudders, which depress the body of the boat under the surface and it remains there as long as the navigator desires. It is meditated that in action such a boat should attack an enemy underwater so as to be safe from attack itself and that it should discharge torpedoes when within about 50 yards of its object, afterwards moving invisibly out of the way . . .[6]

Resurgam was lowered from a 50-ton crane at Birkenhead into the Great Float on 26 November 1879. A reporter asserted that 'Mr Garrett began to test his apparatus . . . at a depth of 25 feet . . . he remained under water for an hour and a half, during which time conversation was kept up with him by telephone . . .'[7] It has been inferred that the reporter watched the 'subaqueous vessel' submerging, but maybe he was talking about Garrett in his pneumataphore apparatus: it is beyond the boundaries of belief to think that the boat ever dived in the accepted sense although, on this occasion, she might have been weighted down and lowered statically by crane. There is no indication on drawings or in specifications of ballast, trimming or compensating tanks, flooding or Kingston valves, depth or level gauges.

In short *Resurgam* had no submarine attributes apart from a sealable hull and slim 'side rudders' amidships which (despite the very slow speed available) may have enabled her to vary exposure between the fully surfaced and low awash conditions or even make a momentary bobbing dip. That would accord pretty well with an observer recalling – in 1916, some thirty years after the event and doubtless encouraged by a prompting press – that he had watched *Resurgam* '. . . being submerged. By the ripple under the surface [sic] you could always tell where she was, and now and then you would see her diver's shaped helmet come to the surface'.[8]

Resurgam set off down the Mersey, at 9 p.m. on the dark, misty evening of Wednesday 10 December 1879, bound for Portsmouth where Garrett intended she should show herself off, singling out the influential Swedish armament tycoon Thorsten Nordenfelt. The ship's company comprised Garrett in command, Capt Jackson (Master Mariner) and Mr George Price, Engineer. The little craft reached the Rock Lighthouse 'without accident of any sort' as Garrett told the *Courier*. At the start, Capt Jackson, as befitted the only proper seaman in the crew, remained on the upper deck where he must have got very wet because the superstructure was only three or four feet above the surface. Garrett took the helm inside the conning-tower. The Master Mariner prudently came below while they were passing through the Rock Channel and, said Garrett, 'we shut ourselves up and fairly started on our way while the boat answered splendidly in the sea way.' The seas 'passed easily over her and caused hardly any motion'.[9]

Resurgam *on completion at the Britannia Engine Works and Foundry, Birkenhead, in late 1879, with Garrett supporting his one-year-old son John William; Captain Jackson on right and Mr George Price, Engineer, on afterpart.* (Garrett family)

Unfortunately, Capt Jackson lost his bearings in Liverpool Bay, and Garrett had to open the hatch to enquire of a passing ship which way to go. He abandoned credibility by informing the captain (according to Price forty-five years later) 'we were a submarine torpedo boat, and had been under his ship for two or three hours' – plainly an impossibility. The captain told Garrett the position but also confided that he and his crew were 'the three biggest fools he had ever met'.[10] By Friday morning 'when the sun rose beautiful and clear' they had been at sea for thirty-six hours, much of which had been spent with the hatch shut. They were understandably 'desirous of making some port, as sleeping on board was not attended with as much comfort as we wished'. This understatement was amplified by Garrett's son: as a small boy he was once taken for a trip because he was small enough to crawl from forward to aft and back, across the 12-in gap above the boiler tubes, to hand his father spanners and other essentials for careful submarine navigation. The temperature owing to the Lamm boiler, he recalled, varied between 100 and 150 degrees F.

In any event Garrett was not happy to continue until certain (unspecified) modifications had been made, and Rhyl, on the north coast of Wales, was adopted as a temporary base. Mr Cochran had long advised the voyage should be made by road – a horse-drawn undertaking of course – but Garrett was determined to go by sea. However, experience in Liverpool Bay had taught him caution and he used the firm's remaining capital to purchase the small steam yacht *Elphin* as a tug and escort for *Resurgam*.

Elphin towed *Resurgam* out of Rhyl Harbour at 10 p.m., in pitch darkness, on 24 February 1880. She headed west along the Welsh coast while the glass was falling. Off Great Orme's Head, *Elphin*'s feed pump for the boiler broke down, and a boat was sent to bring back Engineer Price from the submarine astern. Garrett and Jackson decided to go too, which was just as well because a full north-westerly gale was soon blowing. Price got the pump going again and the tow was resumed, but at 10 a.m. on the following day, 26 February, the towing hawser parted. It was all over in moments: *Resurgam*, probably with her hatch cracked open (no submarine hatch can be securely shut from the outside), foundered and sank. *Elphin* ran for shelter in the River Dee, but was rammed and wrecked by another boat that tried to come to her assistance. It is charitably believed that both losses were accidental. (After many searches, *Resurgam* was located in 1997, and salvage was planned to make her live up to her name.)

The Garretts, father and son, were now in deep financial trouble: Dr Garrett filed for bankruptcy while his wife papered the walls of his study with worthless Submarine Navigation Company share certificates.[11] Garrett junior, however, hastened to establish a formal relationship with Nordenfelt.

Thorsten Nordenfelt (prompted by arms-peddler and part-time guide to Athenian brothels Basil Zaharoff) was convinced that the sales potential for submarines was enormous, especially for those navies which could not match the maritime might of England. He shrewdly perceived that submarines and 'fish' torpedoes were natural allies although intricate torpedo mechanisms would best be kept *inside* a submarine, or at least in a watertight tube, until the moment of firing.

The Swede uncharacteristically accepted Garrett as a sound and level-headed engineer without question. The disastrous joint efforts that resulted were categorized as 'Nordenfelt boats', but the machinery owed something to the recalcitrant curate from Manchester. When the partnership was firmly established Garrett abandoned parochial allegiances altogether: big business was beckoning. The name of George William Garrett was stricken from the Bishop of Manchester's Clerical Register in 1882.[12]

Unfortunately, the two inventors did not stick by Garrett's intuitively sensible lozenge-shaped design. Instead, their boats grew longer and thinner, more like foreshortened eels than the porpoises or fat salmon which ultimately successful submarine designers chose to copy. *Nordenfelt I*, laid down near Stockholm late in 1882 and launched in July 1883, was reasonably

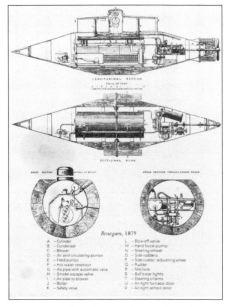

Resurgam *drawings*. (The Engineer)

proportioned with a mainly circular pressure-hull 64 ft long and a maximum beam of 9 ft – by chance almost the ideal seven-to-one ratio for underwater manoeuvrability – but other features were against her. The torpedo was carried in an external tube, which protected it, but the torpedoman stood a good chance of being washed overboard. Maximum safe depth was reckoned at 50 ft (15 m).

The steam plant was a sort of Lamm and most of the boat's interior was occupied by a marine boiler, a steam accumulator and a compound main engine driving the (too large) 5-ft propeller. The engine had exceptionally large-bore cylinders to accommodate low-pressure steam as the pressure dropped. A major snag was that the boiler had to be fired, in harbour, for no less than twelve hours (one account says three days) to get the system up to speed. Replenishment at sea, so to speak, was out of the question.

Nordenfelt did not aim for neutral buoyancy submerged. He wanted to retain some positive buoyancy, to be overcome by vertically shafted propellers:

> I feel confident that previous attempts have proved unsuccessful mainly because either they depend upon varying the displacement of the boat by taking in water to submerge her, and to regulate the depth at which they desire to operate, or they descend by steering downwards. My objection . . . is that . . . when the boat has lost its buoyancy at the surface, it has also no buoyancy at any given depth, and the risk is thus very great of suddenly descending beyond a safe depth. Further . . . they relied upon some mechanical means for ascending by ejecting water. In case such mechanical means failed the boat would be lost . . . .[13]

It is easy enough to criticize Nordenfelt's policy now; but people were still wondering at iron ships floating on the surface, let alone careering about below.

Submergence was therefore achieved by two downhaul propellers which overcame constant positive buoyancy of between 600 and 800 lb. The downhaul screws were operated by separate 6-hp three-cylinder steam-engines. A counterpoise weight worked against sea pressure to regulate the position of the steam valve on these engines and shut off steam if the safe depth was exceeded. The boat would then rise by natural buoyancy until sea pressure decreased to a point where the valves reopened to admit steam to the downhaul engines again. At least, that was the intention.

Nordenfelt I had bow planes but no diving rudders. The planes, like the vertical propellers, were automated. By the action of a plumb weight, according to the inventor, 'they were always held in the horizontal position, and therefore, should the boat for any cause tend to take a direction other than the horizontal, these rudders will immediately bring the boat back to the horizontal position'. The system resembled Whitehead's 'secret' for controlling the depth of his torpedoes but he would not have been flattered by Nordenfelt's ineffective imitation. It is certain that the gear would never have worked in a submarine which, at best, could only make two knots submerged.

The boat was surfaced either by shutting off steam to the downhaul screws, or pumping water from the main ballast tank, or by using steam pressure (if enough was left) to blow out the main ballast, although the constant positive buoyancy was enough by itself to regain the awash condition.

Secondary armament (a reason for rapid surfacing) was provided by a 1-in Nordenfelt gun on the deck just forward of the access tower: it was to be fired by the captain – a busy man in *Nordenfelt I*.

Sea trials at Landskrona in September 1885 attracted thirty-nine distinguished spectators from the major European naval powers, Japan and Mexico. The good news was that the boat was not lost during the demonstration. It succeeded in swooping (like the *Hunley*) under the gunboat *Edda* which carried the observers; but the longest period dived was only five minutes, and then the boat hit the bottom. Nobody was enamoured of the vessel; but Lord Sydenham of Combe was moved to write in *The Times*: 'It is certain that the Nordenfelt boat, as at present existing, will effect no revolution: but it seems equally clear that we shall shortly have to face possibilities which we have hitherto been able to neglect . . .'[14]

The other *Nordenfelt*s that followed became bigger but not better. Giant 3-in diameter candles provided a glimmer of light but heat and humidity were almost unbearable; and a briquette coal-fired boiler, with carbon monoxide escaping in significant quantities through the furnace door to mix with coal-dust, resulted in a thoroughly unpleasant and dangerous atmosphere. Garrett was once ill for three weeks after being gassed and if, as seems likely, carbon monoxide was to blame, it probably contributed towards his premature death at the age of fifty.

The first Nordenfelt *at Landskrona, September 1885.*

However, the operation of these boats submerged was so absorbing that breathing difficulties were scarcely noticeable. Before diving, the furnace was shut down, the telescopic funnel lowered and the funnel sealed (a foretaste of the calamitous steam-driven 'K' boats of 1917 whose diving orders included the tongue-twisting 'shut funnel flap valves'). The ballast tank, a 4-ton affair amidships, was then flooded and the stationary boat settled into the water while the crew devoutly hoped she would do so on an even keel. When only the conning tower was showing above water, and with a positive buoyancy of about one-quarter of a ton remaining, the craft was then clawed fully under by the downhaul propellers: on *Nordenfelt I*, these were either side of the hull amidships but on later models they were in faired recesses at each end. The best submerged performance recorded was a 300-yd run at a depth of 5 ft below the normal waterline.

Whatever its shortcomings, *Nordenfelt I* was bought by the Royal Hellenic Navy for no readily apparent reason other than to bluff Turkey; but the stealthy agency of Zaharoff, 'mystery man of Europe', lurked in the shadows. The submarine reached Piraeus safely and the Duke of Edinburgh, flying his flag in HMS *Temeraire*, sent the young Lt Sydney Eardley-Wilmot to investigate. He reported that 'she had some ingenious qualities, one being a greater difficulty to submerge than to come to the surface, reversing the procedure in early submarine boats'.[15]

Greece paid 225,000 French francs (a trifle less than £9,000, reduced from £20,000) for the so-called submarine boat. The amoral Zaharoff advised Nordenfelt: 'Let this sale go through cheaply. Once we have sold one, we can sell others. And once we have sold to two countries we can force up the price.'[16]

The boat had been sectioned and shipped to Greece in the American SS *Toledo*; but, typically, Garrett spun an absurdly romantic yarn of steering the submarine himself, undetected by night, through the Royal Navy's gathering off Salamis, so close to the ships that he could hear voices. The shade of Sgt Lee must have smiled sardonically.

A trial in the Bay of Salamis on 26 March was 'esteemed a great success', but this was disinformation passed to *The Times* by the Garrett-Zaharoff combination.[17] In truth the Greek Navy was so embarrassed that the boat was quietly laid up at Piraeus. All the same, Greece made much of having a secret weapon.

The price paid by Greece was money wasted. This, though, was not the view taken by Lt Gen Sir Andrew Clarke, Inspector General of Fortifications in Britain; he was supported by Sydenham who, in *The Times*, advised the government that:

> . . . such boats could . . . await the enemy [fleet] in placid serenity . . . indefensible towns, such as Brighton, would possess a means of defence ready to their hand . . . their mere presence would probably suffice to deter the approach of hostile ships. Coast defence [provided by the Army in Great Britain and most other countries until the early 1900s], already very formidable, would be rendered less expensive and its sphere would be extended.[18]

Adm Jacky Fisher, discussed in Chapter 1, read *The Times*! Gen Clarke's assurance that submarines would be preferable to 'a large expenditure on land fortifications and a corresponding increase of military personnel' carried weight, although the £20,000 he recommended for purchasing a Nordenfelt boat was equal to the entire estimate for mines, stores and associated infrastructure for the defence of British mercantile ports in 1885.[19]

Meanwhile, it was rumoured that Russia was acquiring a fleet of fifty 2-ton electrically-driven (actually pedal-powered) midget submarines from Claude Goubet of Paris. Their purpose was unclear; but anyway the Tsarevitch changed his mind and the craft were ignominiously converted into pontoons and buoys. However, Sultan Abdul Hamid II ('Abdul the Damned') was alarmed by the dual submerged threat from Greece and Russia, and in January 1886 the Turkish Admiralty ordered two *Nordenfelts*: to be built amongst the swans at Chertsey on the River Thames.

The craft could not fail to be an improvement on the previous Turkish submarine venture in 1719 when Ibrahim Effendi constructed his *Timsah* (Crocodile): this new vessel was equipped with such a noticeable breathing tube that one of the Sultan's courtiers thought he was looking at the stovepipe of an undersea kitchen. The 'kitchen' disappeared off Seraglio Point while helping to celebrate the circumcision of Sultan Ahmed III's son; but the five-man crew escaped.[20]

The first *Nordenfelt*, in seven sections, was shipped in SS *Trinidad*, arriving in Constantinople on 17 May 1886, short of several important parts but otherwise ready for reassembly under the honorary Commander Garrett's supervision. The second boat, *Abdul Medjid*, was delivered later. The *Abdul Hamid* was half as long again as *Nordenfelt I* and the steam engine was a good deal more powerful, offering a theoretical 10 knots on the surface and 5 knots submerged; but it only achieved a fraction of these speeds. The armament comprised two internal torpedo tubes, mounted one above the other, and two 1-in guns. Such a vessel must have seemed to the Turkish Government an attractive and powerful addition to its forces. It was better (on paper) than anything that the Greeks or Russians had so far recruited to their fleets.

The submarine was launched at the Tashkizak wharf on Saturday 18 September 1886, flying the flag of Sweden at the foremast and of Turkey at the mainmast. Capt (Army rank) P.W. D'Alton representing Nordenfelt, and a future Chief Engineer of the Central London Railway, witnessed the subsequent trials:

> Nothing could be imagined more unstable than [this] boat. . . . The moment she left the horizontal position, the water in her boiler and tanks surged forward and backwards and increased the angle of inclination. She was perpetually working up and down like a scale beam, and no human vigilance could keep her on an even keel for half a minute at a time.[21]

The Turkish Commission concluded an entirely negative report: 'The boats are very dangerous to the crews. . . . They cannot be used to protect ports or the Bosphorus . . . they have *no* naval use'.[22] In the end two (meagre) cheques were handed over – one to Nordenfelt for £1,488 and one to Garrett for £2,000. Garrett's cheque bounced.

Undismayed, Garrett and Nordenfelt constructed yet another submarine, even longer at 125 ft and with a maximum beam of 12 ft. Diving depth was doubled to 100 ft. *Nordenfelt IV* displaced 245 tons submerged: the Lamm system was revived and modified, and engine power was quadrupled to 1200 hp. Nine separate diving tanks held the 35 tons of water required to submerge: Garrett at last realized that divided tanks would prevent the 'free surface' effect of surging water although he neglected the contents of a half-full boiler.

Garrett, apparently as a joke, pictured in USN enlisted man's uniform, with a sailorlike pipe, at Galveston, Texas, 1897. (Garrett family)

An obvious market for the improved design was Russia where the Minister for Coast Defence had been interested in underwater defences for several years, latterly coming close to adopting the plans of a Polish engineer remembered chiefly for the impossible English spelling of his name – Drzewiecki. The Russians had very little idea of what they wanted, so the last and largest *Nordenfelt* was built 'on spec' at the Barrow Shipbuilding Company's Works (later Vickers) and launched as Job No. 149 in March 1887, some thirteen years before work was started on the Royal Navy's first submarine boat.

Number 4 got off to a bad start. At launch, as soon as she slid into the water, it was obvious that somebody had made a serious error in calculating the trim: she settled heavily by the stern, drawing 9 ft aft and only 4 ft 6 in forward. Garrett suffered a kind of seizure and was laid up for six months. The mistake was rectified by adding ballast forward but the extra weight robbed the boat of speed. *The Times* told readers that although the boat was slow it was apparently sure; should she 'sink deeper than is desirable or safe, she would ascend as naturally to the surface as a runaway horse makes for the

Engine room of a Turkish Nordenfelt *during re-assembly, 1886/7.* (RNSM)

stable door'.[23] The upper part of the turtle-back and the two glass-ported conning towers were plated with 1-in-thick steel, implying that the boat was expected to go into action awash.

Nordenfelt IV had a range of 1,000 miles and carried eight tons of coal. The forward conning tower contained a depth gauge, inclinometer and compass which was not compensated for deviation due to the vessel's constantly changing magnetic field. There were nine men in the crew and, for internal communication, speaking tubes obviated the need for any movement which might upset the delicate fore-and-aft trim. There was a bunk for each man and a primitive galley.

The boat was demonstrated on the surface at Queen Victoria's Spithead Review a few months after launching, and the Tsar was captivated: without demanding proof of the pudding he decided forthwith to buy. The low silhouette certainly made the boat hard to see: at full speed the minimal superstructure, painted a dull grey, was actually below the bow-wave when viewed from ahead. Nordenfelt calculated she offered only one-

Garrett's final appearance, centre, with hand on heart (before he died on 26 February 1902) as a Corporal in the US Volunteer Engineers, probably while training in June/July 1898 at Peekskill NY, prior to embarkation for Puerto Rico. (Garrett family)

thirteenth the visible area of a first-class torpedo boat. He told Fred Jane, the naval commentator, that the bow-wave alone 'deflects bullets upwards at such an angle that they clear the hull'.[24]

Nordenfelt IV set off for Krondstadt escorted by the yawl *Lodestar* in November 1888. While passing up the North Sea she ran aground off Jutland on an ebb tide. Judging by the recollections of John W. Garrett, the inventor's son, the ill-fated voyage took a turn for the worse after calling at Amsterdam where two of the crew, Jim Arm and 'Bosun George' made young John walk the plank 'after sampling the sweet champagne of that town'.[25] The submarine was refloated two weeks later but the Russians wisely refused to complete the purchase.

At this point, Garrett and Nordenfelt parted. Garrett's money was gone, his hopes were gone, and the Church showed no signs of taking him back into the fold. He emigrated to America where he served with the Unites States Army Engineers during the Spanish–American War. He died in New York City on 26 February 1902, practically destitute.[26]

CHAPTER 12

An Irish Invention

1845–1850 Ireland: The Great Hunger
1866 Locomotive torpedo: Whitehead
1868 New London, Connecticut Navy Yard established

Occasionally, in this unfair life, the best man wins. While the flamboyantly erratic George Garrett (half-Irish and Protestant) deceived himself and others in the submarine world, the modestly quiet John Philip Holland (wholly Irish and Catholic) was glimpsing victory while neither dissembling about his work nor exaggerating its worth. Indeed, the bespectacled little inventor, pictured at the height of his fame with a walrus moustache and a sober Derby hat, was too honest and straightforward for his own good in the worldly sense. Granted he had a fair share of human frailties: at times he was pernickety, ultra-critical and neurotic; but his personality was knitted together by a kind of dependable Irish quirkiness and softened by a shy inquisitive smile.

Holland had none of the important political and commercial contacts enjoyed by Garrett and, as an obedient, lifelong follower of the Catholic Church, he eschewed Freemasonry.[1] He complained that: 'the results of individual efforts [in submarine design] were . . . hidden to prevent the competition of other inventors. As each designer was thus compelled to face the problem without the knowledge that had been accomplished by his predecessors, he had to discover for himself the main requirement of a submarine vessel, and to foresee and to provide against difficulties.'[2] But this is exactly why Holland got it right! He started with an open mind.

John Holland – he took the name Philip in religion – was born on 24 February 1841 in a single-storeyed cottage off Castle Street, Liscannor overlooking the desolate, windy Atlantic coast of Co. Clare.[3] He was the eldest son of a family resulting from his coastguard father's second marriage to Mary Scanlon:[4] his first wife Anne had died in 1835 aged 25. His stepbrother Alfred was some six years his senior and he had two younger brothers, Robert born in 1845 and Michael Joseph born in 1848.[5]

John Holland Sr retired in 1853 and the family moved to Limerick where John Jr attended the Christian Brothers' school in Sexton Street. The household subsisted on a small military pension and, when young John engaged himself 'in the service of Michael Paul O'Riordan, Superior of the Christian Brothers . . . requiring no other remuneration . . . than whatever food and raiment he may please to give me . . . ,' he was admitted free to the Novitiate in 1858. Had his eyesight been better he would have preferred to join the Merchant Navy; but at the age of seventeen he duly took the initial vows of the Teaching Order of the Irish Christian Brothers.

Coincidentally, a notably less monastic association, the Irish Republican Brotherhood – well known on both sides of the Atlantic as the IRB – had been founded three months earlier on St Patrick's Day. Holland was to be linked financially with the IRB, but for the next fifteen years he would receive no stipend for his work with the Order: he took the habit on 30 June 1858.

Holland, as a boy, saw poverty and disease all round him. The Hungry Forties, at their worst during the 'Great Hunger' from 1846 to 1850, caused by failure of potato crops due to blight originating in America, was followed by widespread 'Famine Fever'. Unfortunately famine arose at the same time as a monetary crisis in Britain; much too little was done to alleviate Ireland's plight. Throughout these long hard times the wicked landlords (or more often their agents), portrayed as moustache-twirling villains on the Victorian stage, were real enough on Irish soil. They were all too ready to evict defaulting tenants from their cottages and strip the thatch from the roofs to prevent their coming back: this was known as 'levelling', and young John saw plenty of it. Before he was ten years old, he watched Robert dying of cholera, and lost two uncles from the same disease.

Thus from his earliest years John profoundly believed, like so many of his countrymen, that England was to blame for Ireland's pitiable condition. All true Irishmen sought some means of throwing off the intolerable English yoke which, in John Holland's view, was largely imposed by a dominating British fleet. He was, of course, considering much the same situation that had angered David Bushnell in the previous century. Word of renewed American submarine activities reached Ireland where Holland quietly absorbed them. Submarines might be poor Ireland's future answer to England's present might.

Thus, Br Philip, now a young schoolmaster, daydreamed, allowing a naturally inventive mind to revolve around mechanical matters instead of keeping proper order in his classroom at the North Monastery, Cork. Encouraged (or abetted) by Br James Dominic Burke, a noted science teacher, he developed surprising talents for mechanics, draftsmanship and applied mathematics, as well as teaching music by the tonic solfa method on his own account. Diffident but witty, and obviously very intelligent, he continually entertained his classes with scientific and musical demonstrations; out of class he never ceased to be fascinated by Br Burke's rather surprising experiments with propulsion for underwater vehicles and the remote detonation of mines ('torpedoes') by electricity.[6] John Philip sketched a submarine which Br Burke transformed into a wooden model for him.

According to Br John Norris, Br Philip 'was a complete failure as a teacher . . .

and had to leave the Congregation in consequence of his lack of control'.[7] In 1865 he was transferred to Drogheda where he spent four years endeavouring to improve his teaching methods. He could hold attention 'for hours at a time talking about and demonstrating mechanical things' such as the artificial duck which he constructed: it 'could walk about in the garden and when put in water could swim, dive and come to the surface again'.[8] All the same, the *Scrutiny Book* for 1868 comments: 'Br Philip Holland should be admonished on the inefficiency of his school and the very reduced attendance of children compared with its condition in care of former years – the cause appearing to be his occupying his mind with things quite foreign to his obligations.'[9]

In 1869 Br Holland was moved to the school at Dundalk where he was described as 'a man of medium height, about 5ft 8in slim and dark, with a pleasing open countenance . . . of a cheerful and happy disposition . . . admired and loved by his pupils'.[10] This was surely as good as being an iron disciplinarian but not, it seems, in the eyes of all.

In 1872 the lengthy period of Br Philip's annual and triennial vows ended. Earlier that year, Holland's family, apart from stepbrother Alfred, had taken ship to America. Michael, a vehement separationist (that is, rebel) had already emigrated (escaped) during the openly rebellious anti-English years 1865–7. John Philip might have resisted the temptation to follow and stayed in Ireland if Dominic McDonnell, newly elected assistant to the Superior General, had not launched a heavy-handed crusade for efficiency in schools, bruising Br Philip in the process;[11] he declined perpetual vows at Christmas 1872. On 26 May 1873, he sailed from Liverpool as a steerage passenger with little in his pocket apart from some drawings of a submarine.

Soon after arriving at Boston in November 1873, he slipped on ice, broke a leg and was laid up with enforced time to reflect on his design. He concluded that his idea was sound, but he had to make a living and was lucky to resume teaching, in a lay capacity, with the (French) Christian Brothers at Paterson, New Jersey. (The Christian Brothers in the USA were of the De La Salle Order and not of the Irish congregation.) Like a number of immigrants from the old country, Holland found his genuine sense of patriotism strengthened by distance. There was plenty of Irish revolutionary fervour in America to encourage him. The Fenian Brotherhood, American counterpart of the IRB, was powerful and militant; but it was divided and confused within itself about how to take action against the British, whether in Canada or Ireland, at sea or on land. However, the Fenians seized on Holland's submarine proposal, the *Irish World* launched an appeal for funds, and money from Irish-Americans started to roll in.

In 1876 Holland built a 30-in model submarine and demonstrated it to prospective Fenian supporters at Coney Island. It was enough to convince them that a full-size 'wrecking boat' should be built. (At that time 'wrecking boat' described, contrarily, a recovery vessel. The term was used by the Fenians to conceal the submarine's true purpose.) Considering the degree of thoroughgoing

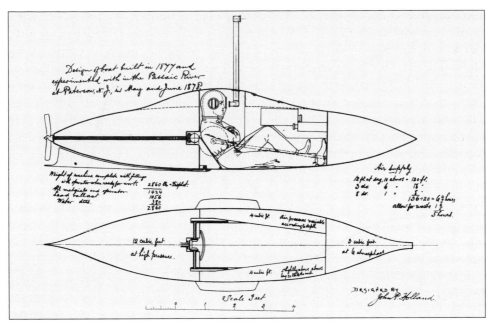

Holland's drawings for his first submarine. In the event he did not wear a diving suit and did not have a periscope. Eventual success was largely due to his diving under way with a bow down angle – a daunting prospect – rather than statically and level, like most of his more cautious competitors, while experimenting although his 'coffin' was stopped on this occasion. (Morris collection).

Irish enthusiasm and alcoholic encouragement which attended the project, the precise nature of the secret was remarkably well kept. Holland's first submarine was lozenge-shaped, 14 ft 6 in long and 2 ft 6 in high with a squat turret-like attachment on the top.[12] She was completed, after being laid down at the Albany Iron Works, by J.C. Todd and Co. on Van Houton Street, Paterson in the spring of 1878, for a total cost of about $4,000. Construction was funded by Jacobs, Snr of Jacobs & Company, codename for the leading Fenian, Jeremiah O'Donovan Rossa, and his 'Skirmishing Fund'. On 22 May, the dwarfish craft was winched onto a wagon and drawn, reportedly by eight pairs of stallions, to the water's edge close by the Spruce Street Bridge on the right bank of the Passaic River. Somebody looking down from the bridge cheerfully remarked, 'I see the Professor has built a coffin for himself.' The quotation is believable; the newspaper report of stallions (why stallions?) is less so. The craft weighed two-and-a-quarter tons. When hauled and tipped off the wagon, she settled rapidly into the water and, in a moment, sank out of sight. Holland was still on the bank: the coffin, fortunately, was empty.

Holland had built the craft so that its manned weight (2,480 lb +380 lb water ballast) was equal to the weight of salt water displaced when fully submerged. But the upper reaches of the Passaic River were fresh: the water was significantly less dense and hence less buoyant. The prototype was hauled up by means of strong lines prudently attached before launching. A week later, she was floating with the correct surface draught after adjustments and repairs had been made. Unfortunately, the very early Brayton two-cylinder engine, patented by George Brayton in 1874, intended to run on gasoline, would not start. Holland put on a brave show of being undismayed though he knew full well that a serious defect at this stage could lead to bankruptcy as well as accusations of incompetence or even sabotage by Rossa and the rest. Spurred by necessity, he adapted the engine to alternative power: steam was passed through a rubber hose from a hired steam launch alongside. It worked. Chugging along under borrowed energy at 3 knots, the submarine and her attendant launch, together with a quorum of prominent Fenians, soon reached a stretch of water unencumbered by other craft.

The steam supply was disconnected and Holland squeezed himself into a cockpit 3 ft wide, 3 ft 8 in long and only a little more than 2 ft high, with his head protuding into a sealed conning tower. Deadlights allowed limited vision ahead and abeam. A diver's helmet (envisaged in his initial sketches) was not needed because he reckoned he had air (compressed and stored) for five hours. When he was ready to go, the steampipe's female joint was brutally forced back on to the submarine's male connection.

Holland, seemingly fearless and replete with faith, flooded the two principal ballast tanks and pushed forward the lever which controlled a single pair of diving rudders pivoted at the centre of buoyancy just forward of the turret. Slight positive buoyancy, a feature of all Holland's early designs, was retained by leaving small tanks forward and aft empty: if power failed the craft should automatically rise to the surface.

The little boat obediently tilted her blunt nose downwards at the first attempt and slid beneath the water to an estimated depth of 12 ft, reappearing safely a few yards farther on. A further trial, during which Holland stayed on the bottom for one hour, was equally reassuring. On this occasion the dive was made 'standing' without forward propulsion, by ballasting alone, and therefore without assistance from the awkwardly placed horizontal rudders. He soon decided that diving rudders were much better positioned right aft.

The Trustees of the Fenian Skirmishing Fund now agreed that financial support was merited for a bigger and better boat. At thirty-seven years of age, Holland looked to a bright engineering future. He ceased teaching in 1878 and shifted direct allegiance from the Christian Brothers to the Fenian Brothers, although he maintained a fond correspondence with former mentors in the Irish Order.

From hereon it was neither politics nor religion – nor even self-interest – that really pushed him to the heights or, rather, to the depths. Submarines were utterly absorbing, and he was not the only man to find them so. Fascination was enough to sustain John Holland's single-minded devotion to 'submarine navigation' for a further score of years before his work was generally acclaimed.

CHAPTER 13

The Salt Water Enterprise

1878 First telephone exchange: Connecticut USA
1880–1 First Boer War

The Fenian factions in America were supposedly united in the *Clan na Gael* (United Brotherhood), but by the beginning of 1878 rivalries, loose talk and liquor were starting to split the association and threaten the success of the Irish submarine project codenamed the 'Salt Water Enterprise'. On 6 February, the prominent Fenian John Devoy wrote to a colleague 'I do not propose to fritter away my life in endless squabbles, nor do I think it safe to go into serious revolutionary work with men who cannot keep a secret.'[1]

Secrecy seemed paramount because the Brotherhood, encouraged by Holland's younger brother Michael, intended to commission a new craft to attack the British fleet as soon as the opportunity offered, for example, if Britain went to war with Russia. Holland himself was so cagey that when he approached the Delamater Ironworks on West 13th Street, New York City, the managers would not undertake the submarine project until they knew who the backers were. They eventually yielded to a promise of cash payment, and produced an estimate guaranteeing that the cost would not exceed $20,000.

One of the problems, complained the unremittingly Irish Holland, was the same that he later encountered among staff officers of the United States Navy: 'they were, almost without exception, of English, Welsh or Scotch descent':[2] they appeared 'to know by intuition that the project was absurd'.

There were a number of foreign visitors to the Ironworks while Holland's second submarine was under construction – so much for secrecy! Mostly Swedes, Russians, Italians and Germans, the envoys included two representatives from Turkey. Holland was consistently reticent and the Turkish contract went to Nordenfelt and Garrett. The meeting confirmed Holland's suspicion that the world, including America, was distrustful of any naval proposal that did not originate in England.

Construction was completed for $18,000, well below estimate, although this did not include some auxiliary machinery. The submarine was launched in May 1881 and towed across the Hudson River to the Morris Dredging Company's Dock, Jersey City. The three-man, 19-ton boat was 31 ft long, 6 ft broad at the

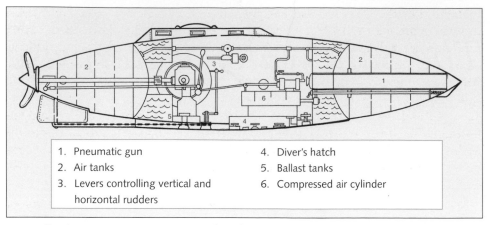

1. Pneumatic gun
2. Air tanks
3. Levers controlling vertical and horizontal rudders
4. Diver's hatch
5. Ballast tanks
6. Compressed air cylinder

J.P. Holland's Fenian Ram, *1881. Length 31ft, max beam 6ft, 19 tons. Hull 11/16in charcoal flange iron.*

widest point and drew 7 ft 4 in. A Brayton 15 hp twin-cylinder, double-acting petroleum engine gave a maximum speed of 8 or 9 mph.

The British naval attaché, Capt William Arthur, and the Consul General at New York, Edmund Archibald, paid ingratiating calls on the shipyard. Archibald charmed Cornelius Delamater into allowing Arthur to copy Holland's drawings,[3] and the consulate was assured by Mr Robertson of US Customs, New York, that a watch would be kept on the submarine.[4] The Salt Water Enterprise cover was finally blown in the summer of 1881 by a reporter for the *New York Sun*, Blakely Hall, who (although denied access by Holland) published a comprehensive account of what he called a mysterious 'Fenian Ram'; the name stuck.

The little boat was propelled in all conditions by its air-dependent engine, though the precise nature of the fuel, and the method of igniting it, is uncertain; when submerged it was supplied with air under pressure bled from storage cylinders. The boat's porpoise-shaped hull, typical of all Holland's designs, provided excellent streamlining. The hydroplanes and rudder were just forward of the single propeller.

Pressure against the exhaust underwater was obviously liable to stop the engine – like the old trick of plugging a motor car's exhaust pipe with a potato. It was a problem that would recur when the *Schnorchel* was introduced in the 1940s; Holland had anticipated the eventual solution by fitting a flap-valve outboard. Later, for larger boats and engines, he designed a chest of spring-loaded non-return valves for the same purpose.[5] Holland (dependably truthful) said he dived the Ram underway to about 45 ft, but probably only for a few moments. When he took the boat down to the calculated maximum safe depth of 60 ft he stopped the engine first.

Meanwhile, the notorious English (and Canadian) spy Maj Henri Le Caron (alias Thomas Beach from Braidwood, Illinois), circled like a jackal around

Holland and the *Clan na Gael*, hoping to pick up saleable titbits and cause dissension among the Irish militants at the same time. His efforts in the latter direction were unnecessary: the United Brotherhood was forever disuniting without any encouragement from outside. It was Le Caron who alerted Consul Archibald, but his attempt to persuade Congress to halt outright the Fenian submarine threat failed on the rightful grounds that it was a private concern. Nevertheless, the British Vice-Consul, Mr Drummond, optimistically told the Foreign Office that 'The American government will do anything to carry out the wishes of Her Majesty's Government with regard to these and any other such plans.'[6] The Foreign Office did not enquire of Drummond to whom he had spoken.

Privately, Holland was not displeased by Hall's newspaper article: the disclosure simplified business dealings and, with the boat's 19-ton hull built of 11/16th charcoal flange iron, the inventor reckoned her 'ramming power' at 49–50 tons, which justified the name. The effectiveness of this tactic was inadvertently demonstrated on trials when the *Ram* hit the end of a pier at 6 knots 'owing to my bad steering or forgetfulness at the time'. A 12-in pile was split and a solid horizontal tie-bar, with 4 ft of stone ballast stacked on it, was forced upwards. The *Ram* was tough: 'Nothing but the engineer's respect for good English' was hurt.[7]

The *Ram*'s crew consisted of the pilot (Holland), the engineer (George M. Richards of Erie, Pennsylvania) and a gunner not yet appointed. There was plenty to keep two men occupied.

The first dive in the summer of 1883 was entirely satisfactory. In Holland's words, 'I drew back the little iron levers on either side of my head' thereby opening Kingston valves through which water was admitted to the two internal ballast tanks amidships and

. . . almost immediately the boat began to settle, giving us the suggestion of slowly descending in an elevator. I looked through the ports in the superstructure and observed that the bow had entirely disappeared and the water was within a few inches of the glass. A second or two later everything grew dark and we were entirely submerged, and nothing could be seen through the ports except a dark green blue.

The boat obviously dived with no way on because 'Our next sensation was a slight jar, when the vessel struck the bottom. It might also be mentioned here that we had no light except the glow that came through the conning tower . . .' The depth was a little over two fathoms – perhaps 15 ft. Richards made the rounds in the dark (they resolved to carry a lantern for the next dive) and discovered no leaks. It was enough for the day. Holland opened the blowing valve and heard the reassuring hiss telling him that compressed air was driving water out of the tanks.

Fenian Ram *looking aft towards the gearing driven by the 15-17hp Brayton petroleum engine.* (Paterson Museum)

The ballasting arrangements called for the after tank to be filled completely and the forward tank likewise except when compensating for relatively minor weight changes or the discharge of a missile. The *Ram* was not plagued by the free-surface surging which worsened the longitudinal instability dogging other inventors. With a fixed centre of gravity and a five-to-one length-to-breadth ratio, the *Ram* was relatively stable and had enough speed in hand to make the diving rudders effective.

The next trial was to show that the *Ram* could dive with the engine running:

For this occasion I [took] my place in the conning tower, while he [Richards] went forward to start the engine. After a little kicking and muttering [Richards was the archetypal submarine engineer] he succeeded in getting it started. We then let in the clutch and the boat started forward . . . we then made sure that everything was tight and opened the Kingston valves. When the water reached the observer's ports in the conning tower, I closed them again.

We then proceeded along awash; that is, with only the little tower showing above the surface. I found that from this position I could observe objects quite a distance ahead, and my vision was obscured only occasionally when a wave washed against the glass. I next threw forward the lever on the right side of my seat [controlling the diving rudders aft]. Immediately the nose of the boat went down and before I realised it our gauge showed a depth of about 10 feet. I now drew the lever back to centre, and the boat straightened out on an even keel. There was very little or no tendency to buck or be cranky; in a word I had no difficulty in preventing her nose from rising or dipping down. After running about 100 yards submerged I steered the boat up, and in a few seconds the superstructure of the boat was again above water . . .[8]

The boat could also be used as a diving bell: it had a hatch in the base of the hull for a diver's exit and re-entry, after first building up sufficient internal air pressure to hold the water at bay. George Richards determined to test the practicality of this: one day, all alone, he settled the *Ram* down on the bottom while alongside the dock and opened the lower hatch. He was not wearing a diving suit, so he stood in the hatchway, on the harbour bed, and passed his hands under the hull on either side to lift the boat 'slowly and with little exertion about one foot from the bottom'. The unauthorized experiment was successful; but Richards was insatiably curious, and his next solo effort was expensive. He decided, early one morning, to take the boat out for a run. Holland arrived a few minutes after he had slipped and found a gaggle of onlookers excitedly pointing to an uprush of foam and bubbles on the surface about 200 yd off the pier. There was no sign of the *Ram*. One of the spectators said that a barge and a tug had just passed very close to the submarine, washing water down the conning tower. It transpired that Richards was only just below the hatch when the water started pouring in. He was able to bale out with the escaping air, reappearing on the surface 'still a bit pale'. The accident cost the Skirmishing Fund some $3,000 to raise the *Ram* and dry her out.

More advanced trials were conducted across the Narrows below Stapleton. Before diving, Holland made sure that no ship in the vicinity was drawing more than 30 ft. Excursion steamers, fishing boats and small yachts could be ignored because he intended running at a depth of not less than 20 ft when close to them. The paddles of the excursion steamers could be heard underwater quite a long way off, and Holland found he had no difficulty in avoiding other vessels by changing course or going to a greater depth until they had passed. On one occasion he 'frightened the devil' out of the steamer *St Johns* by porpoising across its bows. There is enough evidence of this kind to confirm beyond doubt that the *Fenian Ram* was able to navigate several feet below the surface, with the engine running, keeping level or changing depth by using the diving rudders for steering up or down or at a slight angle. In 1883 the Irish submarine was years ahead of any rivals.

However, Holland was bothered about not being able to see underwater. The *Ram* had no periscope and her single propeller caused her to veer to one side. It was simple enough to correct this tendency when the conning tower viewing ports were above water, but equally easy to wander when submerged.

One excursion, on 3 July 1883, was made even more difficult when Holland found his view of Staten Island ahead and Bay Ridge to port 'obscured by what seemed to be a pair of brown rags hanging on either side of the turret'. It turned out that the rags were trousers belonging to a small boy who had managed to drop down on to the conning tower when the craft was leaving the dock. Holland opened the hatch and, typically, invited the stowaway inside to avoid him being swept off. The boy politely refused the invitation and said he was 'puffecly safe' where he was and that he would 'hold on like grim death'. Holland was not going to risk drowning the lad, and he resignedly headed back to the shore. But time had been wasted and the sun soon set. It was too dark to make for the usual moorings; but, while the craft was heading up towards the Bay Ridge Ferry landing-place, two well-spoken boys in a rowing boat came alongside. Holland, always the schoolmaster at heart, showed the astonished youngsters around the boat. His natural kindness bore dividends: one of the boys announced he was the young brother of Mr Vanderbilt Bergen, a noted shipyard owner, and he arranged for the *Fenian Ram* to berth at Bergen's very convenient dock at Bay Ridge. It became the submarine's base for the next two months.

The time now came to test the *Ram*'s extraordinary armament. Robert Whitehead's torpedoes were quite well proven but discharging them underwater was still fraught with problems and external 'Drzewiecki' cradles would have upset the *Ram*'s handling qualities.

Holland's weapon system was a gun, although it resembled a torpedo tube of the future. The bore was a standard 9 in diameter, large enough to hold a projectile up to 6 ft long tipped with a 100-lb charge. It was fired pneumatically by high-pressure air. Holland had long admired Capt John Ericsson for his *Monitor* of Civil War fame and, by chance, found that the Captain was building the new *Destroyer* in Delamater's Ironworks. Ericsson's missiles fortuitously fitted the *Ram*'s gun and the Captain generously agreed to let Holland have some dummies to use for discharge trials.

Holland trimmed the *Ram* down until the gun was horizontal and 3½ ft below the surface. There was a floating dock about 150 yd ahead of the bows, so firing pressure was reduced to 300 lb per sq in to avoid hitting it:

> When the firing valve was opened the projectile passed out and travelled about six or eight feet beyond the muzzle of the gun. Then it turned upward and climbed into the air to a height of 60 or 70 feet before falling point-foremost into the water where it buried itself so deeply in the mud that we could never find it again.[9]

For the second shot, the *Ram*'s bow was depressed a few degrees and swung to port. The firing pressure was doubled to 600 lb per sq in and the shell travelled about twice as far underwater before it 'rose 15 feet in the air and passed over the

The Fenian Ram *at New York State Marine School 1916–27, later moved to the Paterson Museum, New Jersey.* (Morris collection)

wall limiting the Basin, striking a pile that projected above it, and frightening a fisherman who was dozing thereon'. Holland, wary of adverse publicity, was quick to point out that 'the fisherman was in no danger as the pile and the stringer – a piece of heavy pine – afforded him protection'.[10]

The weaponry looked promising, but unfortunately a lawsuit was pending against Trustees of the Skirmishing Fund alleging misuse of monies and non-payment of a debt. John J. Breslin, adventurous editor of the *Irish World*, hastily resolved with a few colleagues to prevent the submarine being sequestered. Forging Holland's name on a pass, they manoeuvred a tug alongside the *Ram* and took her in tow, together with a 16-ft model test-vehicle, and headed away up Long Island Sound – all without a word to Holland. The model sank, never to be seen again; but the *Ram* arrived safely at New Haven. Here the Fenians, who knew nothing about shiphandling, made such a hash of things that the harbourmaster declared the submarine a menace to navigation. Breslin beached the boat and endeavoured, but failed, to sell her to Russia.

Holland's reaction was predictable: 'I'll let her rot on their hands.'[11] In the event, the *Ram* did not rot, although she never entered the water again. She was exhibited at Madison Square Garden in 1916 to help raise money at the time of the Irish uprising, and is now preserved, alongside Holland's first boat, in the Paterson Museum, New Jersey.

PUNCH, OR THE LONDON CHARIVARI.—June 9, 1877.

"FIAT EXPERIMENTUM—!"

Britannia. "ALLOW ME TO INTRODUCE A YOUNG GENTLEMAN WHO HAS JUST MADE HIS DEBUT ON THE DANUBE, AND TO WHOM YOU AND I WILL, I RATHER THINK, HAVE A GOOD DEAL TO SAY."

Punch, 9 *June 1877*

Holland had no more commercial dealings with his fellow Irishmen. From now on, he was intent on designing submarines for the United States Navy, although he soon became 'totally sick and disgusted' with the Navy Department's inaction and was seriously tempted to abandon all further attempts to convince and 'awake it from its lethargy'.[12] Meanwhile he noted that submarine designs in Europe were greatly inferior to his own.

Holland made some useful friends outside the *IRB* during the *Ram*'s brief career: one was the young naval officer, Lt (later Rear Adm) William W. Kimball. Despite his junior position, Kimball promised to prod head office into taking a more active interest in submarines. He underestimated the resistance of bureaucracy: as Capt Edward Simpson at the Newport Torpedo Station opined, 'to put anything through in Washington is uphill work'.[12]

Holland could not wait for Washington. With very little capital left and no income, he was obliged in 1883 to accept a position as a draftsman with the Pneumatic Gun Company where he encountered the ambitious ordnance expert Capt Edmund L. Zalinski of the US Army. Zalinski was anxious to promote a new 'dynamite gun' and he believed that a wooden submarine boat was the best vehicle in which to mount it. The gun was not to be used fully submerged as in the *Fenian Ram*: instead the bow of the submarine would be made to break surface, just before firing, at an angle appropriate to the range of the target, which could be up to half-a-mile distant. In other words, the submarine would serve as an extraordinarily flexible gun-carriage, training and elevating the gun barrel to any required degree. In practice it would have been *too* flexible: precision would have been unattainable unless the sea was flat calm. As it happened the gun was never tested: the submarine itself, chaotically launched on 4 September 1885, was a total failure.

Holland ruefully remarked, towards the end of his career, that the misguided 'Zalinski Boat' held him back for at least ten years. In the meantime, recently married to Margaret Foley of Paterson on 17 January 1887 and financially embarrassed, he had to read galling newspaper stories about well-supported competitors at home and in Europe.

CHAPTER 14

The Reason Why Not

1897 Compression ignition engine: Diesel
1898 German naval expansion: Tirpitz

Submarine development from the American Civil War up to the *fin de siècle* quickened in pace with emerging technology and growing competition between naval powers. Yet the greatest of all naval powers continued to stand aloof.

No less than 290 submissions concerning submarines were received by the British Admiralty between 1865 and 1900. There were peaks during the Russo–Turkish War of 1877–8 when torpedo boats became prominent, in 1885–6 resulting from Nordenfelt's publicity, and from 1893 when France lengthened her stride in the field.[1] But, with a few exceptions, generally where Masonic influence can be inferred, the Admiralty showed little patience with 'projectors'.

Even while the Foreign Office was receiving reports on the *Fenian Ram*, the Director of Naval Construction judged: 'There seems no reason to anticipate that this boat can ever be a real danger to British ships . . . [and] we should not recommend the spending of any money to obtain information.'[2] In January 1887, the Naval Lords declined an invitation for representatives to witness trials at Annapolis, Maryland, of Professor Josiah Tuck's *Peacemaker* with a Honigman fireless natron boiler generating steam by vast amounts of caustic soda; and in November 1888 they refused to send officers 20 miles to Slough to inspect the 'Patent Submarine Ship' built by Mr Henry Middleton. There was concern about the political ramifications of underwater warfare but scant interest in submarine practicalities. Few, if any, upper deck officers or Admiralty officials knew anything of submarine principles, and engineers were seldom asked for advice, partly because technical expertise was (literally) beneath the quarterdeck and partly because those who practised it might have 'left their aitches in Newcastle' – an absurd situation which Adm Jacky Fisher was determined to remedy by making engineers equal to executive officers.[3]

In any case, there was no evident need for the nineteenth-century Royal Navy to have submarine boats when ordinary torpedo boats were fast, fairly well proven and not overly expensive. Moreover, in 1893 the Admiralty Intelligence Department observed that 'the idea of attacking under water actually is not believed to be practicable.'[4] This pessimistic view resulted from the alarming

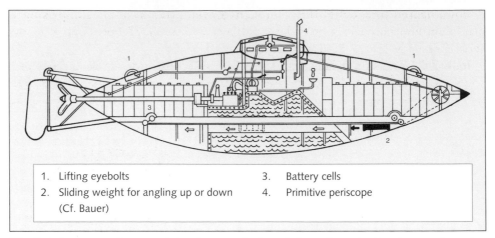

1. Lifting eyebolts
2. Sliding weight for angling up or down (Cf. Bauer)
3. Battery cells
4. Primitive periscope

The Polish engineer Drzewiecki's submarine built at St Petersburg for Russia, as a first of class, in 1879. Intended for carrying on board battleships, the design, pedal-operated, was not nearly so advanced or capable as Holland's Fenian Ram.

tendency of submersibles such as the *Nordenfelt*s to pitch violently in response to any change of weight, such as the discharge of a torpedo, forward or aft. John Holland alone amongst the pioneers perceived that the dangers of longitudinal instability could be markedly lessened by a shape that was short and fat rather than long and narrow: by avoiding long partially filled tanks and surging ('free surface'); by fitting diving rudders aft and having enough speed available to make them effective; and by having a fixed centre of gravity, directly below the centre of buoyancy, which could immediately be restored by transferring water between tanks when displaced by a shift of weight internally.

While submarine practicalities were seemingly in doubt the Admiralty's hesitation was entirely justified, but there is no evidence of delay for moral reasons. Nor was France, or any other nation, afflicted by conscience. The use of submarines was not even mentioned when the Hague Peace Conference conventions were signed on 29 July 1899, although Capt A.T. Mahan, one of the American representatives, had described the submarine as 'inhuman and cruel'.[5]

The British Government, looking around in the late 1890s, could distinguish ten nations with a supposed capability for submarine warfare. France had boats that appeared realistic and the United States soon would have. On the other hand, Greek and Turkish *Nordenfelt*s were 'practically useless'.[6] Spain's 87-ton all-electric *Peral* (invented by the (subsequently ennobled) Lt Isaac Peral) with accumulators was by 'general opinion . . . a complete failure . . . [it] went down three times, but was never able to move more than a few yards'.[7]

Brazil, anxious to keep up with distant Joneses, bought the first of Monsieur Goubet's boats. A feature of the design was 'an undue tendency to suddenly dive'.

A complicated and delightfully French preventative system, comprising a pendulum and pump in a pear-shaped dome, was provided but 'control in the vertical plane by this method was not successful'.[8]

Italy's 107-ton *Delfino*, launched in 1895, was electrically driven for a speed of 5 knots on the surface and 2 knots submerged. She owed much to Nordenfelt with two vertical propellers, a pair of 14-in torpedo tubes and two quick-action firing

Lt Isaac Peral and his 87-ton all-electric boat, launched on 8 September 1888, but rejected by the Spanish navy on 27 September 1890. (RNSM)

1-pdr guns. (After reconstruction, *Delfino* re-emerged in 1901 with a higher capacity battery and an 'explosion motor' for surface propulsion. Thus modified she could make 8 knots on the surface and 6 knots dived. She shed her 'downhauls', becoming quite handy with hydroplanes, and became the proud possessor of a cleptoscope extending about 15 ft above the hull with a 60-degree field of view.)

Portugal completed her 100-ton *Fontes* in 1892, designed by Lt Don Fontes Pereira de Mello. He was from the school which steadfastly refused to dive a submarine at an angle, and insisted on it being clawed under, while still not solving the seemingly intractable problem of keeping it on an even keel.

The state of play in Russia was vague. Stefan Drzewiecki's importunate efforts are best remembered for drop-collar external torpedo cradles which were quite widely adopted. The Tsar had a handful of very small submarine boats, equipped with drop-collars, but it is doubtful if they functioned properly. Russian procurement worked on a commission basis, agents being paid a percentage of the price paid; not surprisingly, costs were kept as high as the market would bear. The British naval attaché at St Petersburg, Capt Ernest Rice, reported 'the fact of this order [for a Drzewiecki boat] being given points more to the anxiety to make money on the part of some official . . . than to any conviction on his part of the actual success or value of the invention'. Rice was sure that 'little will be done by the Russians in actual warfare with an invention so intricate and so dangerous to the principal actors'.[9] The captain of HMS *Vernon*, the torpedo school, was more blunt: 'it has been observed by the Russians themselves that no-one, except in a state of drunkenness, would go into this boat.'[10] However, in 1904, Russia bought the German-built *Forelle* and ordered two more 'Karp'-class like her: designed by d'Equevilley-Monjustin, a former associate of Laubeuf, the boats had good points.

No less than 181 submarine projects were offered to the various German navies between 1861 and 1900, but only two were put into effect. The first did not survive its first trial in the Elbe. The second, mysteriously titled *Construction Number 333* and built at the Howaldt Yard, Kiel in 1897, was a curious mixture of old-fashioned wooden planking and a brand new electrical system hampered by a very wet interior. *Number 333* was quickly concealed under a cover until finally scrapped in 1902.

The German Technical Ship-building Society, established in 1899, was chaired by Professor C. Busley who, at the insistence of Adm von Tirpitz, lectured at great length on the subject of submarine boats, pointing out how dangerous they were to their crew, how expensive they were to build (520,000 marks or £26,000 for the latest French boat *Morse* exclusive of armament), and how much cheaper was a three-times-larger torpedo-boat destroyer at 200,000 marks. He concluded that submarines

> . . . give no great promise for their future . . . nothing but commendation . . . can be bestowed on the German naval authorities for having hitherto not being

led astray into costly and wearisome experiments with submarine boats, and for having simply confined themselves to building line of battle ships, cruisers, and seagoing torpedo craft.[11]

None the less, on 16 December 1906, the *Reichsmarineamt* accepted into service the overdue *U-1*, a considerably modified *Forelle*, and forged steadily ahead thereafter. Britain could relax at the end of the century because as the Director of Naval Construction, Sir William White, recalled: 'There was no difficulty in undertaking here the design of construction of submarines [before 1900] had it been desirable to do so . . . but it was decided to await developments elsewhere before making a start.'[12]

However, on 20 December 1886, White and two influential officers, Capt Lord Charles Beresford and Capt Sidney Eardley-Wilmot went down river to Tilbury to attend trials of the privately-built electrically-powered *Nautilus*. The visit may well have contributed more to the Royal Navy's 'wait and see' strategy than any logical pronouncements.

Nautilus was warranted 'extra special safe'.[13] Her displacement was varied by cylinders in her sides which could be pushed out or withdrawn – rather like Garrett's 'Egg' (see Chapter 11). Naval and military men, with journalists by the score, watched from the jetty as Beresford and Eardley-Wilmot walked aboard to be welcomed by the inventors, Messrs Ash and Campbell. They knowingly admired the cylinder-trimming arrangement which, Mr Campbell (wrongly) assured them, enabled a depth to 'be kept for hours or days in any position without using a fraction of the stored propelling power'.[14]

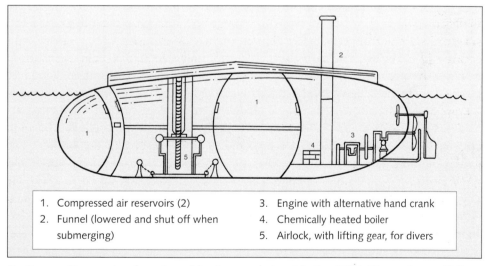

1. Compressed air reservoirs (2)
2. Funnel (lowered and shut off when submerging)
3. Engine with alternative hand crank
4. Chemically heated boiler
5. Airlock, with lifting gear, for divers

Dr Prosper Payenne's submarine with a 'pyrotechnique' boiler, 1884. The craft mercifully never put to sea, but was welcomed as a diving bell at Brest, Cherbourg and Paris.

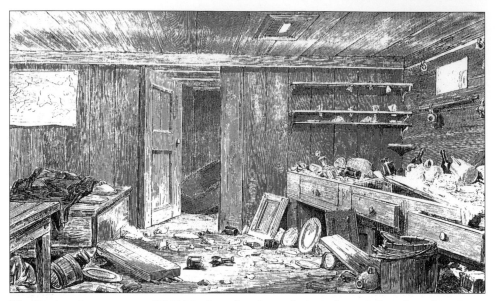

The Engineer's mess-room, HMS Merlin, *after the explosion of two 'infernal machines' under the ship.* (sketched by J.W. Carmichael for the *Illustrated London News*, issue 23, June 1855).

The boat was made ready to dive; the hatch was shut and clipped; and the mechanism for withdrawing the cylinders was set in motion. Only 10 in of the upperworks had been visible at full buoyancy and now the whole boat rapidly disappeared down into the basin where she thudded on to the bottom at a depth of 25 ft. So far, so good. The spectators ashore – including Eardley-Wilmot for whom there was no room on board for the dive – became a trifle anxious when *Nautilus* had not reappeared after an hour or so.

Down below, all was calm until the captain, who had a heart condition, collapsed when his order 'Out cylinders' could not be obeyed. Glutinous mud had jammed them. Somebody (Beresford claimed credit) had an inspiration. All hands – crew and distinguished passengers alike – were ordered to take off their coats and rush backwards and forwards as a body. The ruse succeeded. The mud released its grip, the cylinders slid out, and *Nautilus* sprang to the surface. The boat's engineer, unconcerned by a vista of white faces, flung open the hatch and announced excitedly to the watchers ashore that they were going to dive again. He was forcibly pulled down by his legs to make way for those, including Sir William White, who wanted out.

It cannot be entirely coincidental that both White and Beresford displayed an active dislike of submarines from that time: fifteen years later Sir William earnestly advised the Inspecting Captain of Submarine Boats 'never to go below water'.[15]

CHAPTER 15

Misfits

1829 Stephenson's *Rocket*
1843 Brunel: SS *Great Britain* iron-screw ship
1858 Lourdes miracles

There was a general feeling in the nineteenth century that we were all going somewhere quickly – but we did not quite know where. Perhaps that is why some weird and wonderful submarine designs emerged. These designs covered every aspect of submarine navigation, and some were echoed or actually developed in modern times. For example, both *Le Plongeur*, designed by Capt Bourgois and Naval Constructor Brun, and launched at Rochefort with the exceptional displacement of 450 tons, and the 740-ton submarine proposed by the Swedish Lt Hovgaard in 1887, incorporated sealed rescue craft in their superstructures, accessible through a hatch from inside the submarines. This was precisely the means of escape utilized by survivors from the Soviet nuclear *Komsomolets (K278)* which sank accidentally on 1 April 1989 in the Norwegian Sea.

In 1877 Mr Jos Jones, a Liverpool shipbuilder, 'known for his advanced and practical views upon certain questions connected with naval warfare', built a model which could 'move forwards or backwards in a straight line at any level and, starting out of sight of the enemy, lodge a torpedo [mine] under the bottom of an enemy ship'. The model was not enlarged but the 'advanced and practical views' were adopted in 1918 by a pair of gallant Italians riding a converted torpedo, and they were put to good effect in the Second World War by British X-craft (midget submarines), Italian *Maiali* ('human torpedoes') and British 'chariots'. In the same year Mr A.A. Olivier patented plans for a fish-shaped submarine with a glass conning tower. It had wings, instead of diving rudders, which folded back into the hull when not wanted. The craft was to be jet-propelled by gases, generated from the ignition of high explosives.[1] Happily for all concerned, Olivier's design never left the drawing board although the idea of jet engines for submarines and underwater weaponry is still under consideration.

In 1879, a Mr Leggo suggested an equally inventive and marginally less hazardous method of progression. The submarine was to move through the water on the principle of a switch-back. Resembling a large kite, it was tilted by a moveable weight until it slid gracefully down an inclined curve to a predetermined

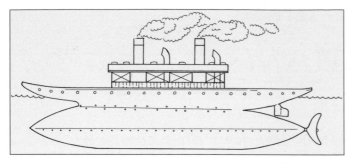

'High speed semi-submersible'
patented by Vogt in 1898. Why the
vessel was expected to be fast, or what
its advantages were, is not apparent.

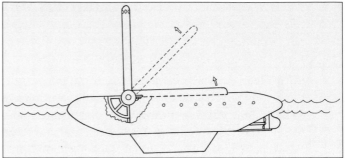

Mr C.H. Homan's proposal, 1898.
A man could either climb up to the
portholes for observation or trigger a
camera.

depth at which point gases produced by heating liquid ammonia with a hydrocarbon were admitted into a large leakproof mattress. The machine would then ascend; gas from the mattress would be released at the top of the trajectory, and another downward glide would commence, and so on *ad infinitum*. The proposal was entirely serious.[2]

For a long time, a substantial (and sensible) minority advocated a semi-submersible rather than a submarine. Messrs Berkley and Hotchkiss (of quick-firing gun fame) had a simple notion for reducing freeboard rapidly. Two long, cork floats were attached on either side of a steam-driven torpedo boat. The floats were on adjustable arms depressed in the fully surfaced position, so that the craft rode high in the water, but elevated when going into action so that all but the funnel, conning tower and air intakes dropped below the surface.[3]

In July 1881 Monsieur Jenoud drew up plans for a gas engine fuelled by hydrogen produced by adding iron filings to sulphuric acid, not the safest of chemical combinations in a confined space. (It would be several years before submariners learned, the hard way, that a 4-per cent concentration of hydrogen in the atmosphere, reached at certain stages of battery charge or discharge, is explosive.) A rather disappointing top speed of 5 knots was predicted from this kind of energy, but the inventor patiently explained that higher speeds were undesirable because they would be 'dangerous in the vicinity of rocks, rendered invisible owing to the impenetrability of water to the human sight'.[4]

Another fantasy was put forward by the respected French engineer Monsieur

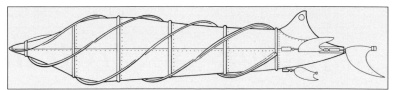

Twister proposed, with minor differences, by Apostolov (Russia, 1889), Lacavalerie (Venezuela, 1894) and Scheuseck (Chicago, patent 1896).

Boucher. He thoughtfully provided three means of propulsion: a screw beneath the keel amidships, automatically feathered oars, and a wriggling tail fin *à la poisson* at the stern. Gloomily predicting accidents, however, he provided four underwater telescopes, one fitted in the bows, one astern, one for looking upwards and the last for examining the seabed. If, despite these safeguards, a collision or a grounding did occur, strong spring buffers were fitted at the bows and beneath the keel – a boon to careless submariners. Boucher was far-sighted in one respect: he proposed to extract air from sea water by 'energetic pulverisation' through perforated metal plates: in other words, he was thinking on the lines of osmosis which is used in modern boats, not as a rule for creating oxygen, but as an alternative to the distillation of fresh water.[5] Another idea, incorporated by Mr Wynam in his 250-ft semi-submersible launched on the Thames in 1864, was a propeller at the bow to create a moving vacuum into which the ordinary propeller at the stern would drive the vessel.[6]

One of Napoleon Bonaparte's unfulfilled schemes was to invade England through a Channel tunnel. In 1869 Dr J.A. Lacomme submitted to Napoleon III plans for a submarine railway across *La Manche* – for purely commercial purposes. In the unlikely event of an accident, the submersible car would detach itself automatically from the track and (having a healthy reserve of floatability) rise safely to the surface. Monsieur Goubet suggested a 'submarine ferry' on similar lines. Nobody thought the proposals absurd then, and nor did they in 1985 when, as a 1 April spoof, the BBC interviewed a submarine commentator who leaked the news that redundant Polaris nuclear submarines were to be converted to cross-channel car and passenger ferries.[7]

The resistance of water, which has 832 times the density of air, has challenged Russian submarine designers since 1889 when a young student named Apostolov explained that it could easily be overcome, for a speed of 140 knots, by building a hull in the form of a huge blunt Archimedean screw. It was pointed out that passengers might find a revolving hull uncomfortable so Apostolov obligingly arranged that the convolutions would stop short of the stern, allowing the passenger area aft to remain stationary. The Venezuelan dentist Sebastian Lacavalerie, inspired by his foot-pedalled drill perhaps, put forward an almost identical scheme in 1894.[8] Eighty years later, Soviet scientists began experimenting with a form of propulsion achieved by rippling the outer hull of a submarine in the same way that a skate flies effortlessly through the sea, a notion which Apostolov and the dentist would doubtless have deemed ridiculous.

CHAPTER 16

Jamais . . . trop de sous-marins[1]

1865 L. Pasteur: germ theory
1895 Lumiere brothers: cinema

Submarine warfare in France was a child of *la jeune école*, the New School, whose early exponents included Simeon Bourgois with his monstrously clumsy compressed air-driven *Le Plongeur* built in 1859, five years before the simpler Confederate *Hunley* was hand-cranked into action. France subsequently lost interest during nearly twenty years of reasonable relationships with England; but then colonial rivalries, and renewed recognition that she could not engage in regular warfare against the greatest naval power in the world, encouraged a submarine revival.

Foreseeing huge profits, of the kind envisaged by Nordenfelt and Zaharoff, private inventors were willing to busy themselves without a contract. Claude Goubet went to work in 1885. He never enjoyed success, but his first boat (sold to Brazil) is memorable for its net-cutter – an extendable 3-m steel bar with a pair of clippers at the end. At such close range, Claude Goubet feared that the whining of his craft's electric motor might be heard, so there were a couple of paddles for what today is known as 'quiet routine'. The paddles imply that the inventor did not contemplate diving to attack; but his second boat dived in Cherbourg Harbour in 1889 and, although depth-keeping was erratic, the remotely operated scissors cut mooring ropes of buoys laid for the demonstration. In May of that year two crewmen remained in the boat, on the bottom, for eight hours: this was considered a great feat. However, they were not inconvenienced except by extreme boredom, and irritation caused by continual calls on the telephone connected from the dockside. *Goubet II* was eventually sold for a few thousand francs to a Swiss entrepreneur who employed her for passenger trips on Lake Geneva.

The renowned naval architect Dupuy de Lôme died in 1885 before his submarine concepts – notably a submersible troop-transport for expediting an invasion of Britain – could be translated into hardware; but his protégé Gustave Zédé grasped the great man's baton in January 1886 when a *jeune école*

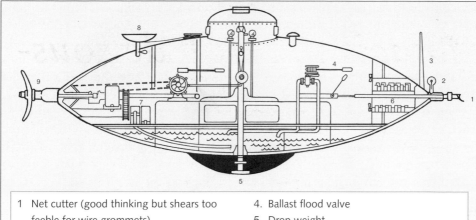

1. Net cutter (good thinking but shears too feeble for wire grommets)
2. Lamp (no help)
3. Submerging batten (watched from conning tower eyelet to help judge depth and pitch).
4. Ballast flood valve
5. Drop weight
6. Battery cells
7. Pumps
8. 'Torpedo' (primitive limpet mine)
9. Steerable propeller

Goubet I, *1886. Length 5m, weight in air 11 tons.*

Gymnote *building, Arsenal du Mousellon at Toulon, mid-1888.* (RNSM)

administration led by Minister of Marine Vice Adm Hyacinthe Théophile Aube took command of naval affairs.[2] The small 31-ton all-electric *Gymnote* was launched as a trial vehicle in September 1888.[3] Old-school naval officers violently opposed Aube's patronage of submarines and their hostility continued well into the 1900s by which time *Gymnote*, part of Toulon's *défense mobile*, had suffered a battery-gas explosion and several inadvertent groundings while running sea-saw fashion submerged. On one occasion she hit the bottom at 20 m with sufficient force to unseat the crew. Her 1891 successor, *Gustave Zédé*, was given what the English press was now calling 'hydroplanes' amidships and right forward (both pairs operated by hydraulics) as well as manually operated diving rudders aft, to curb these alarming excursions.[4]

The 266-ton *Gustave Zédé* was launched on 1 July 1893 at Toulon. The hull, built of non-corrosive and non-magnetic Roma bronze (primarily for the sake of the compass), was 148 ft long with tapering ends. *Gymnote*'s good points, such as they were, were adapted to *Zédé* by the constructor M Romazzotti; but it took ten years to complete the new boat, not least because of constantly changing opinions in the Navy: there were thirty-two Ministers of Marine between 1871 and 1905, some of them for and some against submarines. Aube himself was forced out of office in 1899, and for most of the 1890s *la jeune école*, and with it the submersible torpedo boat, was out of favour.[5]

As for *Zédé*, the worldly-wise British Director of Naval Ordnance, Capt Jeffries RN, explained: 'Of course, for political reasons she was bound to succeed, and they said she did so, but she is not worth much.'[6] This may have been in answer to an unlikely French claim that discharging a 525-lb Whitehead torpedo would 'scarcely affect the longitudinal stability, a caution to the man on the diving levers being alone necessary'.[7] The crew consisted of one lieutenant, a sub-lieutenant and ten men; according to *Le Matin*, she was undetectable (with just her cupola exposed) by the battleship *Magenta* beyond 2,000 yards. The *Magenta* was duly torpedoed without 'being able to bring a single gun to bear on her'. The *Marceau* and *Neptune* were also present and 'the unbiased opinion in the three battleships was that in time of war the submarine would not have been touched by gun-fire.'[8]

'High Freeboard', writing to *The Times*, assured readers that *Zédé* was an almost exact reproduction of *Peral* and that 'there is nothing to make it at all certain that above-water seaman will be unable to sleep o'nights'.[9] But the British Naval Attaché was by no means dismissive when reporting to the Admiralty in January 1899:

The *Gustave Zédé* proceeded to sea, unaccompanied by any vessel until out of sight of the fleet. She then turned and steamed towards the fleet, well out of the water, at 10 knots speed, with her bridge raised and 4 men on it; she was observed from the *Magenta* at a distance of about 3,500 yards. The men on the bridge instantly went below, and the bridge was lowered, and the boat sunk until only her conning tower remained above water.

Gymnote, *ready for launch, 24 September 1888.* (RNSM)

When at about 1,500 yards from the *Magenta* the wash from the *Zédé*'s screw, but not her conning tower, could be observed. The *Zédé* then submerged herself to a depth of about 10 feet.

At a distance of about 450 yards the *Zédé* came to the surface for a moment. The captain of the *Zédé* observed his distance and corrected his course; then, diving again, he fired his torpedo at a range of 270 yards, striking the *Magenta* fairly amidships, while the *Zédé* herself passed under the *Magenta*, coming to the surface about 200 yards on her opposite beam, and thus completing the trial.[10]

Monsieur Lockroy, Minister of Marine, was well pleased. The British Admiralty reluctantly stirred itself, sat up and began to take serious notice. However, there was still no reason to hurry while the French were building so few submarines, although *Morse* – a small and improved *Zédé* – was laid down in 1897 and so were the longer-range dual-propulsion boat *Narval* and her immediate successors, the latter owing their construction to the designs of Monsieur Laubeuf, the extraordinarily able Naval Engineer-in-Chief.[11]

It was not necessarily apparent to outsiders that France was considering two entirely different kinds of underwater boat. One was the submarine, electrically propelled from storage cells with no other source of power, and therefore very limited in range. Its *raison d'être* was harbour defence, and it never surfaced on patrol because an incoming enemy would be fully alert with only a small area to scan. It returned to base for recharging the battery. The other underwater boat

Gymnote *with new conning tower after 1898 refit.* (RNSM)

was the submersible, which had an air-dependent engine (steam with an oil-fired boiler) enabling it to roam at will and recharge its batteries at sea. More aggressive and independent, it was well suited to *La Guerre de Course* – commerce-raiding. There was also the semi-submersible torpedo boat with a variable freeboard, and finally, of course, the standard torpedo boat which was only intended to attack by night at high speed.

The submersible, or the semi-submersible as second best, was what Aube and his journalist friend Gabriel Charmes would have chosen if *la jeune école* had still held sway at the end of the century. As it happened, Lockroy agreed with the New School that destroying merchant shipping was the optimum offensive strategy, although he preferred fast cruisers to *les submersibles* for the purpose. He agreed that *les sous-marins* were an economical means of defence close inshore; but eventually submersibles supplanted *les sous-marins* by reason of their flexibility, but not before a further twenty-six all-electric boats had been ordered, a couple of which were absurdly small (and cheap) at 45 tons.

Charmes, for the press, declared that giant battleships no longer reigned supreme but would be replaced by myriads of tiny torpedo craft – *la poussière navale* – mere specks of dust; and the PR campaign was sustained by reporters such as M Calmette describing for *Figaro*, on 9 January 1901, a trip in *Morse*, a *sous-marin*, 186 ft long, 146 tons, and completed in 1897. The translated report was in *The Times* on the next day:

. . . turning to the crew, every man of which was at his post, the Commandant gave his orders, dwelling with emphasis on each word. A sailor repeated his orders one by one and then all were silent. The *Morse* has already started on its mysterious voyage . . . to say that at this moment . . . I did not have the tremor that comes from contact with the unknown would be beside the truth. On the other hand, calm and imperturbable, but keen and curious . . . General André [Minister for War] had already taken his place near the Commandant on a folding seat. There were no chairs in this long tube in which we were imprisoned . . . [but] the Minister for War was too tall to stand upright beneath the iron ceiling, and in any case, it would be impossible to walk about [and upset the trim].

The only free space was a narrow passage, 60cm broad, less than 2m high and 30m long, divided into three equal sections. In the first . . . reposed the torpedoes with the machine for launching them . . . in the second . . . were the electric accumulators which gave the light and power. In the third, near the screw, was the electric motor. . . . Under all this, beneath the deck, were immense water ballasts which were capable of being emptied or filled in a few seconds [for 'seconds' read 'long minutes'] by electric machines in order to carry the vessel up or down. Finally, in the centre of the tube, dominating these three sections, which the electric light inundated, and which no partitions divided, the navigating lieutenant stood on the look out giving his orders.

There was but one thing which could destroy in a second all the forces of authority, initiative and responsibility in this officer – that of failure of the accumulators. Were the electricity to fail, everything would come to a stop. Darkness would overtake the boat and imprison it forever in the water. To avoid any such disaster there have been arranged, it is true, outside the tube low down, a series of lead weights that are capable of being released from within to lighten the vessel. . .

The *Morse* after skimming along the water outside the port was now about to dive. The Commandant's place was no longer in the helmet or *kiosque*

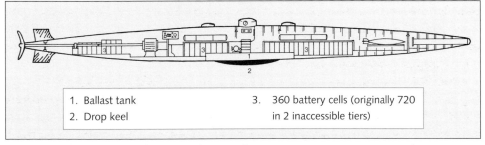

1. Ballast tank   3. 360 battery cells (originally 720
2. Drop keel   in 2 inaccessible tiers)

Gustave Zédé, launched 1893 at Toulon, 148ft, 266 tons; 1 + 2 14-in Fiume 'short' torpedoes (3.68m, wt 856lbs, range 800 yds at 28.5kts).

whence he could direct the route along the surface of the sea. His place was henceforth in the very centre of the tube, in the midst of all sorts of electric manipulators, his eyes continually fixed on a mysterious optical apparatus, the periscope. The other extremity of this instrument floated on the surface of the water. . . .

. . . I hastened . . . to get the impression of total immersion. The lieutenant by the marine chart verified the depth. The casks of water were filled . . . and . . . a most unexpected spectacle presented itself . . .

The plunge was so gentle that in the perfect silence of the water one did not see the process of descent and there was only one instrument capable of indicating, by a needle, the depth to which the *Morse* was penetrating. The vessel was advancing, while at the same time it descended, but there was no sensation of either advance or roll. As to respiration, it was as perfect as in any room. . . .

Morse was all-electric; but in *Narval* and her steam successors, it took fifteen minutes to shut down the boiler and it was impossible to dissipate the heat after diving. A shift toward internal combustion engines was made from 1902, but steam had not been abandoned by 1914, and although seventy-six boats, of various types, were then listed in the French Order of Battle, there were few significant technical or tactical advances after 1905.

Ironically, after setting such a brisk pace at the beginning, political enthusiasm for underwater warfare soon declined. The French submariners were poorly prepared for war when it came, and the results made that disappointingly apparent. Maybe *The Engineer*'s contributor on 1 March 1901 was correct when remarking on the *Zédé*'s torpedo exploits: 'the conditions have nothing whatever in common with naval warfare' and 'To do those who most favour the submarine boat justice, they do not pin their faith on France.'[12]

CHAPTER 17

Success in the States

1889 Eiffel Tower
1897–99 Klondike gold rush
1898 Spanish–American War

The Navy Department in Washington, DC was a good deal more concerned with the prospect of falling behind overseas submarine developments than John Holland knew. Between 1888 and 1893 it announced three successive open competitions for boats with specifications markedly more advanced than any envisaged in Europe: speeds of 15 knots on the surface and 8 knots submerged were demanded, the latter for two hours and with provision for 90 hours at minimum power.[1]

Holland's competitors in 1888 were Nordenfelt, Professor Josiah Tuck with his fireless steam *Peacemaker* (see Chapter 14), and George Baker, a manufacturer of barbed wire in Chicago. Baker's 75-ton steam and electric boat was distinguished by tiltable propellers on either side amidships for changing depth as well as normal propulsion; the system was scarcely more satisfactory than Nordenfelt's downhauls. It was also the first of many boats to suffer a hydrogen explosion. Goddard, the electrician, shut the hatch to keep out heavy rain while charging batteries from a shore station near Lake Erie in the summer of 1892 – and struck a match to read the hydrometer.

The plans which Holland submitted via Cramps Shipbuilding Company, of Philadelphia (which also represented Nordenfelt) were judged the best, but Cramps were unable to guarantee all six of the Navy's detailed requirements. The competition was annulled, which was bad news for Mr and Mrs John Holland, now living at 185 Court Street, Newark with a baby on the way.[2] It was a relief to find the contest renewed in 1889; but hopes were dashed when a new Secretary of the Navy, Capt Benjamin F. Tracy, reallocated the monies to surface ships already under construction.

Holland went to see his old friend Charles A. Morris of the Morris and Cummings Dredging Company at New York and found he was still a submarine supporter, albeit unable to find hard dollars for a new project. In May 1890 Morris found him employment with the company at the modest wage of 4 dollars

---

a day; and while the Wright brothers were deciding whether to open a bicycle shop at Dayton, Ohio, Morris and Holland together devised a flying machine which foreshadowed vertical take-off.[3] Holland calculated that the petroleum-fired steam boiler driving the piston engines (with petroleum at 4 cents a gallon) would propel the two-man machine at 63 mph for four-and-a-half hours for the remarkably low cost of 34 dollars and 12 cents. No one wanted to know.

However, Holland talked submarines perpetually and made chance acquaintances thereby with a young company lawyer, Elihu B. Frost ('E.B.' to his friends), who was advising Morris. Frost, a shrewd judge of circumstance and character, had contacts in Washington and probably knew about a forthcoming submarine policy. He took to Holland straightaway and moved swiftly to incorporate the John P. Holland Torpedo Boat Company in New York early in 1893, while seeking patents for Holland's designs in Europe, South America and Japan, as well as the United States where a major patent for a 'submersible torpedo boat' was already pending. From the start, Frost, company secretary-treasurer, had his eye on exports. The US Navy duly decided to adopt the

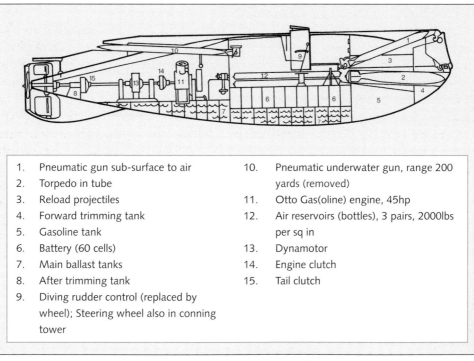

1. Pneumatic gun sub-surface to air
2. Torpedo in tube
3. Reload projectiles
4. Forward trimming tank
5. Gasoline tank
6. Battery (60 cells)
7. Main ballast tanks
8. After trimming tank
9. Diving rudder control (replaced by wheel); Steering wheel also in conning tower
10. Pneumatic underwater gun, range 200 yards (removed)
11. Otto Gas(oline) engine, 45hp
12. Air reservoirs (bottles), 3 pairs, 2000lbs per sq in
13. Dynamotor
14. Engine clutch
15. Tail clutch

Holland VI *(later USS Holland) before winter 1898–9 alterations which included repositioning of propeller forward of control surfaces and removal of underwater gun at stern. Length overall 53.3ft. Max diameter 10.3ft. 63/75 tons. Max diving depth 75ft. Crew 6.*

submarine as an inexpensive weapon of defence, and the competition was reopened on 3 March 1893. Holland won again.

There was the usual bureaucratic delay – two years in this case – while interested parties battled in Washington, but on 13 March 1895 a $200,000 contract for Holland's patented design was signed. Success was in sight, but obstacles remained – notably the 15-knot speed requirement on the surface. Steam was the only answer, and Holland was uneasy about that.

William T. Malster at the Columbian Iron Works, Baltimore, contracted to build the 154/168-ton,[4] 85-ft boat which the government tritely elected to call *Plunger*. The keel was laid on 23 June 1896 alongside, as it happened, a 36-ft submersible of a quite different type – Simon Lake's bottom-crawler *Argonaut*.

Two 1625-hp triple-expansion steam engines turned two outboard propellers at 400 rpm for the 15-knot surface speed, and there was a 70-hp electric motor (supplied from batteries charged by an independent steam engine) for the centre propeller used submerged. A huge Mosher boiler amidships, raising steam to 2,000 lb per sq in, obliged the boat to be much larger than Holland thought desirable. He embarked on the project against his own better judgement, but personal economics left him little choice. At least he now controlled (he thought) a soundly based company and had some freedom of manoeuvre.

Moreover, he had suddenly become quite famous, not least due to the extraordinary loyalty and enthusiasm of a young naval officer, Lt Cdr William (later Rear Adm) W. Kimball, who had for long – based on a fortuitous meeting with Holland – aired his ideas in Washington and among the fleet. In the same year that the steam-driven *Plunger* started growing on the stocks, Kimball (a candidate for *la jeune école*, had he been French) boasted before the Senate Committee of Naval Affairs: 'Give me six "Holland" boats, the officers and crew to be selected by me, and I will pledge my life to stand off the entire British squadron ten miles off Sandy Hook without any aid from the fleet.'[5]

Amidst mounting public interest, Holland persuaded his board to finance another submarine built entirely to his own specifications and independent of government support. Frost insisted that its sale would not be restricted to the United States Navy alone, and he astutely secured an Amendment to the Act of Congress which had granted appropriation for *Plunger*: it allowed two boats to be built 'similar to the submarine boat "Holland"'. The Amendment was carefully phrased under Frost's gentle guidance. Thus Holland's much-preferred design, known as 'Holland VI', could be substituted for *Plunger* if, as Holland predicted to himself, the latter monstrosity were to fail. In the event, although *Plunger* was launched in 1897, she was never commissioned although the name was used again, confusingly, for a totally different USS *Plunger (A-1)*, launched in 1903. Holland meanwhile turned his full attention to what would be his epoch-making sixth boat.

Holland VI, the forerunner of all modern submarines, was built at Lewis Nixon's newly established Crescent Shipyard, Elizabethport, New Jersey, between

1896 and 1897. Nixon, who had been unable to meet specifications for the first competition when chief constructor at Cramps, at first declined to have anything further to do with submarines when Holland approached him in the fall of 1896; indeed he would 'not touch the boat with a ten-foot pole'. But the chief constructor at Crescent, Mr Arthur L. Busch, came round to Holland's way of thinking: when Busch had transformed Holland's sketches into readable engineering plans, Nixon agreed to take the job on board.[6]

As a prominent commentator remarked: 'Of this vessel perhaps more has been heard than of any other ship or boat in the world. She is . . . also, without doubt, the commencement of the "really successful" submarine.'[7] *Holland VI* was 53 ft 10 in long with a diameter of 10 ft 3 in amidships (a 5.25:1 length-to-breadth ratio). She displaced 74 tons submerged, with a 10.7-ton reserve of buoyancy on the surface. Plating and general arrangements would not look out of place in a modern shipyard drawing office. Propulsion on the surface and power for recharging the batteries was provided by an Otto gasoline 45-hp engine, giving 7 knots at 340 rpm. A 50-hp electric motor offered a similar speed submerged but, due to battery limitations, rather less than 5 knots was achieved. A tail clutch and an engine clutch permitted the engine to drive the propeller direct or to recharge the battery by using the motor as a generator with or without the propeller being turned: that is, a 'running' or 'standing' charge could be applied. However the engine could not be reversed: the electric motor had to be used for manoeuvring in harbour.

The diving rudders on either side of the propeller could, in theory, be controlled automatically by a pendulum and pressure-diaphragm system (like Whitehead's torpedo 'secret') but in practice they were worked by mechanical-linkage gearing from a position at the bottom of the stubby glass-eyeletted conning tower which contained the controls, gauges and instruments now found in a submarine control room.

The main armament was a single 18-in torpedo tube.[8] Two reload torpedoes could be carried. There were compensating arrangements for maintaining trim automatically when firing a torpedo, and an elegant bowcap, lifted upwards by worm gearing, was made watertight with a rubber gasket, as was the rear door of the tube. *Holland VI* was also equipped with a Zalinski-type upwardly inclined pneumatic gun (range 1,500 yd) above the torpedo tubes forward, and initially she had an underwater gun *à la Columbiade* aft as well.

Holland believed that his new submarine boat was right in all respects, but he should have realized that even the most patriotic Irishmen are not exempt from Murphy's Law. On the night of Wednesday 13 October 1897, one of Nixon's workmen left open a hull valve while the boat was still on the slip. At high tide, the machinery was flooded and, when the boat was pumped out, full grounds (earths) remained on the electrical circuits. The accident might well have put paid to the entire endeavour, but it called onto the stage a brilliant young electrician who was destined to put British and American 'Holland' boats successfully

John Phillip Holland and Charles A. Morris, loyal Superintending Engineer of the Holland Torpedo Boat Co., at Perth Amboy, New Jersey, 4 April 1898. (Morris collection)

through their trials. Unencumbered by rules or red tape, Frank T. Cable, the electrical expert who saved that day and many more, recorded: 'After an examination I decided that there was only one way of remedying the trouble.'[9] With nothing to lose, he simply reversed the current in the field circuits, abusing all principles of recognized motor management, and soon the wiring generated ample heat to dry out the wiring. The drastic remedy worked, but electrical faults recurred throughout the little boat's lifespan.

Cable was a generally unassuming man, but he did not hesitate to state his mind to Holland (or, later, to British naval officers) although he was only on loan from the Electro-Dynamic Company of Philadelphia who had supplied the motor-cum-dynamo. He never claimed the right to call himself the first real submarine captain, but that is what, *de facto*, he became. (William T. Cox was the other captain, on Holland's behalf, of *Holland VI.*) Calm, thoroughly practical and unflustered at any time, Cable was the ideal submariner although in the winter of

1897 he was by no means anxious to submerge himself in a steel tube:[10] 'Not for anything,' he said, 'would I attempt to do so.'[11] He was persuaded in due course but, for the moment, putting things right on the surface was enough.

Holland VI showed how thoroughly – indeed uniquely – the inventor understood the art of submarine construction. The capacity of the (internal) ballast tanks was such that when flooded, the boat was brought down to an awash condition. A final adjustment was then made by slowly admitting water to a small tank, enabling the boat to dive completely when she went ahead, at an angle dictated by the diving rudders, while retaining a small reserve of buoyancy. There was no instability due to water piling up at one end of the tanks and shifting the centre of gravity: the main ballast tanks were either empty or full as they are in submarines today.

The dozen deadlights in the conning tower were made of heavy glass, and the maximum depth was calculated as 100 ft although Holland had no intention of going so deep. Depth was measured by a manometer (depth-gauge) connected directly through a small-bore pipe to the sea and set against the hull at a convenient height. This happened to be the level of the water when the boat was on the surface, so diving depth was measured from the surface waterline and continued to be so until the 1960s, when it was universally decided that keel-depth would be a more meaningful measure.

Provided that the operators were well drilled, the boat proved sound and obedient under most conditions. She was good value at $150,000 (approx. £1.23M at 1999 values) although the true cost to the Company (calculated by Frost) was $236,615.

The first surface run on 25 February 1898 went well under the expert guidance of Superintending Engineer Charles A. Morris. Frank Cable, not yet attached to Holland's company, wrote in congratulatory terms when he read reports in the *Philadelphia Press*. But Holland was not ready to seek publicity: he made a first static dive to the bottom of the basin in Nixon's Yard, where the depth was only 20 ft, on 11 March, with just four crew members and no fuss.

On 17 March 1898, *Holland VI* made her first successful dive under way off Staten Island. It had been drizzling miserably throughout the morning and early afternoon but, as Holland went below and pulled the hatch shut after him, the sun shone through and a rainbow arched over the western sky.[12]

Official observers were sent by the Navy Department to witness formal trials on Sunday 27 March in Raritan Bay off Perth Amboy, New Jersey where 32-year-old Frank Cable joined as permanent electrician.

The trials were as successful as anyone could have wished. Lt Nathan Sargent USN did not much care for the stern coming out of the water when the boat dived, but Holland politely pointed out that seabirds also show their bottom sides when plunging. Privately he noted that Sargent was of the despised school which preferred a boat to dive on a level keel.[13] (In due course, when submarines came to

Bow view of the 'Holland' showing mouth of aerial torpedo gun. (Scientific American, 9 April 1898)

be fitted with two sets of hydroplanes – one aft and one forward – a compromise would be reached whereby minor depth changes could be made by inclining both planes the same way to 'squeeze' a boat up or down without an angle; one pair of hydroplanes amidships above the centre of buoyancy could theoretically achieve the same. But angles would always be used to drive a boat up or down when diving or changing depth substantially – as Holland strongly advocated.)

On 10 April 1898, Assistant Secretary of the Navy (and future President of the United States) Theodore Roosevelt wrote to Secretary of the Navy John D. Long:

My dear Mr Secretary,
I think that the Holland submarine boat should be purchased. Evidently she has great possibilities in her for harbor defense. Sometimes she doesn't work perfectly, but often she does, and I don't think in the present emergency we can afford to let her slip . . .[14]

Roosevelt had in mind Spain's declaration of war on the United States over Cuba four days after the trial run of *Holland VI*. On 30 April, the boat left Perth

The Holland, *seemingly unmanned (possibly on the occasion when carbon monoxide overcame the crew) with ventilators rigged and hatch open, virtually stopped at her berth.* (Morris collection).

Amboy under tow and on 1 May crossed New York Harbor to berth at the Erie Basin. On that same day, Adm Dewey's Squadron steamed into Manila Bay: the Admiral's Flag Secretary was Ensign Harry H. Caldwell, destined to become the first submarine commanding officer in the United States Navy.

Holland declared that if the government would transport *Holland VI* to a point near the entrance of Santiago he would sink the Spanish fleet if it was still there. He added that he would then expect the Government to buy his boat.[15] However, the offer was not taken up. Worse, the naval officers who replaced Holland and his principle crewmen for subsequent trials were, not surprisingly, slow and inept. It is difficult to understand how the Navy expected them to put an unfamiliar vehicle through its paces and arrive at rightful conclusions. After a dubious evaluation, the Navy Department demanded extensive modifications. To be fair, some of the changes were sensible. The hydraulic gun aft, for instance, intended for firing a projectile through water out to 200 yd, was removed on the grounds of being needless and possibly impractical. The propeller was shifted forward a little with some rearrangement of the rudders and hydroplanes (a debatable improvement), and extra, very handy, little trimming tanks were added. The engine exhaust system was led externally to a higher point to avoid flooding on the surface, and a better kind of fouling paint was applied to the hull.

Articles in newspapers were wholly positive, but there were worrying private moments. On one occasion, Holland and some distinguished guests were watching the submarine returning to her berth with Cable in charge on deck. They heard him order the (non-reversible) gasoline engine to be stopped and the (reversible) motor to be backed – but nothing happened. Two crewman, also on deck, vanished below to investigate, but the boat continued heading for the berth. Cable shouted 'Cut the motor!', but evidently there was no response because he himself then dropped down the hatch. With no one on deck, the submarine collided with the jetty, fortunately doing little damage. Engineer Morris raced on board where he found the crew collapsed with Cable, who had managed to throw the motor switch, lying beside them. Carbon monoxide poisoning from leaky exhaust piping was to blame.[16]

On 23 July 1899, Holland suffered a different kind of setback when the 78-year-old Clara Barton, first President of the American Red Cross, went out for a trip which the inventor thought would give her pleasure. It did not. At the end of the day, which was cold and rainy, she turned to Holland and sharply reprimanded him for developing a dreadful weapon of war. He reiterated that he saw the submarine as a deterrent to warfare but was unable to pacify the indignant lady.[17]

The final trial took place in Little Peconic Bay off New Suffolk, Long Island on 6 November. Holland himself was not on board – there was no room – but two senior naval officers were crowded into the little boat with seven crew members and three torpedoes embarked. It was a tight fit. Capt John Lowe USN was the principal observer and his subsequent report carried an impassioned argument for submarines in an over-the-top style which Adm Jacky Fisher on the other side of the Atlantic would have approved:

> We need right off and right now 50 Submarine Torpedo Vessels in Long Island Sound to preserve the peace and give potency to our diplomacy. The French in this matter are much more alive in their needs than we are. What we have left to a private company the French have taken up as a National affair . . .[18]

Lowe's opinion as the Navy's Chief Engineer was valued. On 11 April 1900, *Holland VI* was bought for the United States Navy. Headlines described her as the 'Monster War Fish', 'Uncle Sam's Devil of the Deep' and 'The Naval "Hell Diver"'. She took her place in the United States Navy as USTB or USS *Holland (SS-1)*.

Isaac L. Rice, founder President of Electric Boat Company (7 February 1899), financier, lawyer and a very much smarter businessman than John Holland. (Morris collection)

In August 1900 the Government ordered six modified boats of the 'Adder' class, including a new *Plunger*, with *Fulton*[19] as their prototype. They had their drawbacks by modern standards, but endurance submerged was not one of them. Due to their uncluttered porpoise-like shape and minimal auxiliary electrical 'hotel' load, they were able to make their full speed of 7.1 knots submerged for three hours, drawing around 500 amps from the battery while voltage fell from 115 to 107. By comparison, no British submarine in the First or Second World War could sustain top speed of about eight knots for more than one hour dived.

It was, as it happened, his boat's batteries which brought about dramatic changes in Holland's business career. While the inventor concerned himself with perfecting designs, a German-American patent lawyer and battery manufacturer, Isaac Rice, who had supplied Holland with storage cells, took over the Holland Company as a subsidiary of his newly incorporated Electric Boat Company.

Rice (incidentally a leading member of the Peace Society) predicted expansion for a new submarine service and multiple sales overseas. Every submarine would require batteries which Rice was already well placed to supply. As president of Electric Boat, he persuaded the trustful Holland to transfer personal patents to the new company, and, while being careful not to upset the Irish political vote by offending the inventor's susceptibilities too openly, Rice steadily eased Holland out of what was becoming a powerful concern. Holland's salary never exceeded $90 per week ($187,200 or £39,000 (1899 rate of exchange) p.a. today) and when he finally resigned from the company, on 31 March 1904 at the age of 63, he held just one-half of one per cent of the company's share value, stock worth about $50,000. John Philip Holland was not a Freemason, he was not a member of the Jewish business community, and he did not even belong to the influential Irish lobbies in New York and Washington, DC. Despite more than three decades in the United States he was no match for American businessmen like Isaac Rice and 'E.B.' Frost.

Late in 1899 the British Naval Attaché in Washington, Capt Ottley, reported that the submarine company 'does not hold itself in any way bound to manufacture solely for the American Govt., nor do I gather that there is any present desire on the part of the authorities to monopolise the invention.' Ottley, rather patronizingly, thought that any major defects in the 'Holland' design could soon be perfected by British naval expertise.[20] In July 1900 Isaac Rice visited England. Lord Rothschild (whose merchant bank held shares in Electric Boat) ensured that he was properly received at the Admiralty. The Royal Navy's submarine story starts from there.[21]

Meanwhile, John Holland had an unusual competitor in Simon Lake (1866–1945), a quarter-century younger and more of a 'go-getter'. By the time that USS *Holland* was at sea, Lake's first boat, *Argonaut Jr*, was an obsolete hulk, but she had only been built as a prototype for the specialized kind of submersible which he intended to employ for commercial purposes. He predicted a profitable future in salvage, oyster gathering, underwater mining and cable maintenance.

In character, as well as aim, Lake could hardly have been more different from the earnest Holland. He had a head of fiery red hair with temper and high humour to match. His written records make light reading, compared with Holland's, although it is advisable to check the details.[22] He had a demonic sense of the absurd and a recognition of good theatre that would be memorable even if he had never invented anything.

Simon was only a schoolboy when he started experimenting underwater. He constructed a canvas canoe, along lines described in the magazine *Golden Days*, and deliberately turned it upside down in the stream running through his New Jersey village, Toms River. It worked well enough as a drifting diving bell although spectators thought the boy had drowned. At the age of fourteen, in 1880, he sketched a proper submersible and this drawing was the basis for boats that followed. In Lake's own words, the first of these, *Argonaut Jr*, was built of:

John Phillip Holland at the time his submarine was commissioned into the US Navy, 1900. (Morris collection)

. . . yellow pine planking, double thick, lined with canvas laid between the double layers of planking, the outer seams caulked and payed. She was a flat-side affair . . . propelled on wheels when on the bottom by a man turning a crank on the inside. Our compressed air reservoir was a soda-water fountain tank. The compressed-air pump was a plumbers hand-pump, by which means we were able to compress the air in the tanks to a pressure of about 100lbs per square inch.

My diving suit I built myself by shaping iron in the form of an open helmet which extended down as far as my breast; this I covered with painted canvas. I used the deadlight from a yacht's cabin as my eye glass in front of the helmet. I tied sash weights to my legs to hold me down on the bottom when walking in the vicinity of my boat . . .[23]

Lake had barely $15 in his pocket when he built *Argonaut Jr* and he had to do things on the cheap. However, the little wooden vessel functioned adequately and, with an air-lock and a diver's compartment, the two-man crew 'had a lot of fun running around the bottom of New York Bay picking up clams and oysters'. The press made sport of the craft – 'Fun for the Merry Mermen' headlined the *New York Herald* on 8 January 1895 – but any publicity is good publicity thought Lake, and he was right. A number of wealthy citizens – Vanderbilts, Astors, Goulds – bought stock in a company promoted on Lake's behalf by a certain Mr H. who did very well for himself but not a lot for the inventor. After a good deal of legal wrangling, the unscrupulous promoter was ousted, and Lake was relieved to find that sufficient monies remained to build a full-size bottom-crawler. *Argonaut First* was launched from cradles alongside Holland's *Plunger* and made a well publicized passage from Norfolk to Sandy Hook in September 1898.[24]

The new *Argonaut* was 36 ft long and 9 ft broad. She displaced 59 tons and was built of ⅜-in steel plate. A 30-hp gasoline engine drove a propeller, or it could be connected to two toothed driving wheels forward for running on the bottom: a third wheel, directed from inside or out, steered. Air for the engine was initially sucked in through a canvas hose connected to a floating buoy above, but this dangerous contrivance was later replaced by two long intake and exhaust masts: if these were 50 ft tall (as Lake asserted) they were a good deal longer than a modern snorkel and, unsupported, were liable to fracture, to say nothing of the danger from surface vessels running them down. The craft was remodelled and enlarged at Robins Dry Dock Company, Brooklyn in 1899 and finally completed with a length of 66 ft in July 1900. The *Argonauts* operated only on the surface or the seabed – never in between.

The usual method of diving was to lower two anchor-weights and flood in water until buoyancy was reduced sufficiently for the anchor cables to haul *Argonaut* down to the bottom when wound in. More water was then let into the ballast tanks and the weights were drawn up into pockets.

Lake's second boat, known as Argonaut First, *at Malster's yard on Locust Point in Baltimore Harbor, 1897. See also the drawing in Chapter 3.* (RNSM)

Lake loved *Argonaut First*. One day his log recorded: 'The spirits of the crew appeared to improve the longer we remain below; the time was spent in catching clams, singing, trying to valse, playing cards and writing letters to wives and sweethearts.'

In 1900, Capt Charles Ottley, Royal Navy Attaché, accepted an invitation for a trip during which Lake was clearly determined to discomfort the Limey officer.[25] Ottley enquired, after the boat had dived, whether the heavily vibrating *Argonaut* was actually proceeding along the bottom of the harbour. It was too dark to see anything through the glass scuttles and the electric searchlight in the bows did not help. By way of reply, Lake took his visitor into a chamber in the bottom of the craft where there was a large hatch, secured with butterfly nuts. He blasted compressed air into the compartment until water ceased to flow from a test-cock, showing that internal pressure had equalized with external sea-pressure. Satisfied, Lake dropped open the hatch with sublime confidence. Shells and starfish could be seen lying on the bottom as the intruder rolled over them. 'Mr Lake,' said Ottley, 'you can close the door as soon as you like, I have seen quite enough.'

Unfortunately, at that moment the submarine took a sharp down-angle. 'Mr Lake turned very pale' (according to Ottley) and announced that they had dropped into a hole in the seabed, implying doubt about whether they would ever get out. The visitor responded with gratifying concern. However, after some thought Lake announced that he could release a 10,000-lb weight (it actually weighed 4,000 lb) as well as blowing water from the tanks; if they all rocked the boat it would come to the surface. Everybody on board participated in this performance (almost certainly contrived and unnecessary) and the submarine bobbed up above the waves. The impressionable British Naval Attaché penned a full report to the Admiralty about his grim experience, concluding with the remark 'we were all very thankful to land'. It may be mere coincidence that Capt Ottley invented the anti-submarine towed sweep known as the 'Otter' in 1901 and, as a Rear Admiral in 1905, asked the RN Design Committee, '. . . whether it is worth while building a [submarine boat] which costs as much as a destroyer with less than half a destroyer's speed, and a third of its radius of action, and incomparably worse sea-keeping . . .'[26]

Lake had put the Captain off submarines for life; but nevertheless the bottom-crawler met all of his barbed questions, except for speed. She was inexpensive and a commercial earner. She covered more than a thousand miles on the surface during a two-month voyage in the summer of 1898, going to the bottom when the weather turned nasty.

Mr Ray Stannard Baker (evidently an influential friend) was treated more seriously than the unfortunate British attaché when he went on a short excursion with Lake on 12 October 1898:

[We] felt a faint jolt, and Mr Lake said that we were on the bottom of the sea. Here we were running as comfortably along the bottom . . . as we would ride in a Broadway car, and with quite as much safety. Wilson [Engineer], who was of a musical turn, was whistling 'Down Went McGinty', and Mr Lake, with his hands on the pilot-wheel, put in an occasional word about his marvellous invention. . . . Once . . . there was a sudden, sharp shock, the pointer [inclinometer] leaped back and then quivered steady again. Mr Lake said that we had probably struck a bit of wreckage or an embankment, but the *Argonaut* was running so lightly that she had leaped up jauntily and slid over the obstruction.

. . . there was 30 ft of yellowish green ocean over our heads. Mr Lake suddenly ordered the machinery stopped. The clacking noises of the dynamo ceased, and the electric lights blinked out, leaving us at once in almost absolute darkness and silence. . . . It lasted only a moment, but . . . we realised completely the meaning and joy of sunshine and moving winds, trees, and the world of men.

Lake entertained the gentlemen of the press lavishly. 'Klondike is nowhere' said the *New York Herald*, and entrepreneurs were quick to see the money-making possibilities. 'You mustn't confuse the *Argonaut* with other submarine boats', said the inventor, 'she is quite different and much safer.'

Simon Lake – 'stout-shouldered, powerfully built' – exuded confidence. He soon decided to construct the multipurpose (minesweeping/laying and with three torpedo tubes) *Protector* on *Argonaut* principles. She was launched at Bridgeport, Connecticut on 1 November 1902 and, stealthily circumventing American neutrality laws, delivered to Russia as the *Osetr* in 1904. It was not until 1910 that Lake's name became associated with submarines (of the standard type) in the United States Navy (the USS *Seal* was built 1910/11 and accepted 29 July 1911). No significant developments seem to have been directly due to Lake apart, of course, from the very useful bottom-crawling functions of his early craft. Frequent references to his advocating a level trim for diving originally derive from 'levelling valves' which he installed in *Argonaut* to compensate for shifting weights when embarking cargo on the surface or seabed: he was not the first to suggest or to install hydroplanes forward as well as aft. Laubeuf was the first to design this arrangement in practical form; British C-class (and following) boats from 1905 were so equipped, and some earlier boats were then retrofitted. A submariner's natural scepticism must be suspended to credit the claim for *Protector*: 'No great skill required to control depth of submergence'![27]

All in all, John Philip Holland – Irish and American patriot, formerly of the Christian Brothers, shockingly unsuspicious businessman – emerges as the clear winner of a long race. The modern submarine really is an Irish invention: *Erin Go Brach*.[28]

CHAPTER 18

Britannia Takes the Plunge

1900 Airship: von Zeppelin
1901 Electric car-lamps

The furore in the press following the firing of a torpedo by *Gustave Zédé* at the anchored battleship *Magenta* on 7 January 1899 was due to well-presented French flim-flam; but the British Ambassador in Paris told Whitehall that 'belief in success of the invention is very likely to encourage Frenchmen to regard their inferiority to England as by no means so great as it is considered to be in the latter country.'[1] Naval Attaché (later Admiral of the Fleet) Capt Henry Jackson (1855–1929), one of Fisher's favourites in 'The Fishpond', warned that 'a vessel of this type . . . is capable of crossing and recrossing the English Channel from Cherbourg to Portland unaided.'[2] That was nonsense: the total distance was 126 nautical miles and *Zédé*'s maximum range was 48 miles at 6 knots;[3] but supposed threats were grist to the Admiralty mill while the Naval Defence Bill, aiming to equal any other two navies combined, was in the offing. (The Bill came into law on 8 March 1899.)

In February 1899 the First Lord of the Admiralty, George Goschen, was questioned in the House about French progress in the underwater field: wisely he was 'not at present prepared to make any statement'. However, on 26 October the Admiralty was given genuine cause for concern by the launch of *Narval*, a submersible clearly intended as an all-weather commerce-raider and designed with some wholly new features by M Maxime Laubeuf. *Narval* had a double hull – a light steel shell surrounding the thick pressure hull with space in between for ballast, compensating and fuel tanks. Besides an exceptional 42 per cent reserve of buoyancy on the surface (*Morse* had only 4 per cent and the British A-class 9 per cent) external ballast tanks meant that, when flooded, sea pressure was exerted on the outside of the circular pressure hull rather than the inside of flat internal tanks. For running on the surface (her prime purpose), she was better proportioned than *Plunger* – 111 ft long against 85 ft with a similar beam; and she was lighter at 106/200 tons against 154/168. Her best speed was 12 knots

Gustave Zédé , *a particular cause of the commotion.* (RNSM)

against *Plunger*'s hoped-for 15 knots, but for that a 250-hp steam plant sufficed against *Plunger*'s 1625 hp. *Narval* suffered from hidden snags, for example, gross discomfort and taking fifteen minutes to dive, but when she ran her trials in the early part of 1900 she was evidently seen by Britain as the last French straw.

It was time for Britannia to take the plunge herself. However, there was face to be preserved. A further question to Goschen, by Capt Norton MP, on 6 April 1900 drew a lofty answer to the effect that 'submarines were a weapon for Maritime Powers on the defensive', and anyway 'we know all about them'. This assurance was intended as a sop to anyone who thought that the Government was dragging its feet; but a month later Goschen was noting against a batch of reports from abroad 'they are not pleasant reading for clearly great strides are being made in the submarine boat'.[4] On 22 May Adm Lord Walter Kerr, Senior Naval Lord (title changed to First Sea Lord in 1904), minuted 'the matter of submarine boats cannot be ignored and must be taken up by us. Our first want is a design.'[5] It was now too late for the latter to be home-grown and, obviously, it could not be French. The United States was the only realistic alternative and a discreet approach was duly prepared.

When Isaac Rice of the Electric Boat Company was introduced to the Admiralty by Lord Rothschild in July, he became aware that Rothschild had a major financial interest in Vickers, Sons & Maxim at Barrow-in-Furness. Rice therefore sought out Charles Craven of Vickers privately to explore possibilities. Craven told him that, in the firm's opinion, there was no chance of the British Navy building submarines, whereupon Rice responded with the exceedingly private news that, on the contrary, the Admiralty had already decided to order five submarines, provided they could be built in British yards.[6] The shipyard at Barrow had spare capacity; submarines (in those days) demanded very little special shipbuilding infrastructure, and a marriage with Electric Boat would save Vickers a great deal of research and development.

Taking these conditions into consideration, Vickers agreed with Rice to build 'Holland'-type submarine boats under licence; but the Admiralty insisted that the intention, as well as the wheeling and dealing, be kept secret. Presumably because money and political reputations were at stake (not simply national security), secrecy was most strictly maintained throughout negotiations which culminated in a formal Admiralty order for Vickers on 18 December 1900, right up until March 1901 when Parliament was at last informed.

Secrecy was a prime reason for the Admiralty conceding a virtual monopoly of submarine construction to Vickers: seeking tenders from other firms would inevitably result in Whitehall's undercover plans becoming parliamentary and public knowledge. In light of the derogatory remarks and innuendo about submarine warfare which had previously been circulated – partly to discourage other nations and partly to excuse Britain for taking her time – a change in

The Holland *in dock at Atlantic Basin, Brooklyn, New York, summer 1898. Count Lieutenant Kosuke Kizaki IJN, at right, is talking with the inventor: he took a trip in the boat later in the year.* (Morris collection)

opinion had to be announced without unseemly haste. It could be conceded that, against the British rules of boxing, submarines hit below the belt – the armoured belt indeed – but the advice of the Controller, Adm Sir Arthur ("ard 'eart') Wilson (1842–1921) that submarine crews captured in wartime 'should be hanged as pirates', together with a general opinion that the submarine was 'unfair, underhand and a damned un-English weapon', needed softening round the edges.[7]

Meanwhile the secret agreement was to build five 'Holland' boats at Barrow at a cost of £35,000 apiece, including delivery to naval ports. A royalty of £10,000 would be paid to Vickers if any boats were manufactured by what were called 'private firms', and £2,500 if built in HM Dockyards. Vickers, however, had to pay Electric Boat a half-share of profits on all submarines built at Barrow of whatever type.[8] Nevertheless, Vickers' profit margin averaged 70 per cent for the first half-dozen British boats – five 'Hollands' and *A1* and the monopoly was not terminated until 1911. On the other hand, the quality of production was undeniably high, one might say unrivalled.

The contract with the American company, for five boats referred to as 'Type Number VII', included the provision of a trained American crew 'which will be at the service of the Admiralty for the purpose of instructing a British Navy crew in the working and general operation of the boat under all circumstances of service'.[9] The Navy, whatever the politicians may have said, did not 'know all about submarines'. Vickers were prepared to guarantee some seemingly tough specified conditions because 'guarantees by the Holland Torpedo Boat Company in America were considerably exceeded at the official trial'. There was 'every reason to believe that better results than those we have mentioned will be obtained'.[10]

The agreed specifications included speeds of 8 knots in fine weather and 7 knots in ordinary (English) weather on the surface with a range of 250 nautical miles, and 7 knots for 25 miles submerged. (In later classes with sundry excrescences, of the kind which Holland complained bitterly about, the range dived was generally no more in miles than the speed in knots.) Diving time was 2–10 minutes 'according to the skill of the crew'. Maximum safe depth was 100 ft; but calculations made by naval architects, when HM Submarine Torpedo Boat *No. 1* ('Holland I') was salvaged for the RN Submarine Museum in 1982, indicate that it would have been wise to stay above 60 ft.

Meanwhile USS *Holland* (SS-1) was formally commissioned on 12 October 1900; and Congress agreed to the construction of six more boats, of the 'Adder' class including a new *Plunger*. The first was launched in July 1901; it was this design, not that of USS *Holland*, which the five British 'Hollands' copied with sundry modifications. Such was Britain's trust in American engineering that the Royal Navy's contract negotiated by Isaac Rice was signed without any Admiralty official inspecting the hardware.

HM Submarine *No. 1* was laid down in February 1901. Secrecy was still paramount but the Government must have 'leaked' some hints to *The Times*,

Launch of HM Submarine Torpedo Boat No.1, 2 October 1901, as pictured by the Illustrated London News *on 12 October.*

No. 1 *immediately after launch at Barrow, 2 October 1901, disproving the persistent rumour that she capsized on entering the water.* (RNSM)

because on 10 January a leader appeared with the obvious intention of acclimatizing British citizens to the thought of formerly ignoble underwater warfare. It concluded:

> Our Navy, it is true, has always been rather slow to adopt appliances and engines of war that have found favour with other Powers. Slow and sure is a good maxim, but sure and ready is better . . . .we shall be surprised and disappointed if the Admiralty have neglected to provide the Navy with a few submarine boats of the best type yet produced to be employed on an experimental study of the whole problem.

Thus, when the Naval Estimates were published on 1 March, it came as no great surprise that they included costings for five submarine boats of the 'Holland' type. Hugh Arnold-Forster, Parliamentary Secretary to the Admiralty, told the House of Commons on 18 March 1901:

> I will not say much about submarine vessels, but I will say I am glad that the Admiralty, under the advice of Lord Goschen [recently ennobled], took the view that it was wise not to be found unprepared in regard to this matter. We have a great deal of information about these boats, but . . . we believe that an ounce of practice is worth a ton of theory. . . . We are comforted by the judgement of the United States and Germany, which is hostile to these inventions, which I confess I desire shall never prosper.[11]

At this juncture, Cdr Young MP said that if the Admiralty built any submarine boats, all he would ask is that he might not be ordered to serve in one.[12] So what was the British public, or the Royal Navy, to think?

CHAPTER 19

Setting up Shop

1901 Assassination of President McKinley; Theodore Roosevelt President

The *Holland*'s reception in the US Navy was lukewarm;[1] in two important camps, it became actively hostile when a sizeable number of successors to 'SS-1' was nominated. Rear Adm O'Neil, Chief of the Bureau of Ordnance, was singularly uncomplimentary about the boat when he reported to the Congressional Committee on Naval Affairs in January 1901. He was right to complain that the main motor armature had burned out five times (no surprise) in a few months; but, as the official under whose jurisdiction *Holland* had operated since her purchase nine months before, his condemnation of submarines generally boded ill for their proper support in the United States Navy. They were 'ingeniously-contrived craft of an eccentric character which mark a step in the development of an interesting science, but nothing more'. He was unable to accept 'the sum total of her [*Holland*'s] performances' as 'sufficient evidence that such boats are useful and efficient instruments for naval purposes'; and their only use was 'to discharge torpedoes', adding that 'no weapon is more erratic and uncertain in its flight'.[2] Opinion was one thing, but the last statement was pernicious. Granted, there were plenty of torpedo failures but the weapon was steadily improving in determined hands. Gyroscopic steering had been introduced in 1898 and the Royal Navy's 18-in RGF Mk V was performing well out to a healthy 800 yards. HMS *Vernon* was turning out keen, well-trained young torpedo officers; but it would be surprising if a negative attitude at the top of BuOrd was not reflected throughout the Naval Torpedo Station at Newport, Rhode Island. Moreover, as *The Engineer* observed, Rear Adm Melville USN, Chief of the Bureau of Steam Engineering, took the same view as O'Neil.[3]

If there was no enthusiasm for the US Navy's submarine service and its weaponry at the beginning, and scant stimulus during the First World War in which USN submarines scarcely played a role, it seems fair to wonder if the appalling performance of American submarine torpedoes for the first eighteen months of the Second World War can be traced back to a speech made some forty-two years earlier.

The Engineer went on, however, to instance Rear Adm Hichborn, Chief

Constructor, United States Navy, as a submarine protagonist, but then markedly weakened his reportedly positive view by explaining that:

> . . . he favours submarine boats, not so much because he is sure they are really good for anything, as because he thinks they could comfort nervous people. Asked if he thought two submarine boats for each port in case of war would be enough, he replied that they would not, but 'they would be a help to nervous people. We had a little experience of that during the last war [1898]. The people on the New England coast raided the Navy Department from morning to night for old monitors that had been condemned for more than thirty years; and we took them down there, and the people kept quiet after that. The submarines would be as good a cure for nervous prostration as anything you could get.' It seems to us that just the same end would be answered by official assurance that the submarine boats were really there, whether they were or not . . .[4]

Quite so. The mere possession of submarines was enough for most countries; and it can be assumed that bluff featured largely in their proclaimed capabilities during the early 1900s – and, in some cases, long after that. Few American officers had faith in submarine boats 'except as being small beginnings from which great things may come'.[5] Funds were grudged, especially when they threatened programmes intended to make the United States Navy second to none.[6] Nor were the 'Adder' follow-on boats given all the ancillary equipment that they needed: periscopes were fitted late, the first type being combined with a ventilator tube, and they were inferior to British instruments.

Lt Harry H. Caldwell, commanding the US Torpedo Boat *Holland* and previously aide to pro-submarine Adm Dewey, was sternly denied an initial success that was his by right. The setting for the first US Navy submarine exercise was a blockade off Newport by ships of the US North Atlantic Squadron (Rear Adm Farquar). USTB *Holland* rumbled away from the base at sunset on the second night and headed for open waters where Caldwell instructed Acting Gunner Owen Hill to trim the boat right down, so that only the tiny conning tower and a few inches of hull remained above the surface. Capt Cable had declared the crew of nine sufficiently trained barely four weeks before – they had no operational experience.

The blockading vessels, three battleships supported by two gunboats, were darkened. The only light came from a scatter of stars in the clear September sky. Manoeuvring awash with no navigation lights, and unable to submerge fully in less than five minutes, the little submarine was in a very dangerous position. No modern submariner would, in peacetime anyway, take such a risk of being rammed. Caldwell was unworried because, as yet, there had been no serious submarine collisions in any navy.

When the boat was out to sea, a vast black shape suddenly appeared ahead. It was the battleship *Kearsarge*, flagship of the Squadron and commanded by Capt

William M. Folger. The ship was probably stopped when, half-a-cable off, Caldwell pointed straight at his target, waved a lamp and shouted across the flat calm water: 'Hullo *Kearsarge*! You are blown to atoms. This is the submarine boat *Holland*.'[7]

The umpire meanly refused to allow Caldwell a dummy sinking because *Kearsarge* had already been 'torpedoed' by the torpedo boat *Dahlgren* and shelled by defending surface ships. Caldwell insisted that he had not been seen by any vessel of the blockading fleet, nor by its escorts, and that his attack was wholly successful. Furthermore, he could have gone on to torpedo the other blockading battleships had he chosen to do so. Folger acknowledged that *Holland* was undetected but snidely remarked that a submarine in the middle of a fleet stood a good chance of being run down. How right he was!

O'Neil commented characteristically on Caldwell's achievement: '. . . the *Holland*, on a very fine evening and under exceptionally favourable circumstances, steamed 7 miles, as a surface boat only, outside Newport Harbor . . . she did no more . . . than might have been accomplished by an ordinary steam launch . . .'[8] Adm Farquar pointed out, rather ingenuously, that the *Holland* did not reach an attacking position until after several other torpedo boats 'so that so strict a look-out was probably not being kept as would otherwise have been on board the *Kearsage*.'[9] The only winner in the make-believe battle was the umpire. It could take a very long while to realize that in a shooting war it is impossible to cheat or be cheated.

Recrossing the Atlantic, and moving only three years further on, some prototype submarine and anti-submarine exercise rules were devised for the Royal Navy by Capt Reginald Bacon after counter-blockade manoeuvres in the summer of 1904.[10] The manuscript rules are indicative of actual submarine and anti-submarine abilities:

> Rules for putting out of action, by submarines, vessels other than those against which they can fire [real] torpedoes:
>
> (1) Such a vessel is to be considered out of action if 'A' class sm, having two loaded torpedo tubes, can rise at any distance between 150 and 450 yards, on any bearing between 4 points before the beam and the beam.
>
> (2) If a *Holland* type boat, having one loaded torpedo tube, can arrive in a similar position, the vessel is to be claimed, but only half the total number of such claims will be allowed . . .
>
> The above rule is based on the experience obtained in the late manoeuvres, *viz*, a sm has a 50% chance of hitting a destroyer target from above named positions . . .
>
> Rules for putting a submarine out of action:
>
> (1) For a submarine boat to be put out of action by any vessel: she must have been under fire with her conning tower above water for at least one uninterrupted minute within a range of 300 yards, or

(2) She is to be considered out of action if the number [painted on lower part of] her optical tube can be read.

 . . . the numbers on optical tubes . . . should be of such a size as to be read with a service telescope 150 yards off.

A 'War Game' devised in *Jane's Fighting Ships* (1905/06 edition), is equally revealing. When the submarine player was on the surface or awash, he made his moves on a huge chessboard with the other players, indicating his position with a small pin. He was allowed to take any reasonable means not to attract the enemy's attention to his pin! But he was not allowed to conceal it. When submerged, he was obliged to retire from the table and sit with his back to it, with only a tiny board of his own on which the umpire located his position. The submariner was thereafter not allowed to use a pencil for drawing lines on his board and he was only permitted to look at the play through 'a small fragment of looking-glass, not exceeding half-an-inch in diameter'. Having fired a torpedo, he could not reload inside half-an-hour and he had to do that either on the surface or on the bottom. A submarine on the surface was to be regarded as defenceless: 'diving time varies, but in no case is there any such thing to be allowed as popping up and down again at once. No submarine in existence can yet do this.'[11]

HM Submarine *No. 1* was launched on 2 October 1901 at Barrow where naval personnel joined her. The cast was headed by an officer who had distinguished himself in torpedo work, Capt Reginald Bacon DSO. Appointed Inspecting Captain of Submarine Boats he demanded the services of a support ship for which HMS *Hazard*, an 1894 torpedo-gunboat, was immediately provided. The little 1,070-ton vessel was less than ideal, but a submarine depot ship had not yet been conceived; and at least she ensured that Bacon received command pay.

The captain of *Number 1* was Lt D. Arnold-Forster, who just happened to be the nephew of Hugh Oakley Arnold-Forster (1855–1909), the Parliamentary and Financial Secretary to the Admiralty of the same name, and a Fisher confidant and collaborator. He was kept on a tight rein; Bacon himself took practically all command decisions.

Arnold-Forster came, like most young naval officers of the period, from a good upper middle-class family. He had just completed the specialist torpedo course at HMS *Vernon* and could look forward to steady progression in the Royal Navy while enjoying all that society had to offer ashore and afloat. He was thus hesitant about going to a brand-new service at the outer fringe of society, or quite possibly beyond it, which would not provide the sparkle of overseas cruises. His 1901 diary suggests he would be a less than dedicated submariner:

Sunday 13 January. Yarn with Uncle Oakley [Arnold-Forster]. He is apparently anxious that we should start building submarine boats as a reply to the French. Perhaps we ought. It seems to be a matter of policy more than anything else . . .

Saturday 23 February. Read about submarine boats . . .

Sunday 24 February. . . . I have an idea of fitting [Lyddite fuses for shells] to fire with small charges from six-inch guns at submarine boats. Phosphide of Calcium to light fuse after it has sunk a certain depth [possibly the first 'depth-charge' concept] . . . Practised banjo.

Sunday 24 March. Wrote to Uncle Oakley volunteering for submarine boats . . . I don't believe in them [Uncle Oakley, of course, desired they 'shall never prosper'[12]] but I suppose somebody will be wanted to do preliminary experiments and it might be a useful experience. Anyhow no harm in asking . . .

Thursday 9 May. Wrote letter to Captain applying for submarine boat. Have no idea what will come of it, probably nothing.

Monday 17 June. Wrote to Allen asking him if he would exchange and let me go to *Implacable* for Mediterranean.

Wednesday 26 June. Skipper . . . told me . . . confidentially that he was forwarding my application for submarine boats. . . . In some ways I would rather go to sea [*sic*] but if I get in alright I think the job ought to be good for me from the Service point of view.[13]

Arnold-Forster had rather feeble reasons for joining submarines (and, as things transpired, quickly leaving), but the officers who came soon after him wanted to escape the dreary routines of big ship life and stand a chance of early command. Most volunteers from the lower deck (initially drawn from the battleships *Jupiter* and *Anson*, together with some officers) had a similar dislike of capital ships, but extra pay in submarines was the principal attraction for all. Hard-lying money in submarine boats at sea was 6 shillings a day for officers and 2 shillings for able seamen; with submarine specialization pay (never, contrary to public opinion, 'danger money'), the total could double an average pay packet. (In the US Navy a submarine sailor was paid 5 dollars a month extra and received an additional dollar for each day his boat dived up to a maximum total of 20 dollars per month.)

On 20 August 1901, Arnold-Forster was appointed to HMS *Hazard* 'For Special Service': the word 'submarine' was studiously omitted. He went straight to Vickers but nobody in the yard had heard of any submarine. Eventually he discovered his command in a building labelled 'Yacht Shed', where she was being put together in utmost secrecy. Only selected, trustworthy men were allowed inside. All frames and other parts made for her in the yard were marked 'Pontoon No. 1'.

Arnold-Forster was daunted by what he found inside the craft:

. . . the ingenious designer in New York evidently did not realise that the average naval officer has only two eyes and two hands; the little conning tower was simply plastered with wheels, levers and gauges with which some superman was to fire the torpedoes, dive and steer, and do everything else at the same time . . .

. . . and whilst the boat was being made ship-shape and less like a box of conjuring tricks, those with artistic ideas tried their hands at painting periscopes in various ways to make them invisible. The early periscopes were long and bulky [either rigged vertically and stayed like a mast or laid flat along the hull] and there was plenty of surface for paint. A barber's pole gave one enthusiast an idea. He painted a periscope in spiral stripes of all the primary colours. When whizzed round with a small electric motor it ought to have been invisible – but it wasn't, and the periscope painting craze gradually died out. [The anecdote is, of course, nonsense, but it illustrates the decidedly prep. school humour of the times.][14]

The drawings to which Vickers worked were not the same in detail as those for an American *Adder*; but for the fanatical Fenian John Devoy to impute that Holland, out of loyalty to Ireland, altered these and later drawings – and was somehow responsible for disasters in the British 'A' Class which followed – was patently absurd.[15] However, Bacon told the Controller ('hang them') Wilson it was 'simply courting murder to carry out trials with the boat in her then condition and with no-one on board who had any real knowledge of submarine work'.[16] Vickers called on the American Company to send over the promised trained crew forthwith.

The American team duly arrived headed by Capt Cable. He was astonished to find the boat full of 'gimcrack' fittings to which Bacon had rightly taken objection. Bacon described Cable as 'a thoroughly sound and careful captain'.[17]

On 3 October 1901 the *Naval and Military Record* announced: 'It is understood that no ceremony will take place at the forthcoming launch of the first British submarine. . . . The Admiralty regard these boats as wholly in the nature of an experiment and, like all other experiments conducted from time to time, this one will be carried out with every privacy.' Privacy was certainly achieved. HM Submarine *No. 1* had slid down the slipway on the previous day, 2 October 1901, the birthday of the Royal Navy's Submarine Service.

Meanwhile people were still worried about breathing in a confined space. The first of several 'fug trials' took place on 21 October in HMS *Hazard*'s tiny bread room where four men were incarcerated for two-and-a-half hours without any ill effects. Successive tests in the bread room were uneventful: the subjects passed the time with cards and music, and, every hour, the doctor took everyone's pulse and temperature including his own. Something serious was expected to happen, and the medical experts were disappointed when nobody collapsed. Even when eighteen bodies, including Capt Bacon, were shut down in the submarine itself for a whole night, there were no breathing difficulties; but the incarcerated crewmen were called upon to endure something worse than suffocation. An elderly

No. 1 on trials in Ramsden Dock, Barrow, January 1902, precariously attended by Vickers and naval observers with Captain Bacon often steering personally. (RNSM)

representative from Electric Boat brought his flute along to beguile the company, and he played it throughout a long, long night. As Capt Bacon feelingly recalled: 'they all looked upon flutes thereafter with a personal measure of animosity.'[18]

The first surface run on the gasoline (petrol) engine was made up the Ramsden Dock on 15 January 1902. The little boat was awkward to steer although the turning circle was a phenomenally small 130 yd. Once she alarmed the inmates of *Hazard*'s sick-bay by poking her blunt bows right through the ship's side into their berths.

On Good Friday, 20 March 1902, the first dive was made, as it still is today, in an enclosed shipyard basin. Chains were passed beneath the hull to pull the boat up in case she got stuck on the bottom like *Nautilus* in 1887. Arnold-Forster was upset when, on the following Monday morning, *No. 1* went out into the dock for her first free dive and 'the Captain [Bacon] said we could not both go down together the first time . . . so I had to come out and follow on the steamboat in charge of the rescue party.' He was not permitted to dive in his own boat until the afternoon of 3 April 'after waiting seven months and seeing apparently endless difficulties. Captain Bacon tried steering the boat by a new wheel close to the optical tube with successful results. Morell worked diving wheel.[19] Av. depth 3 to 4 feet. Hit the bottom twice but quite soft.'[20]

Submerged trials at sea followed:

Sunday 6 April: A fine day . . . went out to Morecambe Bay for our first deep submarine run. We all went in *Furness* tug, very comfortable, the submarine was towed by steam launch . . . Captain Cable in charge. Morell and three other Yankees, Captain Bacon and myself, Spence [Engineer] TI [Petty Officer Torpedo Instructor] and Chief ERA and Williams, the Yard Foreman. The first run I did understudy for diving wheel. Rather tricky at first but shall soon get into it. Kept her fairly steady at 8 feet. . . . Went back in steam launch. Went to church and wrote letters . . .'[21]

Tuesday 8 April: Decided to go out again to Morecambe Bay. Mrs Bacon came with us in the tug . . . had lunch before going down. . . . Captain Cable went back to America this morning, leaving Morell and one other electrician, so Morell took charge. I worked the diving wheel, Captain Bacon steered with periscope. . . . We had three long [sic] dives about 6 minutes. I am getting more steady on the diving wheel and kept her about 10 feet deep. Said goodbye to Morell as he is off tonight. He is a good sort but some of his yarns are rather too doubtful.[22]

The most important man on board was Cable – 'Boss Diver', as the Americans called him. Whether the boat sank or swam depended on him. His place was to be taken in the Royal Navy by the Diving Coxswain, soon shortened to Coxswain. The first was Petty Officer William R. Waller: it was he who laid the foundations for a coxswain being the rightful 'boss' of a British submarine, responsible for discipline and administration as well as taking over the planes in tricky situations. The later and broadly equivalent designation 'Chief of the Boat' in the US Navy did not usually imply hydroplane control. The French gave by far the best name to their key rating – *Le Patron*.

Capt Bacon, who thoroughly enjoyed himself during trials and was prone to take direct command, 'absentmindedly ran under a low bridge with the periscope up on the surface and carried it away. No damage otherwise.'[23] Being the only senior officer for miles around, he felt there was no need to report the incident; after all the periscope was, he fondly believed, his own invention. Arnold-Forster was left to make repairs.

On 16 April, Arnold-Forster noted something much more serious in his diary: '. . . four gallons of rum adrift somehow. Beastly nuisance.'[24] That was a gentlemanly understatement: many a British submarine officer for years to come was to learn the painful extent of this particular kind of 'beastly nuisance' when a Board of Enquiry, very possibly followed by a Court Martial, resulted.

Trials in the Irish Sea demonstrated that a 'Holland' was too small for proper seagoing: the conning tower hatch had to be shut above Sea State 3. Higher speeds and more torpedo tubes were also needed. A new 'A' class was therefore speedily designed by Vickers to Admiralty requirements; and HMS *A1* was launched on 19 February 1902, a year before the first 'Holland', delayed by technical faults, was finally completed on 2 February 1903.[25] *A1* was 103 ft long with a 7-ft conning tower and a 2-ft freeboard She displaced 190/207 tons and speed surface/submerged was 9.5/6 knots. Endurance dived, with twice the battery capacity of a 'Holland', was a theoretical 4 hours 5 minutes at full speed.[26]

The 'A's' bore a faint family resemblance to the 'Holland's but there was no question of infringing American rights. The British submarine service was declaring independence from America. However, half of all Vickers' profits had to be paid as royalties to Electric Boat *whatever* submarines were built at Barrow.[27]

In the summer of 1902, a small convoy comprising HMS *Hazard*, submarines *No. 2* and *No. 3* with Torpedo-boat *No. 42* as escort, left Barrow for Portsmouth where Nos *1*, *4* and *5* joined them a few months later. Here they were banished for three years, with the ageing cruiser *Thames* as parent ship, to the far reaches of Portsmouth Harbour up Fareham Creek – traditional home to other dangerous and undesirable tenants such as powder barges, prison hulks and quarantine vessels. This meant that, on their way to and from the Solent, they had to pass long ranks of His Majesty's immaculate ships lying at their berths. Thus, twice in every seagoing day, the young submariners were looked down upon, literally as well as figuratively, by gilded officers of the surface fleet striding spotless quarter-decks and doubtless wrinkling their noses as the smelly little submergibles passed by. 'Unwashed chauffeurs' was one of several imprecations muttered from above.

Britain's fledgling submarine service appeared to let insult and innuendo wash over it. Much of it was good-natured after all, and there were more important things to worry about: there was a lot to do and everything to learn. With the Service showing signs of rapid expansion, lessons had to be passed from mouth to mouth and hand to hand. There were no text books. Bacon knew that they were all groping in the dark and he preached care. He had a brass plate engraved with the words 'No one of us is infallible not even the youngest', and presented the plaque in turn to the boat whose captain had most recently offended.

Otto engines were apt to pack up without notice – assuming an engine could be started in the first place; but one of Bacon's ambitions was to circumnavigate the Isle of Wight with all five boats. Three broke down before they passed Spit Fort, four miles from the start, and only one reached Cowes. At times the game seemed hopeless, but patience and dogged hard work gradually eliminated causes of failure and captains began to bring their boats into a reasonably efficient state.

A day at sea was carefully planned. When 'Harbour Stations' was ordered the long horizontal door-like torpedo loading hatch was firmly screwed down while the steering and diving rudders were tested. The Coxswain enveloped himself in an enormous admiralty-pattern oilskin and sat down squarely on the edge of the conning tower with a small, dismountable steering wheel which, like the diving rudder wheel, required considerable strength to turn. Two ventilating tubes

No. 1 *alongside HMS* Hazard *in Fareham Creek, c. 1903. The towing wire running along the port side could be slipped from inside the boat, an arrangement which the Second World War X-craft would copy.* (RNSM)

supplied air when the conning tower hatch was shut while a third was supposed to vent stray fumes.

Following the original *Holland*, like all submarines with alternative diesel and electric propulsion (before diesel-electric systems were introduced), the engine, motor and propeller were mounted on a common shaft: there was an engine clutch between the engine and motor, and a tail clutch between motor and propeller. The 160-hp gasoline engine, which had a large cast-iron flywheel, was started by the electric motor with the propeller clutch in (because the clutch could not be operated while the shaft was revolving). The starting process was thereby jerky and, while the Otto was coughing and spluttering, the submarine itself was helpless.

When and if the boat reached her assigned diving area in the Solent, the Coxswain unshipped the wheel, shed his oilskins (it was impossible to squeeze through the hatch otherwise), shouted 'Diving stations below', and scrambled down the ladder. Meanwhile the Captain, still on deck, lowered and secured the ventilators, checked the periscope rigging and had a good look all round for ships and navigational marks, ordering the engine to be stopped and declutched when he thought he knew where he was. The main motor was tested by the Petty Officer TI in charge of the switchboard; hull valves were checked shut, and the second captain, a Lieutenant or Sub-Lieutenant, sang out 'All correct' to the captain who climbed down the conning tower, shutting the hatch above him and ordering 'Flood the main ballast tanks.' Camp stools were unfolded and the crew – eight plus one or two trainees – took their place while the stationary craft settled in the water until the sea lapped around the conning tower. It was now possible to judge, by watching the inclinometer, the fore-and-aft trim: this was adjusted by blowing water between the forward and after trimming tanks and fine-tuned by instructing a suitably well-built member of the crew to shift his stool a little further aft or forward. The statical diving tank, holding one-third of a ton and equalling the volume of the conning tower, was then flooded and, hopefully with just a tiny amount of positive buoyancy remaining, the Captain ordered 'Go ahead' on the motor. Lt (later Rear Adm) C.G. Brodie described what followed during his first day at sea under training:

> . . . the coxswain started a strenuous yet delicate juggling with the diving wheel which governed the fore-and-aft angle of the submarine. Watching the bubble [in the inclinometer] he revolved the wheel gently against its movement. The silence and immobility of everybody else as *Holland No. 3*, still almost horizontal, gathered way, began to suggest that diving was simpler than we had expected. Suddenly calm was shattered as she plunged steeply by the nose. We passengers, the only people not holding on to a wheel or a valve, slid forward

No. 3, *obviously on a formal occasion and probably due to give a demonstration to VIPs, passing HMS* Victory *on the way out of Portsmouth Harbour.* (RNSM)

along the boards to the rear of the torpedo tube a few feet away. I saw Skinner [second captain] leap to the cause of error, the brass pointer on the indicator arm of the diving helm. It had disconnected – stuck at 5 degrees 'Rise' though the coxswain had turned the wheel against the bubble towards 'Dive'. Instantaneously the motor speeded up, the coxswain hastily put his helm up hard and *Holland 3* gave us an exhibition of her lively diving qualities. Her change to rise was equally rapid as Horton and I [Max K. Horton, to become one of the most famous submariners of all time], trying to look nonchalant, scrambled back to our places. . . . But for the lightning movement of Skinner's the stolid coxswain would have kept his wheel down and, with two or three seconds under dive helm, the angle of the boat could have been disastrous [made worse by Brodie and Skinner sliding forward], spilling the acid from the battery – a more serious danger than hitting the bottom.[28]

Printed instructions to submarine officers emphasized the necessity of mopping up spilt battery acid and keeping bilges dry to avoid the generation of marsh gas – yet another hazard for the white mice ready to 'give warning of noxious gases'. But the mice would probably not have noticed anyway: reputedly credited with one shilling a day for their upkeep they were stuffed so full of food by the sailors – notorious pet-lovers at the best of times – that they were virtually insensible throughout their service careers.

The second captain steered the boat submerged with one eye glued to the eye-piece of the tube where he could see the reflected illumination of the compass. The captain took over when attacking with torpedoes. The most dangerous time for a submarine was coming to periscope depth from periods deliberately spent deep and blind. The periscope broke surface at an indicated depth of 15 ft and the optimum periscope depth for observation was 10 ft: the top of the conning tower was then only about six ft below the surface and there was every chance of being hit by any unseen ship that passed overhead. Propeller noises could sometimes be heard through the hull but there was no indication of range or direction.

A mild case of collision in the vertical plane occurred in the Solent when *No. 2* was 'playing porpoises' for the Princess Royal watching from a nearby tug. The boat had just come up to 10 ft when there was 'a curious scraping noise overhead, a tremor and a slight roll'. An irrepressible able seaman on his stool right forward helpfully sang out 'What ho! She bumps!' as a hollow series of thuds sounded along the pressure hull. The instinct today, unless water was flooding in, would be to go deep again as quickly as possible and wait until any shipping overhead had drawn clear; but in those days the captain was strongly in favour of regaining the surface without delay, so he ordered 'Hard-a-rise' while blowing main ballast and stopping the motor.

No. 2 had hit an anchored brigantine of vintage years but the surface vessel's captain, despite aggrieved gesticulations by his crew, kindly reassured his underwater opposite number by saying that it was 'nothing to hurt'.[29] The periscope was bent into a bow but fortunately the hull was undamaged. If the brigantine had been underway, she would have sliced the little boat in half.

The incident foreshadowed real disasters ahead; and soon they came. But, for the moment, Britain's new Submarine Service was splashing enjoyably in shallow waters and, of course, it was not alone in the paddling pool (or Fishpond as Fisher advocates would have it). Upper-deck seamen became engineers almost before they knew it; and the stench of gasoline, oil and unwashed bodies clung to their clothing.

'The Trade', as Rudyard Kipling christened the Royal Navy's Submarine Service, was in business. Fisher predicted great things for it, but he made one false prophecy: 'My beloved submarines are not only going to make it damned hot for the enemy . . . but they are going to bring the income tax down to threepence in the pound.'[30] If only Jacky had been right!

Submarine sailors escaped dreary big-ship routines, but they still had to polish brightwork as shown on board HMS A1 soon after completion in July 1903. Perhaps it was the extra pay that resulted in only 7.2 per cent of British submariners signing the pledge, and becoming entitled to one penny a day instead of free rum, compared with 13.4 per cent of men in the Royal Navy as a whole being teetotal. (RNSM)

CHAPTER 20

Back to the Future

Submarines and submariners are forever pioneering in one direction or another; but the year 1904 marked, give or take, the end of their beginning in the British and United States navies. Not that they were popular on either side of the Atlantic. British submariners withdrew into their shells, and communication with the Admiralty was tenuous. Very few people in authority understood what submarines could or could not do; so misemployment and

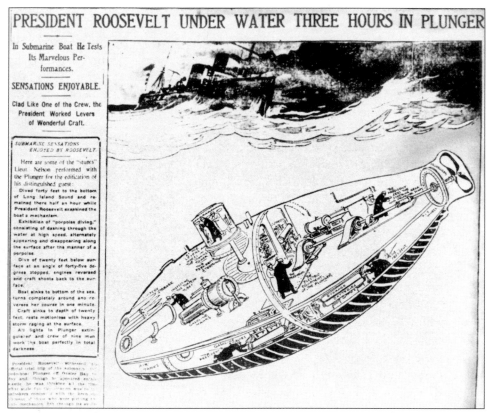

President Theodore Roosevelt took a trip in USS Plunger *(A-1), 25 August 1905, in Long Island Sound near his home on Sagamore Hill (*New York Herald*, 27 August 1905). Afterwards he directed that submariners' pay be increased from shore-duty to sea-duty rate. (Via R.K. Morris)*

inappropriate equipment were bound to follow. In the US Navy, a 'pig-boats' were not rated at all highly until at least another generation of naval planners had come and gone; and crews had to emphasize they were subma*r*iners, to avoid being mistaken for sub-standard mariners.[1]

In France the popularity of *les sous-marins* and *les submersibles* ebbed and flowed according to the current cordiality of *entente* with *la perfide Albion*. *Elan* was noteworthy but the percentage of accidental losses and serious accidents up to 1914 was nearly twice that of the Royal Navy.[2] Meanwhile, Italy's small flotilla displayed interesting technical variations, but purposefulness was less apparent.

Russia was spreading her bets by buying both Lake and Holland types as well as small home-grown produce. The naval commentator Fred T. Jane (1865–1916), of *Jane's Fighting Ships* fame, opined that the Lake type '. . . being able to lie submerged and stationary embodied features considerably superior to any possessed by the *Holland* type'.[3] The usually well-informed Fred had fallen victim to Simon Lake's salesmanship: at the time Lake boats were bottom-crawlers, valuable for mine-laying and sweeping, but not submarines or submersibles in the accepted sense.[4]

Japan engaged in thoroughgoing, more or less overt, espionage and then unhesitatingly purchased five 'Hollands', but not in time to have them fully up and running for the 1904–5 war with Russia which she won anyway. She also captured a tiny Russian 'Peter Koshka' which had reportedly been 'rendered useless before the surrender' – an unnecessary precaution.[5]

'Holland' types were generally accepted as the best except in Germany where the Kaiser and Admiral Tirpitz were watchfully biding their time. The fact that submarines soon became longer, thinner and more buoyant, with substantial conning towers, superstructures, masts and guns had nothing to do with underwater performance: on the contrary the enlargements and additions signified that the boats were to operate primarily as *surface* raiders, which is not what John Holland had in mind, although submarines bearing his name followed the same trend from about 1908, as did Simon Lake's. The ocean-going submarines that fought both World Wars had so many bulky attachments and such high auxiliary electrical loads that they had only about one-third the submerged endurance of Holland's slippery little 'Adders'. On the other hand their speed on the surface was much higher and their range was incomparably greater.

Simon Lake's Protector. (RNSM)

Left: *USS Skipjack (SSN-585) at Portland, England, after her first major NATO exercise.*

Below: *Soviet 'Alfa' class (1971) nuclear attack-type submarine (SSN) capable of about 42 knots.*

It was not until nuclear power became feasible for propulsion in the 1950s that submarine navigation truly merited the name. At that point, naval architects promptly reverted to the uncluttered contours and porpoise-like proportions that Holland had so resolutely advocated more than half a century before.[6] He would have no difficulty in recognizing a modern 'nuke' as one of his own; and he would appreciate the part these leviathans can play in preventing warfare by their very presence, whether actual or suspected. He continually expressed a hope, from the time that Clara Barton rebuked him in 1899 for inventing such 'a dreadful weapon', that his submarines would prevent war;[7] but he recognized this was 'too

No. 1 (aka Holland 1 in British terms) in dry dock at Plymouth immediately after salvage in August 1982 on behalf of the RN Submarine Museum, after 69 years on the seabed. She displays the ideal porpoise-shape adopted by the larger USS Skipjack (SSN 585), commissioned 15 April 1959, and by other nuclear attack-type submarines such as the extremely fast Soviet/Russian 'Alfa' class. (Author's collection)

Utopian for serious consideration' and never made a sales pitch of the possibility in the way that Fulton had.[8] He also noted that 'how the menace of the submarine is to be met nobody has at this time been able to say.'[9] Nor have they said since: submariners continually play leapfrog with the opposition.

Holland was generous in acknowledging pioneers such as Bushnell – too generous. In reality, he scarcely owed a debt to anybody, save to Br Dominic Burke and the Christian Brothers for mechanical and spiritual preparation respectively, and to the Irish Republican Brotherhood and *Clan na Gael* for enabling him to set up shop. In turn the Royal Navy (among others) became indebted for its Submarine Service to Holland's first financiers – a supreme irony bearing in mind that the sundry Fenian factions constituted an ancestral IRA largely funded by North American aid.

Holland died of pneumonia, aged 73, on 12 August 1914. His remains are interred in the Holy Sepulchre Cemetery, Paterson, New Jersey.

Sadly, it may appear inopportune nowadays to recall the words of John Holland's younger brother Michael, writing from New London in 1916 about the *Fenian Ram*, two years after the inventor's death, but the tribute is hard to refute: '. . . to me she will always be "the boat"';[10] and, more generally, 'The submarine in my estimation is a monument to the honesty, ability and earnestness of the revolutionary Irishman.'[11]

Notes

1. Wing Collars and Sea Boots

1. See Chapter 19: there is doubt about who said what, but such epithets did represent social feelings.
2. Powell, Nicholas: 'The Lost Brothels of Paris', *Sunday Telegraph Magazine*, 14 February 1999; and Keith Middlemas, *The Life and Times of Edward VII* (Weidenfeld & Nicolson, 1972), p. 78.
3. Original source uncertain; but John Wells relates the story in *The Royal Navy* (1994), p. 53, and refers to its telling by Peter Padfield in *Aim Straight: a Biography of Admiral Sir Percy Scott* (London, Hodder & Stoughton, 1966) pp. 143–4.
4. Ponsonby, Sir Frederick: *Recollections of Three Reigns* (London, Seeley & Co., 1900), partly quoted in this paragraph, illustrates the King and his companions with admirable discretion. (For the record, Frederick refused the offer in Vienna.)
5. Cf. Vice Adm Sir Louis Le Bailly: *From Fisher to the Falklands* (Marine Management (Holdings) Ltd for the IME, 1991), p. xi and his quoting Professor Arthur Marder.
6. Extensive research has failed to find the source of this phrase; and the author confesses that it could have originated from his own media broadcasts in 1976, on the occasion of the RN Submarine Service's seventy-fifth anniversary, when he may well have coined it as representative of Edwardian views – which indeed it was.
7. Mackay, Ruddock F., *Fisher of Kilverstone* (Oxford, Clarendon Press, 1973), pp. 286–8.
8. Fisher to son Cecil *c*. August 1903, quoted by Mackay, ibid., p. 286.
9. Beresford was Conservative MP for Waterford 1874–80, East Div. Marylebone 1885–9, York 1897–1900, Woolwich 1902, Portsmouth (U) 1910–16.
10. Mackay, op. cit., p. 286 (see note 8).
11. Dash, Michael W. , 'British Submarine Policy 1853–1918' (1990), p. 236 quoting Arnold-Forster to Lyttleton (CGS), 19 May 1904, and memo by Col Ruck, 29 January 1904, both in British Library Mss.
12. Cf. Mackay, op. cit., pp. 285–304.
13. Ibid., p. 299.
14. Fisher to Lord Knollys (Secretary to HM), 20 April 1904, Bacon, Reginald, *The Life of Lord Fisher of Kilverstone* (London, Hodder & Stoughton, 1929), 2 vols.
15. But covert tows of 35-ton X-craft by standard submarines at 8–10 knots were entirely practicable in the Second World War. The purpose – harbour penetration – was the same as Fisher had in mind.
16. Mackay, op. cit., p. 297 quoting Fisher Papers 4702, p. 73, note.
17. Bacon, op. cit.
18. Ibid. Lady Fisher to her son, 25 February 1904.
19. Ibid.
20. Esher, R., *Journals and Letters of Reginald, Viscount Esher*, eds M.V. Brett and Oliver, Viscount Esher, (London, 1934–8), 4 vols, Vol. 2, p. 49.
21. Ibid.
22. Mackay, op. cit., pp. 285–304.
23. Author not known, but his crested notepaper was headed 'Craigendowie, Reigate' (RN Submarine Museum archives).

2. Good Thinking and a Quintessential Chymist

1. Supposedly Archimedes was struck by the notion in his bath and ran naked through the streets of Syracuse shouting '*Eureka*'. The story may be true: a tenth-century

Byzantine palimpsest containing the only known copy of the original Greek text of his work *On Floating Bodies* resurfaced in France in November 1998.

2. Bourne, William, *Inuentions or Deuices. Very Necessary for all Generalles and Captains, or Leaders of men, as well by Sea as by Land* (*c.* 1578, printed for Thomas Woodcock, London, *c.* 1590).

3. Sueter, Cdr Murray, *The Evolution of the Submarine Boat, Mine and Torpedo* (1907), pp. 16–17; and *Gentleman's Magazine*, June 1749. There is confusion between Borelli's work and Symons': nor is it sure that anything practical emerged.

4. Boyle, Hon. Robert, *Experiments on Air*, (Oxford, 1660), pp. 364 *et seq.*, and *New Experiments Physico-mechanical touching the Spring of the Air and its Effects* (1662, 2nd edn).

5. Description by Duke of Wurtenberg on 1 May 1610: cf. *The Dictionary of National Biography*, 1888 edn, vol 16, pp. 13–14.

6. *Dictionary of National Biography*, ibid.

7. Roland, Alex, *Underwater Warfare in the Age of Sail* (1976), p. 24 and quoting Constantin Huygen, Drebbel's close friend, in his 1631 *Autobiography* also quoted by Gerrit Tierie *Cornelis Drebbel, 1572–1633* (Amsterdam, H.J. Paris 1932), p. 61.

8. Sueter, op. cit., says it was the *boat* that was more immersed, but it is assumed he meant the basket. One of the most helpful articles describing Drebbel's work was published in *The Army and Navy Illustrated*, 1 November 1902, but it makes invalid assumptions.

9. Quintessence as explained in *OED*, 2nd edn, vol. V.

10. Sueter, op. cit., p. 10, quoting from de Hautefeuille, *Art de Respirer sous l'eau* (Paris, Bibliothèque Nationale, 1692).

3. Inspiration from Above

1. *Leonardo da Vinci's Notebooks*, arranged by Edward MacCurdy (London, Duckworth & Co., 1906) and *The Notebooks of Leonardo da Vinci* by the same author (London, Reprint Society, 1954), 2 vols, vol. I, p. 109.

2. Ibid., vol. II, p. 480.

3. The name implies a seafarer from the River Seine. Marin was an apt baptismal name.

4. Fournier was a royal chaplain associated with the Navy; he wrote a long discourse on marine matters titled *L'Hydrographie* (1643 edition in the Ministère de la Marine Library, Paris).

5. Patent No. 36 of April 1632. (Patents were adopted in England from 1617.)

6. Chancellor, Alexander, 'Footnote', *Daily Telegraph*, 2 November 1998.

7. Cf. A. Roland, *Underwater Warfare in the Age of Sail* (1976), p. 29 quoting Mersenne as 'the good thief', the honest compiler of the works of others and described by Lynn Thorndike in *A History of Magic and Experimental Science* (New York, Columbia University Press, 1929–58), vol. VII, p. 430.

8. *Mathematical Magick . . . Not before treated of in this language; by the late Lord Bishop of Chester, London: Printed for Edw. Gellibrand at the Golden Ball in St. Paul's Churchyard 1680.* Republished, more accessibly, by J. Nicholson, London 1708 under the title *Mathematical and Philosophical Works of the Right Reverend John Wilkins, Late Lord Bishop of Chester.*

4. Not Going Like Clockwork

1. *Philosophical Transactions* of the Royal Society, vol. I, p. 83.

2. Moggach, Deborah, *Tulip Fever* (London, Heinemann, 1999); Anna Pavord, *The Tulip* (London, Bloomsbury, 1999).

3. Delpeuch, Maurice, *Les Sous-Marins à travers les Siècles* (Paris, 1907), p. 27 quoting a Dutch author of 1669.

4. Ibid, p. 28.

5. Sueter, op. cit., pp 14–15.

6. Delpeuch, op. cit., pp. 28–9 (although he says nothing about the wheel not working in the water), and Sueter, ibid., p. 16.

5. Unhappy Day

1. Oliver, Peter (1713–91), 'Journal of a Voyage to England in 1776 and of a Tour

through part of England'. Unpublished MS in British Library, Egerton MSS 2672/2673 (ff 81b–82a). Summary kindly sent to the author by Dr T.R. Shaw OBE.

2. Beer, Frank: *Day's Diving Disaster in Plymouth Sound*, (Plymouth, PDS Printers, *c*. 1983).

3. Details from Charles Babbage (proposer of mobile diving bells and designer of the first mechanical calculator/computer) writing in the *Encyclopaedia Metropolitana* about a century after Day's attempt.

4. The newspapers who reported the event (and from which quotations are taken here and below) included *The Western Flying Post*, or *Sherborne and Yeovil Mercury and General Advertiser* (4 and 18 July 1774), and *Trewman's Exeter Flying Post* or *Plymouth and Cornish Advertiser* (September 1774). Original research (which pointed to these and other sources) was undertaken by Beer, op. cit.

5. Beer, op. cit., p. 6.

6. Ibid.

7. Ibid.

6. An Effort of Genius?

1. With shame the current author has to admit that, in his previous books, he too has unquestioningly accepted the bulk of the original story.

2. The Bushnell farm home (now demolished, but site indicated by a sign) was on modern Connecticut Rt. 153, not in Westbrook itself.

3. It is not known how Ezra found the money for this transaction.

4. Practically all histories concerning Bushnell derive from a collection of documents and commentaries (including Gale's) assembled by Lt Col (Brevet Brig-Gen) Henry L. Abbot (1831–1927), *The Beginning of Submarine Warfare under Captain-Lieutenant David Bushnell, Sappers and Miners, Army of the Revolution* (Willets Point, New York Harbor, Engineer School of Application, 1882), paper no. III; the collection is a primary source for this chapter: quotations, if not otherwise referenced, are taken from it.

5. *Inter alia* C. Knight and R. Lomas, *The Hiram Key* (Arrow Books, 1997). The point about Freemasonry here is that it aimed for liberty, transcending forbidden subjects of religion and politics, while the Lodge was a forum for the confidential exchange of national and international information, including scientific findings. Masons, numbering many of the best minds and influential men amongst them, were (and are) able – uniquely perhaps – to trust each other.

6. Barber, F.M. *Lecture on Submarine Boats and the Application to Torpedo Operations* (Newport, RI, US Torpedo Station, 1875).

7. Roland, Alex, *Underwater Warfare in the Age of Sail* (Indiana University Press, 1978), p. 76, and Phineas Pratt Jr, letter in the collection of the Connecticut Historical Society, cited by Marion Hepburn Grant in her splendidly readable and enthusiastic, but perhaps over-trusting, *The Infernal Machines of Saybrook's David Bushnell* (1976), which is additionally valuable for research references.

8. Wagner, Frederick, *Submarine Fighter of the American Revolution* (New York, Dodd, Mead & Co., 1963), p. 34.

9. Ibid., p. 35.

10. Abbot, op. cit., p. 9, citing Collections of Connecticut Historical Society, vol. II, *Correspondence of Silas Deane Esq.*, p. 315.

11. Ibid., p. 10.

12. Ibid., pp. 14–15.

13. *The Despatches of Molineux Shuldham*, ed. Robert W. Neisen, (New York, 1913), pp. 41–2, quoted by Grant op. cit., p. 17.

14. Grant, ibid., p. 17.

15. Howe was created Viscount in 1782 and Earl in 1788; from 1783 to 1789 he was First Lord of the Admiralty.

16. William Howe was elected MP in 1758; and created Viscount in 1799.

17. Woodforde, J. *The Strange Story of False Teeth* (London, Routledge & Kegan Paul, 1968), pp. 98–108.

18. *Thacher's Military Journal during the Revolutionary War*, October 1776 (Boston, 1823), p. 63 quoted in Abbot, Lee, Ezra,

p. 23. See also op. cit., *American Biographical Dictionary*, 1824 edition. Lee was afterwards employed by Washington on secret service, fought in the battles of Trenton, Brandywine and Monmouth, was promoted Ensign, and died at Lyme, Connecticut, on 29 October 1821, aged 72. Cf. footnote on p. 16 of Abbot.

19. This first-person narrative is quoted in full by Grant, op. cit., pp. 24–6 but does not appear in Abbot. Grant cites *Naval Documents of the American Revolution* (Washington DC. 1972), ed. William James Morgan, vol. VI, p. 1509.

20. Bushnell, David, October 1787, *Transactions of the American Philosophical Society* (Philadelphia, 1799), vol. IV, p. 303: quoted in Abbot op. cit., pp. 25–6.

21. Grant, op. cit., pp. 24–6 and p. 17.

22. According to C. Griswald in 1820; see Abbot, op. cit., p. 18.

23. HMS *Eagle* Records and Logs, for period 9 February 1776–8 February 1777, Greenwich, National Maritime Museum.

24. Ibid.

25. Sinnott, Col John P. AUS (Retd), 'New York Harbor is to the Submarine as Dayton, Ohio is to the Airplane', *The Submarine Review*, April 1998, p. 27. The Colonel remarks *inter alia* that 'my doubts about the episode were swept away when a full-scale model of the *Turtle* was launched into the Connecticut River on Saturday 10 August 1977': the author, who spoke with those concerned, begs to differ.

26 National Maritime Museum 'Progress Books', HMS *Eagle*, 1782.

27. Cf Note 15: Bushnell's letter to Jefferson (in Paris), October 1787. There is also mention of these abortive attempts, quoted by Grant, op. cit., p. 28 from Revd F.W. Chapman, *The Pratt Family: or the Descendants of Lieutenant William Pratt*, Hartford, 1864.

28. Bushnell to Jefferson; Abbot, op. cit., p. 26.

29. Ibid., p. 29.

30. Roland, op. cit., Note 21 p. 198; James Thacher, *Military Journal of the American Revolution*, 10 February 1778 (Boston 1823 and Hartford 1862); also Symons to Rear Adm Parker, 15 August 1777.

31. Roland, ibid., p. 83 and Abbot, op. cit., pp. 30–1.

32. An example of the floating 'keg mine' is on display at the Smithsonian Museum in Washington DC.

33. *Inter alia* Grant, op. cit., pp. 38–41.

34. Abbot, op. cit., pp. 5–7; Grant, op. cit., p. 44; Wagner, op. cit., p. 113.

35. Morgan, op. cit., vol. VI, p. 1,499, quoted in part by Grant, op. cit., pp. 4–5.

36. Not the current meaning of 'genius': 'distinctive character or spirit' was a contemporary dictionary definition; but 'he had a bent for it' is a close modern equivalent.

37. Abbot, op. cit., pp. 4–5.

38. Franklin and Deane were also joined by Arthur Lee and a little later by John Adams (second US President 1797–1801), who had a very low opinion of Franklin, then in his early sixties, as a statesman despite French reverence for him. Franklin was not officially recognized as the US Ambassador until 1778. See Henry Smith Williams (ed. *The Historians' History of the World* (London, *The Times*, 1908), vol. XXIII, p. 268.

39. Grant, op. cit., for full text pp. 46–8, quoting Morgan (op. cit.), Vol. VI pp. 1501–2.

40. Thacher, op. cit., p. 121; Abbot, op. cit., pp. 15–16 and p. 23 with Footnote.

41. Bushnell to Stiles, 16 October 1787: quoted by Grant, op. cit., p. 49.

42. Roland, op. cit., pp. 86–7, quoting piece in *New York Herald* for 5 September 1897 which said that Fulton (see Ch. 7) sought Bushnell out in Paris.

43. Wagner, op. cit., pp. 119–21.

44. See Note 19. Reference to this and other works is emphatically not intended to imply that Grant, Wagner, Roland et al. reached the same conclusions as the present author about the story's veracity.

7. *Monsieur Fulton and Mr Francis*

1. Cf. Sueter (Portsmouth, J. Griffin & Co), p. 28; and Fulton's *Thoughts on Free Trade* submitted to the French Directory on

9 October 1797 (extracts cited by Fulton's biographers, W.S. Hutcheon, C.D. Colden, H.W. Dickinson, J.S. Morgan *et al.*); and Fulton's own *Torpedo War and Submarine Explosions* (New York, 1810) – his primary statement.

2. Sueter, ibid.

3. 'Carcass' was another new name for a mine (soon to be called 'torpedo') along with 'magazine', 'infernal', 'coffer', etc.

4. Sueter, op. cit., pp. 29–30.

5. Ibid.

6. Roland, Alex, *Underwater Warfare in the Age of Sail* (1976), p. 94.

7. Hutcheon, Wallace S. , *Robert Fulton* (USNIP, Annapolis, 1981) p. 41 names the American and French crewmen.

8. *Naval Chronicle*, January–July, 1802, vol. VII, p. 270. St Aubin's letter came during the brief respite from war between October 1801 and May 1803: the complete text implied, *inter alia*, that by 1801, Fulton was (improbably) constructing a larger boat capable of carrying eight men underwater for eight hours and diving to 100 ft. This project was presumably halted at some point after October 1801 when Adm Decrès rejected Fulton's plan.

9. Cf. Hutcheon, op. cit., p. 41; and see also Sueter, op. cit., p. 33 and Roland, op. cit., p. 105.

10. Dash, Michael W. , 'British Submarine Policy 1853–1918' (King's College, University of London, 1990), p. 19, quotes Admiralty letters and references (all in the Public Records Office), Adm 2/140 with Linzee's reply of 21 September 1800, Adm 1/2067, and précis of miscellaneous secret papers, Adm 1/4362; also *The Keith Papers III*, ed. Christopher Lloyd (London, 1955), pp. 21–2.

11. There are varying versions of this famous remark quoted, amongst others, by G.L. Pesche, *La Navigation Sous-Marine* (1897 & 1906), p. 208 and in a letter from 'F.F.F.', *Naval Chronicle*, vol. XX, 1808.

12. Sueter, op. cit., p. 33 and Roland, op. cit., p. 105.

13. Parsons, W.M. , *Robert Fulton and the Submarine* (New York, Columbia University Press, 1922), p. 96.

14. Hutcheon, op. cit., pp. 72–3, quoting 20 July 1804, Pitt/Fulton contract, Robert Fulton MSS (Montague Collection), New York Public Library.

15. Hutcheon, ibid., pp. 75–7.

16. Ibid., p. 77.

17. Ibid., p. 82.

18. Ibid., p. 87.

19. Roland, op. cit., p. 113, quoting Berkeley (commanding the British Squadron in North American waters) to James Barry, 14 September 1807.

20. *Naval Chronicle*, 1809, vol. XXI, correspondence, p. 411.

21. A reliable original source of this perceptive and well-known quotation has never been pinned down.

22. Hutcheon, op. cit., p. 91.

23. Quoted in part by Hutcheon, op. cit., p. 99. Complete original (as here) is in Jefferson MSS, Micro-reel 63, Library of Congress, Washington, DC.

8. *On His Majesty's Secret Service*

1. Brown, John, *The Historical Gallery of Criminal Portraiture*, 2 vols, (Manchester 1823), Vol. II, pp. 495 *et seq.*

2. Pocock, Tom, *The Chelsea Submarine* (Chelsea Society Report, 1984) and *Sailor King* (Sinclair-Stevens, 1984). An article by Cyril Bracegirdle in *Country Life* (1982) offers some splendid stories about Johnson's love-life but does not append sources.

3. Bracegirdle, op. cit., quoted, with reservations, by Pocock, in *The Chelsea Submarine*.

4. Expedition described in *Naval Chronicle*, 1804, Vol. XII, pp. 313, 418; but there is no mention of Johnson.

5. St Vincent to Lord Howick: Pocock, *The Chelsea Submarine*, p. 42.

6. *Morning Post*, 1 January 1901, reprinting a piece of one hundred years before.

7. Brown, op. cit. There is no supporting evidence for this although £100,000 is the sum which Johnson wanted in 1815.

8. Ibid.

9. Security from Lord Sidmouth 15 October 1813, enclosed in Johnson to Admiralty, no

date (? July), Michael W. Dash, 'British Submarine Policy 1853–1918' (1990), Appendix 2.

10. Johnson to Admiralty (? July 1815) and minute by Lord Paulet (? July 1815), Adm 1/4783; and Admiralty to Johnson, 8 July 1815, Adm 2/919: all quoted by Dash, ibid.

11. Ibid.

12. Dash, ibid., quotes digest cut 59–8, Adm 12/198, noting that the original report (by Sir George Cockburn) has disappeared; Johnson to Admiralty, 28 March 1820 and enclosures, PRO J letters 48, Adm 1/4787.

13. Brown, op. cit., and Pocock, *Chelsea Submarine*, op. cit.; *Naval Chronicle* (1814) p. 287; Arthur Morris, 'A Boom in Submarines', *Nautical Magazine*, issue 71 (Sept.–Oct. 1902), p. 563, all quoted by Dash, ibid.

14. Pocock, *Chelsea Submarine*, op. cit.

15. Ibid.

16. Delpeuch, Maurice, op. cit. pp. 122–8.

17. Clowes, William Laird, 'Submarine Boat', *United Services Journal II* (1888–9) pp. 286–7, quoted by Dash, op. cit.

18. Ibid., and Pocock, *Chelsea Submarine*, op. cit.

19. Pocock, ibid.

20. Pocock, op. cit. quotes the Chelsea artist Walter Greaves who remembered his father telling this story: letter to Director, Royal Naval Submarine Museum (RNSM), 1984 (RNSM archive), and Dash, op. cit., p. 334.

21. Dash, op. cit., quotes Admiralty rough minutes, dated 19 April 1828 (PRO Adm 3/216).

9. *Reaching for Reality*

1. Delpeuch, M., *Les Sous-marins a Travers les Siecles* (1907), p. 133 (Figures), pp. 134–6; and (primarily for weapons) J.-P.M. de Montgéry's *Mémoire sur les mines flottantes et les petards flottants, ou machines infernales maritimes* (1819).

2. The Columbiad cannon or howitzer, known chiefly for its use, similar to the Dahlgren, by the US Army during the Civil War, had an extremely thick cast-iron breech but tapered off gradually from trunnions to muzzle. It was several times considered for underwater ordnance in the nineteenth century.

3. Soviet Shch-421 made sail (with engine covers) when power was lost in 1943.

4. Bacon, Adm Sir Reginald, *A Naval Scrapbook From 1900 Onward* (London, 1940), pp. 51–2.

5. *Dossier Villeroi*, Ministry of Marine, Paris, archives of *Constructions Navales*. The two quotations are from opinions given, at the re-dedication of Smith's restored tomb in Paris on 21 May 1999, by Adm Pierre Sabatié-Garat and Rear Adm Simon Moore respectively (*Daily Telegraph*, 22 May 1999).

6. Delpeuch, op. cit., p. 137.

7. Burgoyne, Alan H., *Submarine Navigation Past & Present* (London and New York, 1903) vol. I, p. 127.

8. A principle revived *c.* 1983 for Maritalia's midget submarine styled ''3gst9''.

9. She was restored and, after several moves, finally displayed in the War Museum at Dresden.

10. Rössler, Eberhard, *The U-boat* (London, Arms & Armour Press, 1981) (tr. Erenburg), gives an excellent account of Bauer's career; Dash also summarizes events in 'British Submarine Policy 1853–1918'.

11. *The Times*, Court Circular, 6 August 1852.

12. Dash, op. cit., quotes Palmerston papers RC/H/59, Albert to Palmerston, 9 January 1856. 'Genius' did not carry the weight of its modern meaning in Victorian times any more than it did when Washington applied the word to Bushnell's 'effort' (see Chapter 6, note 36).

13. Queen Victoria was the last 'executive' British sovereign (after her the monarchy, that is, from Edward VII, became an institution) and Albert was, in effect, her Private Secretary. Source: HRH Prince Philip, reported in an interview with Gyles Brandreth, *Sunday Telegraph Review*, 16 May 1999.

14. Rössler, op. cit., p. 12.

15. Ibid., p. 13, quotes Shipbuilding Department letter No. 12,480, dated 20 November 1857.

16. Ibid., p. 13.

17. Most details are given by John Guthrie,

Bizarre Ships of the 19th Century (London, Hutchinson, 1970); but without full reference to original sources which evidently include a contemporary (1850s) magazine article. There are mentions of Philips elsewhere but they tend to be vague.

18. Dash, op. cit., rightly quotes Admiralty Surveyor's minute dated 2 June 1859 (Adm 92/20 Lot 591); but Philips had gone down with one of his boats some eight years earlier, and the reason for delay is not known.

19. Cf. Edwyn Gray, *Few Survived* (London, Leo Cooper, 1986), pp. 21–2.

10. *Peripatetic Coffins*

1. Roland, *Underwater Warfare in the Age of Sail* (1976), p. 156.

2. Ibid., p. 161. David Ebaugh built the craft which attacked the *Ironsides* and his family has claimed he lent his name; but the biblical connection is more probable.

3. Ibid., pp. 162–3.

4. The former *Merrimac* engaged the USS *Monitor* in epic battle, 9 March 1862, which ended in a draw favouring the *Monitor*.

5. Regan, Mark K., *The Hunley: Submarines, Sacrifice and Success in the Civil War* (Charleston, Narwhal Press, 1995), pp. 18–20. This thoroughly researched book gives a great deal of hitherto hidden detail together with sources. An additional source, not cited by Regan, is Adm David Porter USN, *Naval History of the Civil War*, 1877. A few of Regan's conclusions may be disputed (by the present author, anyway) but he gives by far the most complete, and entertaining, account of the *Hunley–Housatonic* episode ever written.

6. Farragut took the unprecedented step of running his fleet past the defending ports and risking the mines (torpedoes): 'Damn the torpedoes! Captain Drayton go ahead! . . . Jouett full speed!' USS *Tecumseh* was destroyed by a mine.

7. Regan, op. cit., p. 24, quoting Francis Buchanan Letterbook, Southern Historical Collection, University of North Carolina, Chapel Hill, NC.

8. Except where otherwise noted, hereafter most of the figures and quotations (but not necessarily the deductions derived from Regan's invaluable work) result from comparison and selection among marginally differing records cited both in Regan and the archives of the Royal Navy Submarine Museum.

9. Correspondence (in author's possession) passed to the Admiralty, including statements by those concerned, resulting from McClintock's interviews on board HMS *Royal Arthur*, flagship of Vice Adm E.G. Fanshawe, Commander-in-Chief, North American Station at Halifax, commencing 18 October 1872: Adm 1/6236 part 2, X/K 941.

10. Ibid.

11. Ibid.

12. Depths on charts are given for Mean Low Water Springs (MLWS). Modern charts are usually marked in metres, but older versions are in fathoms (1 fathom = 6 ft) or, in shallow waters, in feet.

13. Beauregard, P.G.T., *Torpedo Service in the Harbor and Water Defense of Charleston*, Southern Historical Society Papers, p. 153; also cited by Rogers, op. cit.

14. von Kolnitz, Lt Harry, USN, 'The Confederate Submarine', *US Naval Institute Proceedings*, October 1937; and Engineer James A. Tomb (ex-the '*Ironsides*' David), *Reminiscences in Official Records of the Union and Confederate Navies in the War of Rebellion*, series I, vol. 15, pp. 334–5, quoted by Regan, op. cit. Kolnitz said the triggering line was 150 yd long; but I agree with Regan's suggestion that it was 150 ft.

15. Cf. Regan, op. cit., who includes several original descriptions of the attack as seen from *Housatonic*, pp. 136–40.

16. *Le Navigateur*, quoted by G.L. Pesce, *La Navigation sous-marin* (Paris, 1906). Location of the trial is uncertain.

17. Original letter in Office of Navy Records, Washington, DC.

18. It is not known whence the 'mysterious vessel' reported by the *Bulletin* emanated; but it might have been secretly built in Washington Navy Yard if not in Philadelphia.

19. Letter to *Philadelphia Public Ledger*, 26 March 1862.
20. *The Engineer* (usually reliable) reported a total of thirteen deaths (one entire crew) in its issue dated 17 July 1896.
21. Copy of original in author's possession.
22. Tarpey, Capt John F. USN (Retd), 'A Mine Struck Navy forgets its History', *US Naval Institute Proceedings*, February 1988. The Confederates lost four vessels to Federal 'torpedoes'.

11. The Curate's Eggs

1. The full story is splendidly told in William Scanlan Murphy's thoroughly researched, compelling and entertaining *Father of the Submarine* (London, Wiliam Kimber & Co. Ltd, 1987). I disagree with the title (I believe that the author is not entirely happy with it either) and I go further than Bill Murphy in disputing Garrett-esque submarine claims; but the book's content could not be improved, and I make no attempt to do so. A fair number of source documents and photographs relevant to Garrett were collected by myself, many of them thanks to great-grandson Bill Garrett, and placed in the archives of the RN Submarine Museum, Gosport. But, as well as the fascinating asides and commentaries in his book, Bill Murphy brought much fresh material to the scene: I endeavour to make clear, in the Notes that follow, those areas which were researched or discovered by him rather than by myself.
2. 'So he passed over, and all the trumpets sounded for him on the other side': conclusion of *Pilgrim's Progress*, Pt. 2 by John Bunyan.
3. *Punch* cartoon of 1895 (vol. 109, p. 222), *viz.*, Bishop to curate (at breakfast): 'I'm afraid you've got a bad egg, Mr Jones.' Curate: 'Oh no, my Lord, I assure you! Parts of it are excellent.'
4. On display at the RN Submarine Museum, Gosport.
5. *Manchester Courier*, 7 May 1880.
6. Ibid.
7. *Liverpool Weekly Mercury*, 29 March 1879.
8. Ibid., 29 January 1916, cited by Murphy, op. cit.
9. *Liverpool Daily Post*, 16 December 1879. The Log of the *Resurgam* voyage is among the Cochran & Co. papers in the Glasgow Museum of Transport, cited by Murphy, op. cit.
10. *Liverpool Echo*, interview with George Price, 8 December 1925.
11. Murphy, op. cit., p. 78.
12. Ibid., p. 84.
13. Nordenfelt lecture to the Royal United Services Institute (RUSI), 1886.
14. *The Times*, 1 and 9 October 1885, summarized in Sydenham's *Naval Review* article, 1933, cited by Murphy, op. cit.
15. Sir Sydney of Eardley-Wilmot, Rear Adm, *An Admiral's Memories: Sixty-Five Years Afloat and Ashore* (London, Low, 1927).
16. Quoted by Murphy, op. cit., who is suspicious of the authenticity of the source *Documents Politiques de la Guerre* included in Donald McCormick's *Pedlar of Death: the Life of Sir Basil Zaharoff* (London, Gollancz, 1929) but rightly points out that the quote is by no means out of character.
17. *The Times*, 27 March 1886.
18. *The Times*, 9 October 1885.
19. Nordenfelt lecture 1886, op. cit., questions; and Clarke memorandum, 31 December 1884, War Office papers WO 33/43 PRO.
20. Murphy, op. cit., p. 117.
21. *The Engineer*, 8 February 1901.
22. Turkish Trials report, quoted by Murphy, op. cit., pp. 144, 226.
23. *The Times*, 27 May 1887.
24. *The Engineer*, 29 July 1887.
25. Garrett, J.W., letter to T.J. Arm, 27 November 1933, RN Submarine Museum: Garrett archive.
26. The Garrett family in the US, however, went on to produce some outstandingly good engineers.

12. An Irish Invention

1. Holland's letter from America to Brother Aloysius Yorke of the Christian Brothers, 22 June 1898, accused the Spanish government of being managed by

Freemasons, infidels and thieves, and for Europe predicted a 'whirlwind due to the Reformation and its children, infidelity, socialism and anarchism'. Quoted by Br D.S. Blake in *Christian Brothers' Educational Record* (1986), p. 202. I am deeply grateful to Br Donal Blake for sending me the fruits of his thorough investigation and for so gently chiding me for some monastic solecisms in my *Submarine Boats* (1983).

2. *Cassier's Magazine*, Marine Number, 1897.

3. In the absence of birth or baptismal records the year could be 1840, '41, or '42, and books of reference often give 1840; but the Dundalk Annals of the Christian Brothers and Novice Master Joseph Hearn's note on Holland's novitiate declaration of 15 June 1858 confirm that he was seventeen in that year. (Blake, op. cit., pp. 171–4, see Note 1).

4. John may have been born at his grandmother's house (it was a common custom in Ireland for a wife to await a first birth in her mother's abode) but the Liscannor cottage was his first home.

5. Anne Foley Holland probably died in 1835 in childbirth when Alfred was born; but the date of Alfred's birth is nowhere recorded. Parish records in Liscannor were not kept until 1842.

6. Blake, op. cit., p. 181 citing Burke's 1984 biographer, D.V. Kellher.

7. Ibid.

8. Ibid., p. 186.

9. Ibid.

10. Ibid., p. 187.

11. Ibid., p. 191, quoting a letter from Holland to Br Aloysius Yorke. Br McDonnell was not re-elected assistant to the Superior at the 1880 General Chapter.

12. Morris, Richard K. *John P. Holland, 1841–1914: Inventor of the Modern Submarine* (USNIP, 1966, 1998), Chapter 3. Morris has written the definitive, unequalled work on Holland and his submarines, and has either provided material directly therein, on which I have drawn, or guided me to sources. I have not hesitated (having been privileged to know Professor Morris and his reputation for a score of years) to accept his account 'as is'.

13. The Salt Water Enterprise

1. O'Brien, W. and Ryan, D., *Devoy's Post Bag* (1948), Vol. I, p. 302: Devoy to James Reynolds, 6 February 1878.

2. Lake, Simon, *The Submarine in War and Peace* (Philadelphia, 1918), p. 97.

3. Dash, Michael W., 'British Submarine Policy, 1853–1918' (1990), pp. 67–8, quotes Consul General Archibald to Thornton, 20 December 1880, Foreign Office paper (PRO) FO 5/1746, fols 186–9, and Capt Arthur, NA report No. 90, 2 August 1881, FO 115/673, fols 209–10 et al., including volume of reports fol. 77, Adm 1/6551.

4. Dash, ibid., quotes Drummond (Vice Consul) telegram, 3 September 1881, FO 5/1780, fol. 13.

5. Discovered unexpectedly on HM Submarine Torpedo Boat *No. 1* (colloq. *Holland 1*) when salvaged for RN Submarine Museum, Gosport, in 1982. The implication is that this and boats of similar type could – if they cared or dared – run their gasoline engines submerged.

6. Dash, op. cit., quotes Drummond telegram, 3 September 1881, FO 5/1780, fol. 13.

7. The anecdotes in this chapter are drawn from various mutually supportive sources, but chiefly Simon Lake, op. cit., (who was apt to make the best of a good story) and the invariably reliable Richard K. Morris, *John P. Holland, 1841–1914* (1966, 1998)

8. Lake, op. cit., pp. 98–9.

9. Cable, Frank T., *The Birth and Development of the American Submarine* (New York, 1924), p. 78.

10. Ibid., p. 90.

11. Lake, op. cit., p. 112.

12. Holland correspondence with Simpson, Paterson Museum, New Jersey, quoted by Morris, op. cit., p. 51.

14. The Reason Why Not

1. Dash, Michael W., 'British Submarine Policy, 1853–1918' (1990), p. 35.

2. Ibid., p. 68, quoting Nathaniel Barnaby (DNC minute), 12 June 1880, 'Supposed Fenian Submarine', FO, fol. 7.

3. Dropping aitches was a common disparagement exemplified by the story of a new Chief (Engineer) joining HMS *Amphitrite* in 1899 and being mistaken for a cabby: G.L. Lewis, *Fabulous Admirals* (London, Putnam, 1957), p. 24.

4. Report by Naval Attaché Capt Langley to Admiralty: *United States: Navy Dockyards, materials, etc.*, July 1893; PRO Adm 231/22.

5. Sueter, Cdr Murray, *The Evolution of the Submarine Boat, Mine and Torpedo* (1907), p. xix.

6. NID 577 (British) Naval Intelligence *Confidential* summary *Submarine Boats*, p. 52, issued by the Admiralty as Naval Intelligence document No. 577 in May 1900. The RN Submarine Museum holds copy No. 208 of this invaluable and comprehensive booklet which does not appear to have been much used, if at all, by naval historians – possibly because other copies were destroyed.

7. Capt William May, naval attaché, NID No. 346, April 1893: Adm 231/22.

8. Sueter, op. cit., p. 75.

9. Quoted by Dash, op. cit., pp. 71–2; NA report No. 11, 27 July 1880, Adm 1/6551.

10. Ibid., p. 72: HMS *Vernon* annual report for 1885, p. 61, Adm 189/5.

11. NID 577, op. cit., p. 72.

12. Sir William White, DNC (1885–1902), writing in *The Times Literary Supplement*, March 1905.

13. Press release by Campbell, part-owner and inventor of *Nautilus*, on the day.

14. Fyfe, Herbert C., *Submarine Warfare Past and Present* (London, 1907), p. 286.

15. Adm Sir Reginald Bacon, *A Naval Scrapbook From 1900 Onwards* (London, Hutchinson, 1940), p. 53; Sydney Eardley-Wilmot, *The British Navy Past & Present* (London, 1904), pp. 56–8; *The Times*, 21 December 1886, p. 11.

15. Misfits

1. *Invention*, London 1895.

2. Ibid.; and Lt Col Alan H. Burgoyne MP, *Submarine Navigation Past and Present* (London and New York, 1903).

3. Burgoyne, ibid.

4. Ibid.

5. Ibid.

6. Ibid.

7. The author was the commentator on that April Fool's Day. Not a single viewer rang the BBC to express doubt or disagreement.

8. Burgoyne, op. cit.

16. Jamais . . . trop de sous-marins

1. 'Jamais nous n'aurions pas trop de sous-marins': M.V. Guilouse in *Le Yacht*, 1901.

2. Dash, Michael W., 'British Submarine Policy 1853–1918' (1990), p. 80; and Henri Le Masson, *Les sous-marins Français, de nos origines (1800) a nos jours* (1980), pp. 41–3.

3. Sueter, Cdr Murray, *The Evolution of the Submarine Boat, Mine and Torpedo* (1907), pp. 79–80.

4. Ibid., pp. 81–2.

5. Dash, op. cit., pp. 82–3; NA Captain Jackson's report No. 14, 22 January 1889, Adm 1/7422.

6. DNO to *Vernon*, 27 May 1889, Adm 1/7422.

7. Sueter, op. cit., p. 82.

8. Ibid.

9. *The Times*, 18 January 1899, p. 10.

10. NA report (see Note 5) of trial conducted in the Salins d'Hyeres, east of Toulon, 7 January 1899.

11. NID 577 (British) Naval Intelligence *Confidential* Summary *Submarine Boats*, document, May 1900, pp. 50–1.

12. *The Engineer*, 1 March 1901, p. 218, col. 2.

17. Success in the States

1. *Circular: Showing the General Requirements Desired to be Fulfilled in Design and Trial of a Steel Submarine Torpedo Boat for the US Navy*, 20 August 1888; copy held in the Nautilus Submarine Museum and library, Groton, Connecticut.

2. John Philip, Jr, died in infancy. The next child, born in 1890, was also christened John Philip. Five more children followed 1891–97.

3. Original document (two copies) *The Practicality of Mechanical Flight*, in Holland's own hand, is in the Nautilus Submarine Museum (see Note 1) and the Library of Congress, Washington, DC. The author has a photocopy.

4. Surface/submerged displacement. Where, from now on, only one tonnage is given it refers to submerged displacement.

5. Senate Records 1896, quoted by Richard K. Morris, *John P. Holland, 1841–1914* (1966), p. 79.

6. The major role which Busch, an English immigrant, played in the construction of *Holland VI* and later boats (e.g. *Fulton*, *Porpoise*, etc. and the building, at Fore River Works, Quincy Point, Mass., of the five Japanese 'Hollands', shipping them to Yokosuka and reassembling them) has not before been recognized. The details now given result from the author's 1991 correspondence with great-grandson Mr A.N. der Busch and Professor Morris. Mr Busch is also the source for naming William T. Cox as an early captain of *Holland VI*.

7. Burgoyne, Alan H., *Submarine Navigation, Past and Present* (1903).

8. Strictly speaking, so-called 18-in torpedoes were rather less than 18 in in diameter, usually built to a 450-mm standard (17.72 in). A widespread belief that the 'Hollands' carried 14-in torpedoes is incorrect.

9. Cable, F.T., *The Birth & Development of the American Submarine* (New York, 1924), pp. 109 *et seq.*

10. It is difficult to be sure whether metal for the 'Hollands' was technically iron or steel; but analysis of Britain's *Holland I* concludes that low-grade steel with rather a lot of impurities would fit the bill. Engine supports and suchlike, however, were certainly cast iron.

11. Cable, op. cit.

12. Morris, op. cit., p. 84 describes the scene.

13. Ibid., p. 86.

14. Quoted, with sources, by Morris, ibid., p. 87.

15. Ibid., p. 90, quoting the *New York Sun*, 27 May 1898.

16. Ibid., p. 105, quoting Cable, op. cit., pp. 133–5 and the R.K. Morris Collection

diaries entry for 11 October 1898 and newspaper cuttings in Vol. I (Nautilus Submarine Museum and Library, Groton, Connecticut).

17. Cable, op. cit., pp. 132–3.

18. Burgoyne, op. cit.

19. *Fulton* was sold to Russia 1904, very soon after Lock's *Protector* (see end of this chapter). The Electric Boat Company sold five dismantled Adders to Japan (for reassembly at Yokosaka, Tokyo) at about the same time, prompting Holland to remark on 'the strangely unpatriotic heart which beats in the breast of a corporation'. Morris, op. cit., p. 128.

20. Dash, Michael W., 'British Submarine Policy 1853–1918' (1990), pp. 95–6 quotes NA report No. 9, 18 December 1899, Adm 1/7471.

21. Ibid., p. 96, quoting Rothschild's letter of introduction, 3 July 1900, Adm 1/7515.

22. I endorse the warning, about reliability in detail, by Dash, ibid., p. 21, n. 11, who specifically refers to Simon Lake, *Submarine: the Autobiography of Simon Lake* (New York, 1938).

23. The quotations which follow in this chapter are from Lake, ibid., Ch. 5, and Burgoyne, op. cit., Ch. 7, and from papers in the RN Submarine Museum archives.

24. Sometimes simply *Argonaut* or alternatively *Argonaut 2*, but Lake preferred *First* because he actually conceived her before *Junior*.

25. See Note 22 and RNSM archive A1980/127/005 (L. Honeywell collection).

26. Ottley memorandum, 4 August 1905, National Maritime Museum.

27. Lt John Helligan, Jr, writing in the *Scientific American Supplement*, 2 January 1904.

28. 'Ireland Forever!' Irish Gaelic purists will note that the letterhead watchword of the Fenian Brotherhood was *Erin go Bragh*, and that the equivalent phrase today is different again; but J.P. Holland is most likely to have been familiar with *Erin go Brach* as a rallying cry.

18. Britannia *Takes the Plunge*

1. Dash, Michael W. 'British Submarine Policy 1853–1918' (1990), p. 86, quotes Sir

Edward Monson to Foreign Office, 28 January 1899, Adm 1/7422.

2. Ibid., quoting Jackson report, 22 January 1899, Adm 1/7422.

3. *Jane's Fighting Ships*, 1906–7, p. 182.

4. Dash, op. cit., p. 86, quoting Goschen minute, May 1900, Adm 1/7462.

5. Kerr minute, 22 May 1900, Adm 1/7515.

6. Dash, op. cit., p. 101 with sources. See also J.D. Scott, *Vickers: a History* (London 1960), p. 63.

7. A.K. Wilson was Controller of the Navy when, in his paper 'Submarine Boats', dated 15 January 1901, he recommended hanging as a deterrent, not out of personal animosity. Phrases describing submarines as 'unfair, underhand' etc., have been attributed to him subsequently but there is no contemporary evidence that he coined them. They are simply a part of submarine folklore!

8. Admiralty draft contract, 13 December 1900, Vickers Papers 624/150, Cambridge University Library, quoted by Dash, op. cit., pp. 102, 109, 111 with notes to sources; Richard Compton-Hall, *Submarine Boats* (Conway Maritime, 1983) p. 112; and Harrison, A.N., *The Development of HM Submarines* (1974) p. 3.1.

9. Vickers to Secretary of the Admiralty, 27 October 1900: copy in RN Submarine Museum.

10. Ibid.

11. Parliamentary reports (known as *Hansard* from 1943).

12. Ibid., 18 March 1901.

19. Setting up Shop

1. Lukewarm as noted by the British Naval Attaché in Washington, at the end of 1900. HMS *Vernon*, annual report (Adm 188/21), p. 153.

2. *The Engineer* (an English journal), 1 March 1901, p. 225 contains all these statements and speeches in full, copied from Congressional records.

3. Ibid.

4. Ibid.

5. BNA/*Vernon*, op. cit.

6. Cable, Frank T., *The Birth and Development of the American Submarine* (1924), p. 171. President Theodore Roosevelt was sure that if submarines were advocated, Congress would no longer vote for battleships.

7. Richard K. Morris, *John P. Holland, 1841–1914* (1966, 1998), Chapter 2.

8. *The Engineer*, op. cit.

9. Ibid., quoting the writers in full. Admiral Ferguson's statement was included in his report No. 167, dated 1 October 1900, to the Navy Department.

10. Uniquely in RN Submarine archives.

11. *Jane's Fighting Ships*, 1905–6, Appendix.

12. See Chapter 18 and Note 11 thereto.

13. Original diary in RN Submarine Museum, thanks to the generosity of his daughter Mrs Margaret Barrett.

14. Arnold-Forster, Rear Adm D., *The Ways of the Navy* (London, 1931), pp. 240–1.

15. Cf. Morris, op. cit., p. 120.

16. Adm Sir Reginald Bacon, *A Naval Scrapbook From 1900 Onward* (London, 1940), Chapter 7.

17. Ibid. See also Cable, op. cit.

18. Bacon, op. cit.

19. One of the American crewmen.

20. Arnold-Forster diary, op. cit.

21. Ibid.

22. Ibid.

23. Bacon, op. cit.

24. Arnold-Forster diary, op. cit.

25. Now on display at the RN Submarine Museum, Gosport.

26. Harrison, A.N., *The Development of British Submarines 1910–1930*, BR 3043: 120 chloride cells wt 49.5 tons in 'A' class (60 in a 'Holland', wt 24.75 tons), working voltage 240v (120v); max. charging voltage 324v (162v); 500 amps (500).

27. Vickers Papers (VP, Cambridge University Library) 632/161 fol. 90 (Rice to Naumberg, 9 January 1907); VP 59/135 Royalties payable to EB Co. 1902–1934, all quoted in Michael W. Dash, 'British Submarine Policy 1853–1918' (1990), pp. 106–8.

28. Brodie, C.G., MS in RN Submarine Museum, writing as 'Seagee' in the *Naval Review*, 1962/63 series 'Some Early Submariners'.

29. Arnold-Forster, op. cit., pp. 217 *et seq.*
30. Cf. R.F. Mackay, *Fisher of Kilverstone* (1973), p. 286, and Bacon, op. cit.

20. Back to the Future

1. 'Pig-boats' from sea-pigs, the mariner's name for porpoises, not because of living conditions on board although that was the eventual connotation. The date when the term was first used is uncertain.
2. See Edward Gray, *Few Survived* (London, Leo Cooper with Secker Warburg, 1986) pp. 232–3 and p. 246. France suffered eleven losses and four serious accidents from 1904 to 1914. Britain had eight losses and three serious accidents in the same period among a considerably larger number of fully operational boats.
3. *Jane's Fighting Ships*, 1906–7, p. 125 (Notes).
4. They could also be anchored submerged without bottoming; but research has not uncovered solid evidence that archetypal Lake boats in the *Protector* mould were able to manoeuvre as submarines submerged (e.g. at periscope depth). However, as G.W. Hovgaard points out (*Modern History of Warships*, 1919, p. 301) Lake boats 'developed along the same lines as other types': they probably had similar dive characteristics from about 1908 (e.g., Russian *Alligator*).
5. *Jane's*, op. cit., p. 223.
6. The diesel-electric 'hydrodynamic test vehicle' USS *Albacore*, commissioned in December 1953, prepared the way for high sustained speed from nuclear power plants – first installed in USS *Nautilus*, underway 17 January 1955, and first exploited to the full in 1959 by USS *Skipjack*, a huge replica of Holland's ideal hull and capable of more than 30 knots.
7. See Chapter 17.
8. Holland, J.P., 'The Submarine Boat and its Future' *The North American Review*, 1900, p. 395; see Chapter 7 for Fulton.
9. Holland, ibid.
10. M.H. Holland from 17 Star Street, New London, Conn. to Devoy, undated October 1916, *Devoy's Post Bag*, vol. II, p. 516.
11. M.H. Holland to Devoy, 8 October 1916, ibid., p. 517.

Select Bibliography

Abbot, Henry L., *The Beginning of Submarine Warfare under Captain-Lieutenant David Bushnell, Sappers and Miners, Army of the Revolution* (Willetts Point, New York, Engineer School of Application, 1882).

Arnold-Forster, Forster D., *The Ways of the Navy* (London, 1931). Written long after his brief involvement with HM S/M *No 1* but it cross-checks pretty well with other accounts and includes some entertaining anecdotes.

Bacon, Reginald, *The Life of Lord Fisher of Kilverstone*, 2 vols (London, Hodder & Stoughton, 1929).

——, *A Naval Scrapbook From 1900 Onward* (London, Marine Management (Holdings) 1940). Valuable for less formal submarine quotations and accounts of 1900–1904.

Le Bailly, Vice Adm Sir Louis, *From Fisher to the Falklands* (London, Marine Management (Holdings) Ltd for the IME, 1991).

Beer, Frank, *Day's Diving Disaster in Plymouth Sound* (Plymouth, PDS Printers, *c.* 1983) (available in Plymouth Public Library).

Blake, Br D.S., *Christian Brothers' Educational Record: John Philip Holland: The Father of the Submarine, His Connection with the Christian Brothers*: extract from the *Record* and printed as a pamphlet (presumably within the Order) in 1986. Copy held in RN Submarine Museum.

Blond, Georges, tr. Marshall May, *La Grande Armée* (London, Arms and Armour Press, 1995).

Burgoyne, Lt Col Alan H., MP, *Submarine Navigation, Past and Present*, 2 vols (London, Grant Richards, 1903). Includes the weird and wonderful, and quotes nineteenth-century attitudes.

Cable, Frank T., *The Birth and Development of the American Submarine* (New York, Harper & Bros., 1924).

Compton-Hall, Richard, *Submarine Boats* (London, Conway Maritime, 1983). Profusely illustrated but some of the text has been overtaken by deeper research for the current work.

Dash, Michael W., 'British Submarine Policy 1853–1918' PhD thesis (unpublished) for Kings College, University of London, 1990. An excellent analysis – quite possibly unequalled so far – and an invaluable basis for research.

Delpeuch, M., *Les Sous-marins a Travers les Siecles* (Paris, Société d'Edition et de Publications, 1907). Includes an account of virtually every submarine dreamed of or built up to the *fin de siècle*; but the author makes little attempt to distinguish the practical from the impractical.

Dugan, J., *Man explores the Sea* (London, Hamish Hamilton, 1956).

Dupuy, R.E. and T.N., *The Compact History of the Revolutionary War* (New York, Hawthorn Books Inc., 1963).

Esher, R., *Journals and Letters of Reginald, Viscount Esher*, eds M.W. Brett and Oliver, Viscount Esher, 4 vols, (London, 1934–8).

Field, C., *The Story of the Submarine, from the earliest times to the present day* (London, Sampson Low Marston & Co., 1908).

Forest and Noalhat, H., *Les Bateaux Sous-marins*, 2 vols (Paris, 1900).

Fulton, Robert, *Torpedo War and Submarine Explosions* (New York, William Elliot, 1810).

Fyfe, Herbert C., *Submarine Warfare Past and Present*, 2nd edn (London, Grant Richards, 1907).

Gaget, M., *La Navigation Sous-marine* (Paris, 1901).

Grant, M.H., *The Infernal Machines of Saybrook's David Bushnell* (Bicentennial Committee of Old Saybrook, Connecticut, 1976). Splendidly enthusiastic and patriotic support for Bushnell.

Guthrie, John, *Bizarre Ships of the Nineteenth Century* (London, Hutchinson, 1970).

Harrison, A.N., *Development of HM Submarines 1910–1930*, BR 3043; not in public libraries but available in National Maritime & RN Submarine Museums. Includes technical details not available elsewhere.

Hay, M.F., *Secrets of the Submarine* (New York, Dodd, Mead & Co., 1917).

Hough, R., *First Sea Lord* (London, George Allen and Unwin, 1969). Biography of Lord Fisher.

Hovgaard, G.W., *Submarine Boats* (London, E. & F.N. Spon, 1919).

——, *Modern History of Warships* (London, E. & F.N. Spon, 1919).

Hutcheon, Wallace S., *Robert Fulton* (Annapolis, USNIP, 1981).

Jane, F.T., *Jane's Fighting Ships* (London, 1898–1905 editions).

——, *The Imperial Russian Navy* (London, 1899 edition reprinted by Conway Maritime, 1983).

Lake, S., *Submarine, an autobiography* (New York, D. Appleton Century, 1938).

——, *The Submarine in War and Peace* (Philadelphia, J.P. Lippincott Co. Inc., 1918).

Latané, John Halladay, *America as a World Power 1897–1907* (New York, Harper, 1907).

Low, A.M., *The Submarine at War* (London, Hutchinson & Co. Ltd., 1941).

Mackay, R.F., *Fisher of Kilverstone* (Oxford, Clarendon Press, 1973).

Marder, Arthur, ed., *Fear God and Dread Nought*, 3 vols (London, Jonathan Cape, 1952–9). Correspondence of Lord Fisher.

——, *The anatomy of British Seapower . . . 1880–1905* (Conn., Hamden, 1964; distributed in UK by Frank Cass).

le Masson, Henri, *Les sous-marins Français, des nos origines (1800) à nos jours* (Brest, 1980); similar but titled *Du Nautilus (1800) à Redoubtable* (Paris, Presses de la cité, 1969).

Mersenne, Marin, *Cogitata Physico-mathematica* (Paris, Sumptibus A Bertier, 1644).

Mersenne, M. and Fournier, G., *Questions Théologiques, Physiques, Morales et Mathématiques* (Paris, 1634).

Montgéry, J.-P.M. (*capitaine de frégate*), *Mémoire sur les mines flottantes et les petards flottans, ou machines infernales maritimes* (Paris, Bachelier, 1819).

Morgan, William J., ed., *Naval Documents of the American Revolution* (Washington, DC, Office of Naval Records, 1972).

Morris, Richard K., *John P. Holland, 1841–1914: Inventor of the Modern Submarine* (Annapolis, USNIP, 1966, republished 1998). The definitive work and essential reading (besides being a good read anyway).

Murphy, William, *Father of the Submarine: the life of the Reverend George Garrett Pasha*

(London, William Kimber, 1987). Penetrating, complete and witty review of Garrett, Nordenfelt *et al.*

Naval Intelligence Document 577, *Confidential* summary, *Submarine Boats* (London, Admiralty, May 1900).

Noalhat, H., *Les Torpilles et les Mines Sous-marines* (Paris, 1905).

O'Brien, W. and Ryan, D., *Devoy's Post Bag*, 2 vols (Dublin, C.J. Fallom Ltd., 1948 and 1953). The basis for understanding Holland's relationship with the Fenians.

Padfield, P., *Aim Straight: a biography of Admiral Sir Percy Scott* (London, Hodder & Stoughton, 1966).

Papin, D., *Receuil de diverses Pièces touchant quelques nouvelles Machines* (Paris, Jacob Estienne Marchand Libraire, 1695).

Parsons, W.M., *Robert Fulton and the Submarine* (New York, Columbia University Press, 1922).

Pesce, G.L., *La Navigation Sous-marine* (Paris, 1897 and 1906).

Pocock, Tom, *The Chelsea Submarine* (London, Chelsea Society Report, 1984).

——, *Sailor King* (London, Sinclair-Stevenson, 1984).

Poland, E.N., *The Torpedomen*, apparently published privately or by HMS *Vernon*, ISBN 0-85937-396-7, *c.* 1993. Very good on torpedoes although weak on sources: but, then, one can trust a Rear Admiral!

Regan, Mark K., *The Hunley: Submarines, Sacrifice and Success in the Civil War* (Charleston, SC, Narwhal Press, 1995). Uniquely comprehensive and thoroughly researched besides being a good read.

Roland, Alex, *Underwater Warfare in the Age of Sail* (Bloomington, Indiana, Indiana University Press, 1976). Studiously researched in unsurpassed detail.

Rössler, E., *The U-boat: the evolution & technical history*, trans. Harold Erenberg (Munich, J.F. Lehmanns Verlag, 1975; London, Arms & Armour Press, 1981).

Scott, Percy, *Fifty Years in the Royal Navy* (London, 1919). Excellent for understanding Victorian and Edwardian naval deficiencies.

Sleeman, Lt C. (late RN), *Torpedoes and Torpedo Warfare*, 2 vols (London (?), 1889).

Sueter, Cdr Murray, *The Evolution of the Submarine Boat, Mine and Torpedo* (Portsmouth, Griffin, 1907). The classical compilation but not entirely reliable in detail.

Wagner, F., *Submarine Fighter of the American Revolution* (New York, Dodd, Mead & Co., 1963). The best, and very readable, account of Bushnell's life albeit accepting, more or less, the *Turtle-Eagle* affair 'as received'.

Wells, John, *The Royal Navy* (Stroud, Sutton Publishing for the Royal Navy, 1994).

Index

bold numbers refer to illustration captions, sub = submarine

A-class submarines 9, 137, 148, 150–1
  A-1: 6–8, 8, 151, **155**
Abdul Hamid II, Sultan 91
Abdul Medjid (sub) 91
Adams, John Quincy 53
'Adder' class 132, 140, 144, 157
Admiralty, British *see under* Royal Navy
Albany Iron Works 97
Albert, Prince 61, 81
'Alfa' Soviet sub **158**
Alligator (sub) 76–8
Alstitt, Engineer 68, **69**
American Diver (sub) **68**
American Turtle (sub) 29–40, **31**, **32**
André, Gen 121
Anson, HMS 147
Apostolov (inventor) 115, **115**
Archibald, Consul Edmund 100, 101
Archimedes 13
Argonauts (subs) **19**, 125, 132–6, **134**
Argus, US Frigate 49
Army, British 4–6, 8, 10–11, 52, 90
Arnold-Forster, Lt D. 146–50
Arnold-Forster, Hugh Oakley 142, 146–7
Arthur, Capt William 100
Asha and Campbell (inventors) 111
Aube, Vice Adm Hyacinthe 118, 120

Bacon, Capt Reginald 6, 57–8, **57**, 145–6, 148–51
Baker, George 123
Baker, Ray Stannard 135–6
Baldwin, Abraham 39, 42
Banham, AB 2
Barber, Lt F.M. 29, **31**
Barlow, Joel 42
Barrow-in-Furness 92, 138–40, 146, **149**

Barton, Clara 131, 158
'Battle of the Kegs' 36–7
Bauer, Wilhelm **59**, 60–4
Beauregard, Gen P.G.T. 72–3
Belton, Seaman 74
Beresford, Rear Adm Lord Charles 4, 5, 111, 112
Bergen, Vanderbilt 104
Berkeley, Vice Adm Sir George 48
Berkley and Hotchkiss (inventors) 114
Berwick Castle, SS 7
Birkenhead 84, 85, **86**
Blake, Christopher 25–7
boilers 84, 86, 88, 107, **111**, 125
Boulogne 46, 47
Borelli, Giovanni-Alfonso 14, 20
Boucher (inventor) 114–15
Bourgois, Capt Simeon 113, 116
Bourne, William **12**, 13–14
Boyle, Richard **37**
Boyle, Robert 14
Brandtaucher (sub) **59**, 60–1
Brayton, George 98
Brazil 108–9
Breslin, John J. 105
Brest 44–5
Britannia Engine Works (Birkenhead) 84, **86**
Brodie, Rear Adm C.G. 153–4
Bruix, Adm Eustache 43, 47
Brun, Naval Constructor 113
Buchanan, Adm Franklin 68, 69
buoyancy 12–13, 57–8, 64–5, 88, 90, 98, 137
Burke, Br James Dominic 95, 159
Busch, Arthur L. 126
Bushnell, David 28–40, 52
Bushnell, Ezra 28–34, 37
Busley, Professor C. 110–11

Cable, Capt Frank T. 126–7, 128, 131, 148, 150
Cairo, USS 66
Caldwell, Lt Harry H. 130, 144–5
Calmette, M. 120
Castera, Monsieur **51**
Castlereigh, Lord 47–8
Cerberus, HMS 36
Cervo (inventor) 59
Channel tunnel, early schemes 115
Charles Martel (battleship) **5**
Charleston 66, 69, 72, 73–4
Charmes, Gabriel 120
Chesapeake, USS 49
Christian Brothers 95, 96, **98**, 159
Clan na Gael see Fenians
Clarke, Lt Gen Sir Andrew 90–1
clockwork firing mechanism 29–30
clockwork sub 22–3, **23**
Columbian Iron Works (Baltimore) 125
Construction Number 333 (sub) 110
Coëssin brothers 53
Cochran, Mr 84, 86
Congreve rockets 53
Cox, William T. 127
Craven, Charles 138–9
Crescent Shipyard (Elizabethport) 125–6
Crimean War 59, 62
Crosby, Lt F.K. 75

Dahlgren, Rear Adm John 66–7, 74
Dahlgren (torpedo boat) 145
D'Alton, Capt (Army) P.W. 91
'Davids' (small torpedo boats) 66, 79 *bis*
Day, John 24–7
Deane, Silas 30, 31, 39
Decrès, Adm 45
Delamater, Cornelius/Delamater Ironworks 99, 100, 104
Delfino (sub) 109–10
de Lôme, Dupuy 116
Denmark 54, 61
d'Equevilley-Monjustin (inventor) 110
De Son (inventor) 22–3, 43
Devoy, John 99, 148
Dixon, Lt George E. 70, 73–6

Dönitz, Adm 63
Doolittle, Isaac 30
Dorothea (brig) 47, 49
Drebbel, Cornelis van 14–17, **16**, 52
Drummond, Vice-Consul 101
Drzewiecki, Stefan 92, 104, **108**, 110
duck, artificial 96
Duncan, Capt Henry 35
Du Pont, Capt Samuel 76–7
Duportail, Brig Louis 42
Dutch Republic 22–3

Eagle, HMS 33, 34, 35, 40
Eardley-Wilmot, Lt Sydney 90, 111–12
Edward VII, King 1, 2, 3–4, **3**, **4**
Effendi, Ibrahim 91
'egg', Garrett's (sub) 82–4, **83**
Electric Boat Company 132, 138–9, 140
Electro-Dynamic Company 127
Eliot, Jared 28
Ellis, Chief Eng Josiah 70–1
Elphin (steam yacht) 86–7
Empress of India, HMS 8
Ericsson, Capt John 104
Esher, Lord 4, 6–7
Excellent, HMS **3**

Falck, Dr N.D. 26–7
Faraday, Michael 61
Farquar, Rear Adm 144, 145
Farragut, Adm David G. 68
Fenians *see* Irish Republican Brotherhood
Fenian Ram (sub) 99–105, **100**, **102**, **105**, 107, 159
Fisher, Adm Sir John 'Jacky' 2, 3, **3**, 4–8, **4**, 91, 107, 155
Fitsum, Ivan Ivanovitch 62
flying machine, Holland's 124
Folger, Capt William M. 144–5
Fontes (sub) 110
Forelle (sub) 110, 111
Forfait, Pierre 43
Forth, HMS **9**
Fournier, Fr Georges 18–19, 82
Fox (Revenue cutter) 51
France/French 2–3, **5**, 39, 42–55 *passim*, 58–9, 82, 116–22, 137, 157

Franklin, Benjamin 28, 29, 30–1, 39
Freemasons 19, 28, 29, 61, 81, 82, 107
Frost, Elihu B. 124
Fulton, Robert 41–9, 50, 52

Gale, Benjamin 28, 29, 30–1
Garrett, Revd George W. 81–93, **83, 86, 92,**
    94, 99
Garrett, Jane (née Parker) 81–2
Garrett, Revd Dr John 81, 82–3
Garrett, John William 86, **86,** 93
Garrett Submarine Navigation and
    Pneumataphore Company 82, 84, 87
gassing incidents 89, 131
George V (Prince of Wales) 6–7
German Technical Ship-Building Society
    110–11
Germany 8, 62–3, 80, 110–11, 157
Glassel, Lt 67
Goddard, Electrician 123
Good, Lt H.J.G. **2**
Goschen, Adm Lord George 137, 138, 142
Goubet, Claude 91, 108, 115, 116
Goubet submarines 116, **117**
Gray, Maj M.C. **32**
Great Britain 1–4, 45–9, 52, 61, 108
    see also Royal Navy
Greece 90, 91, 108
Gustave Zédé (sub) 118–19, **121,** 122, 137,
    138
Gymnote (sub) **117,** 118, **119, 120**

Hale, Nathan 28, 30, 40
Hall, Blakely 100, 101
Halstead, Oliver 78
Hardy, Capt 49
Harsdorffer, George 16
Hasker, Charles 69–70
Hautefeuille, Abbé de 17
Hazard, HMS 146–9, 151, **152**
Hichborn, Rear Adm 143–4
Hill, Gunner Owen 144
Holland, Alfred 94, 96
Holland, John Sr 94
Holland, John Philip **1, 127, 133, 139**
    early years in Ireland 94–6

inventor in USA 96–8, 99–106, 108
success in USA 123–32, 136
summary of achievement 157–9
Holland, Margaret (née Foley) 106, 123
Holland, Michael 94, 96, 99, 159
Holland, Robert 94, 95
Holland submarines 140, 142, 143–5,
    150–51, 157–9
    No.1: **2, 6, 9, 10,** 97–8, **97,** 140–2, **141,**
        146–9, **149, 152**
    No.2: 151, 154–5
    No.3: 151, 153–4, **153**
    No.6: (USS *Holland*): **1, 124,** 125–31,
        129, 130, 139
Holland Torpedo Boat Company 124, 140
Homan, C.H. **114**
Hopkinson, Francis 36–7
Horton, Max K. 154
Housatonic (steam sloop) 74–5
Hovgaard, Lt 113
Howe, Vice Adm Sir Richard 'Black Dick'
    33–4, 35
Howe, Gen Sir William 33–4, 36–7
Hunley, Horace L. 68, 70, 72–3
Hunley, CSS (sub) 68–76, **75,** 116
hydroplanes 59, 69–70, 84, 129

Idjalalieh (battleship) 82
Indian Chief, CSS 70, 71, 74
Inglefield, Rear Adm E.A. 78–9
Intelligent Whale (sub) 78–9, **78**
Ireland 81, 94–5
Irish Republican Brotherhood (Fenians)
    95–105 *passim,* 159
    Skirmishing Fund 96, 97, 98, 103, 105
Ironsides, USS 66–7, 73
Italy 109–10, 113, 157

Jackson, Capt 85–6, **86**
Jackson, Adm Henry 137
James I, King 14, 15, 16
Jane, Fred T. 93, 157
Jane's Fighting Ships 146
Japan 89, 157
J.C.Todd and Co. 97
Jefferson, Thomas 37–8, 39, 49

Jeffries, Capt 118
Jenoud (inventor) 114
Johnson, Tom 50–5
Jones, Jos 113
Jupiter, HMS 147

K-boats 90
Kearsarge, USS 144–5
Keith, Adm 47
Kiel 60–1, 110
Kimball, Rear Adm William W. 106, 125
Kingston, Capt 47
Kingston, Seaman Samuel 35
Kingston valves 14, 30, 68, 101, 102
Kizaki, Count Lt Kosuke **139**
Komsomolets (nuclear sub) 113
Kronstadt 62
Küstenbrander (sub) 62–4

Lacavalerie, Sebastian 115, **115**
Lacomme, Dr J.A. 115
Lake, Simon 125, 132–6, 157
Lamm, Eugene 84, 86, 88
Landskrona 89, **89**
Laubeuf, Eng-in-Chief Maxime 119, 137
Le Carron, Maj Henri 100–101
Lee, Sgt Ezra 34–5. 39–40
Lee, Capt (Army) Francis D. 66
Leggo (inventor) 113–14
Le Plongeur (sub) 113, 116
Leonardo da Vinci 18
Leopard, HMS 47, 49
le Pelley, Adm Pléville 43
Lincoln, Abraham 77
L'Invisible (proposed sub) 56
Lockroy, Minister 119, 120
L'Oiseau, HMS 45
London Underground Railway 84
Loring, Elizabeth 36–7
Lowe, Capt John 131

M-class submarines 62
McClintock, James 68, 70, 71
McDonnell, Br Dominic 96
McLeod, Revd Norman 84
Magenta (battleship) 118–19, **137**

Maiali (human torpedoes) 113
Malster, William T. 125
Manchester 81, 82
Marceau (battleship) **118**
Maria (converted sloop) 24–7
Marine Cigar (sub) **63**, 64–5
Martenote, M. 56
Maury, Capt Matthew 71
Melville, Rear Adm 143
Merlin, HMS **112**
Merrimac, USS 67, 77
Mersenne, Friar Marin 18–19, 20, 84
Messenger, The (submersible) 46
Mexico 89
Middleton, Henry 107
midget submarines 58, 91, 113
   Kleinkampfmittel-Verband 36
    'Peter Koshka' 157
    X-craft 7, 37, 113
    see also American Turtle
mines 6–7, 36, 47, 66
Monarch, HMS 47
Monitor (ship) 78
Monson, Adm Sir William 13
Montgéry, Capt Jacques-Philippe M. de
   56–7, 58–9
Morell, Electrician 149–50
Morris, Charles A. 123–4, **127**, 128, 131
Morris and Cummings Dredging Company
   123
Morse (sub) 110, 119, 120–22, **137**
Mute (semi-submersible) **48**, 49

Napoleon I 43, 47, 54–5, 58, 115
Napoleon III 115
Narval (sub) 119, 122, 137–8
Nasmyth, James **54**
Nautile (sub) 53
Nautilus (sub) 42–6, **44**, **46**, 111–12
Naval Defence Bill 137
Neafic and Levy's shipyard 77
Nelson, Adm Horatio 46, 48
Neptune (battleship) 118
New Orleans 68
New York 33–4, 49, 93
Nicholson, Flag Capt 70–1

Nikonov, Efim 61–2
Nixon, Lewis 125–6
Nordenfelt, Thorsten 85, 87, 88, 93, 99, 123
Nordenfelts (subs) 87–93, **89**, **92**, 108
Norris, Br John 95–6
Norwood, Richard 19

Olivier, A.A. 113
O'Neil, Rear Adm 143, 145
Opdam, Adm 23
O'Riordan, Br Michael Paul 95
'Otter' (anti-submarine sweep) 135
Ottley, Rear Adm 132, 135
oxygen 16–17

Papin, Denis 16
Paris 43–4
Park, First Officer Thomas 72–3
Park & Lyons factory 68, 72
Paterson Museum (New Jersey) 105
Payenne, Dr Prosper **111**
Payne, Lt John A. 69–70
Peacemaker (sub) 107, 123
Pearl, HMS 35
Peral, Lt Isaac/*Peral* sub 108, **109**, 118
Pereira de Mello, Lt Don Fontes 110
Perrier Brothers 43
Peter the Great, Tsar 61–2
Petit, Dr Jean-Baptiste 59
Philadelphia 36, 77
Philips, Lodner **63**, 64–5
Pickering, Capt Charles 75
Pioneer (sub) **67**, 68
Pioneer II (American Diver) 68
Pitt, William 45–7, 48
Plunger (sub) 125, 137–8, 140, **156**
Plymouth 24, 25–7
pneumataphore (diving suit) 82, 85
Pneumatic Gun Company 106
Pocock, Tom 50
polar conditions 20, **21**
Poland/Polish 19, 92
Ponsonby, Frederick 4
Portsmouth 1, 151
Portugal 110

Pratt, Phineas 30, 35
pressure 18, 25, 61
Price, Engineer George 85–6, **86**, 87
Priestley, Joseph 16–17
Princess Royal (1902) 154
Protector (sub) 136, **157**
Prussia 62–3
Putnam, Gen Israel 34

Ramillies, HMS 49
Renown, HMS 35
Repulse, HMS 35
rescue craft 113
respiration 22, 148–9
Resurgam 84–7, **86**, **87**
Rhyl 86–7
Rice, Capt Ernest 110
Rice, Isaac L. **131**, 132, 138–9, 140
Richards, George M. 101–3
Robins Dry Dock Company (Brooklyn) 134
Romazotti, M. 118
Roosevelt, Theodore 129–30, **156**
Rossa, Jeremiah O'Donovan 97, 98
Rothschild, Lord 132, 138
Rotterdam 22
Royal Arthur, HMS 70
Royal Naval Submarine Museum 140
Royal Navy 1–11, 42, 111, 132, 145–6, 156, 159
   Admiralty 52, 55, 80, 107, 108, 119, 137–42
Rozhdestvensky, Lt Zinovi 82
Russia 61–2, 91, 92, **108**, 110, 115, 136, 157
Russo-Turkish War 82, 107
Russell, John Scott 61

St Aubin, Monsieur 44
St Johns, SS 103
St Petersburg 62
St Vincent, Adm Lord 48, 51
San Francisco 84
Sandwich, Lord 26, 27
Sargent, Lt Nathan 128
Scheuseck (inventor) 115
Schleswig-Holstein 60, 61

Schnorchel 100
  snorkel/snort (hollow mast) **15**
Schweffel and Howaldt (foundry) 60
Scott, John K. 68
Seal, US Submarine 136
Seeteufel (sub) 62
Shiloh, Battle of 73
Shipp, Seaman 74
Shuldham, Vice Adm Molineux 33
Simpson, Capt Edward 106
Singer, E.C./Singer Submarine Corporation 68
Skinner, Second Capt 154
skins used as ballast tanks **13**, 14
Skipjack, US Submarine **158**
slaves 73
Smith, Adm Sir Sydney 58
Spain 47, 54, 108, 129–30
Spuyten Duyvil (sub) 79–80
steamboats 41
Steele, K.W. 16–17
Stockholm 87
Styles, Ezra 29, 39
Sweden 87–8, 89, 91
Symons, Nathaniel 14, 20

Temeraire, HMS 90
Thames (cruiser) 151
Three Friends (privateer) 50
Thursfield, Sub Lt H.G. **2**
Timsah (sub) 91
Tirpitz, Adm von 110, 157
Tirpitz (battleship) 7
Toledo, SS 90
Tomb, Engineer 74
Torpedo Boat No.42: 151
torpedoes 2, 72, 74, 75, 79, 88, 104, 110, 118, 126
Tracy, Capt Benjamin F. 123
Trafalgar, Battle of 48

Trinidad, SS 91
Tryon, William 33
Tuck, Professor Josiah 107, 123
Turkey 82, 90, 91–2, 99, 107, 108

U-boats 8, 76, 111
United States of America 43, 52, 53, 64
  Civil War 66–80
  US Navy 49, 143–5, 147, 156–7
  War of Independence 28–40
  see also Holland, John Philip

Vatry, Marc-Antoine Bourdon de 43
Vernon, HMS 110, 143, 146
Vickers, Sons & Maxim 92, 138–40, 148
Victory, HMS **153**
Villeroi, Brutus de 58–9, 76–8
Virginia, CSS 67, 77
Vogt semi-submersible **114**

Walker, Maude 3–4
Waller, PO William R. **2**, 150
Warbash, USS 73
Washington, George 29, 33, 35, 37–8, 39
Watson, Baxter Jr 68
Welles, Gideon 67
White, Sir William (Director of Naval Construction) 107, 111, 112
Whitehead, Robert 104, 88
Wilkins, Dr John 19–21, **20**, 22
Wilson, Adm Sir Arthur 140, 148
World War One 62, 132, 143, 157
World War Two 58, 63, 113, 132, 143, 157
Wright brothers 124
Wynam (inventor) 115

Zaharoff, Basil 87, 90, 116
Zalinski, Capt Edmund/Zalinski boat 106
Zédé, Gustave 59, 116–18
  see also Gustave Zédé